# THE POINTER
AND HIS PREDECESSORS

## 'THE POINTER AND HIS PREDECESSORS.'

### SOME PRESS OPINIONS.

'An Arkwright on the Pointer sounds as good as a Westwood on editions of Walton or a Hawker on the Gun; and, indeed, Mr. Arkwright graces with something of the literary taste of Westwood the hard-won knowledge of a Hawker.'—Saturday Review.

'As a monograph on a variety of Dog the work is unique, and the completeness and extent of the Author's researches disarm criticism.'
     The Field.

'Mr. Arkwright seems for years to have devoted a labour of love to its compilation . . . . and he has traced in a very pleasant fashion the history not only of the particular kind of dog, but of the sport with which it has been associated.'—Morning Post.

'Mr. William Arkwright is an enthusiast, otherwise it would have been impossible for him to write this book about the Pointer and its ancestors. . . . . It is a thorough work well worthy of the nine years the author has spent upon it.'—The Times.

'The chapters on shows and working trials, on alien crosses, on breaking, and kennel management, are exhaustive and practical.'
     County Gentleman.

'Mr. Arkwright's book . . . will be useful not only to pointer breeders, but to every gun-man and every lover of a gun-dog of any sort.'
     Land and Water.

'He has followed the proper historic method, first testing, and generally rejecting, traditional stories about the origin of pointers, and then accumulating a quantity of fresh material at first hand.'—Spectator.

'Mr. William Arkwright has added a classic to the books on sport in his *The Pointer and his Predecessors* . . . . Mr. Arkwright's chapter on shooting over pointers does even this difficult subject justice.'
     C. J. Cornish (in Country Life).

'C'est, sans contredit, la plus remarquable œuvre d'art vouée à la description d'une seule race de chiens.'
     Henry Sodenkamp (in Chasse et Peche).

# THE POINTER
## AND HIS PREDECESSORS

An Illustrated History of the Pointing Dog from the Earliest Times

BY
WILLIAM ARKWRIGHT

*POPULAR EDITION*

TO THE
# MEMORY OF MY FATHER
THIS BOOK IS DEDICATED.

'Huic par capiendi quærendique sudor, summusque et idem gratissimus labor invenire.'
*Panegyricus Trajano dictus,* LXXXI.

# PREFACE TO SECOND EDITION

SINCE the publication of *The Pointer and his Predecessors* in its original form, a demand appears to have arisen for a cheaper, more portable edition, which shall be suitable for everyday use.

To meet this demand the present volume has been designed, to synchronise if possible with a similar edition in French. It has been carefully revised throughout and a few additions have been made chiefly to the chapter on kennel management : otherwise it remains unaltered. The general arrangement is identical, with the exception that the descriptions of the illustrations, formerly in a separate chapter, have been distributed, so that each may be opposite the picture of which it treats ; and the forty original plates have been reduced to twenty-two of the most apposite in order to make the book as compact as possible. After consideration, the chapter that deals with Shows and Working Trials has been left untouched because since 1901, the year when it was written, there has been no appreciable change in the policy of the various canine Societies.

One fresh subject alone seems to me to require consideration. The late Mr. C. J. Cornish, in the course of a most thoughtful criticism of this book for 'Country Life,' remarked, 'There is only one bed-rock subject which Mr. Arkwright does not discuss, and that is the history of the growth and transmission of the gift or habit of pointing.' This omission not having been due to any cloudiness in my own mind as to the derivation of the phenomenon, I am now presenting my view of the subject without claiming for it any special originality.

## PREFACE TO SECOND EDITION

The pointing habit is an artificial prolongation of the instinctive pause of a carnivorous animal on first becoming aware of the proximity of prey—a pause for the purpose of devising a stratagem. Indeed it is a quality so readily intensified by selection that in specialised breeds of dogs there is constant danger of its exaggeration, evidenced in false-pointing and in unwillingness to road up the game, both of which habits may be reckoned among the mortal sins for a gundog.

To show that pointing is a trick easily taught there is the well-known case of the New Forest pig, which was taught ' to find and point partridges within a fortnight ;' and, without descending so far as the farm-yard, I myself once broke a fox-terrier to stand partridges perfectly, after she had been accustomed to run them up.

The unflagging range of the Pointer where there may be no game, his statuesque attitude when on point, the presentation of his nostrils to the wind while galloping across it—all these seem to me to separate him from other dogs far more widely than the actual pointing, because they are qualities impossible to teach, the developments of centuries of careful breeding.

# PREFACE

ABOUT nine years ago I said in my haste, 'I will write a complete record of the Pointer.' Ever since I have been hunting up the materials at home and abroad, and to aid the pursuit I have been obliged to learn from its commencement the language of one of the countries involved in my research.

I do not make mention of these labours in a grumbling spirit, but simply to prove that I have worked hard at the historical part of my subject; and, partly to substantiate my claim, partly to help others bent on kindred studies, I have added, in an appendix, a complete list of all the books that I have consulted. In this list I cannot, of course, guarantee that, despite diligent endeavour, my dates are in all cases those of the first editions; but I have myself verified all my references and have made all the translations except the German ones, which are the work of my friend, Miss L. Smythe, a lady in whose accuracy I have every confidence. I believe these selections to be undistorted by any bias, and not plucked unduly from their contexts; while in the renderings of foreign passages, fidelity rather than elegance has been aimed at. It was my wish to place the original texts in an appendix, but I have been dissuaded on the ground of cumbrousness.

I trust that my reiterated introduction of dates and names of reference will not irritate the hyper-sensitive reader; but I myself have suffered so grievously by the absence of such details from the pages of others, that I resolved at any risk to be guiltless of similar sins of omission.

I fear that the matters treated of in my chapters are not all so clearly separated as may be wished, and that

## PREFACE

they often invade each other's territory, in consequence of the quoted passages with which this book abounds. For whenever I have been able to find my opinion anticipated by an old-time author, I have given it in his words in preference to my own : this method certainly entails extra work, and possibly some self-denial, but on the other hand it authoritatively settles all contentious subjects.

I have excluded, as far as possible, comparisons between pointer and setter, because there is a great conflict of opinion about their relative merits, and because, though personally I prefer the former, I have nothing but admiration for excellence in a setter, and, indeed, in all the other gundogs.

My fitness for writing the practical part of this book mainly depends on my having been reared literally from earliest infancy among pure pointers, though afterwards I experimented, on my own account, with the houndy ones. For my father, dying when I was but a few weeks old, left instructions that his pointers were to be preserved for me, instructing Charles Ecob his favourite keeper, to look after my sporting education. His wishes were carried out to the letter, and no child could have had a kinder or more competent tutor. We commenced our studies before my third birthday ; and it is owing to those early years of training that I have a working experience of kennel-management.

In conclusion, let me express my gratitude for the help given me by many kind persons, among whom I must specially mention Madame Riaño, Miss L. Smythe, Señor Alvarez, M. Bouchôt, M. de Chennevières, Mr. Charles Cockburn, Mr. Sidney Colvin, Mr. J. B. Muir, and Señor Vignau.

I must also cordially thank Mr. Craig Annan, who has executed the photogravures that so embellish this volume, for his patient, discerning assistance.

# CONTENTS

| CHAPTER | PAGE |
|---|---|
| I.—EARLY HISTORY | 1 |
| II.—LATER HISTORY | 71 |
| III.—SHOWS AND WORKING TRIALS | 98 |
| IV.—CHARACTERISTICS OF THE POINTER | 115 |
| V.—BREEDING AND SELECTION | 137 |
| VI.—ALIEN CROSSES | 147 |
| VII.—SHOOTING OVER DOGS | 163 |
| VIII.—BREAKING | 190 |
| IX.—KENNEL MANAGEMENT | 223 |
| LIST OF BOOKS | 251 |

# ILLUSTRATIONS

Plate
- I.—From an Etching after Tillemans
- II.—From a Pencil-sketch by Pisanello
- III.—From a Painting by Titian
- IV.—From a Painting by Velazquez
- V.—From a Painting by Desportes
- VI.—From a Painting by Oudry
- VII.—From a Painting by Wootton
- VIII.—From an Engraving after Stubbs
- IX.—From an Engraving after Gilpin
- X.—From an Engraving after Reinagle
- XI.—From a Painting by Jackson
- XII.—From a Painting by Newton
- XIII.—From an Engraving after Lewis
- XIV.—From an Engraving after Laporte.
- XV.—From a Painting by Alken
- XVI.—From a Painting by Shayer.
- XVII.—From a Painting by G. Earl
- XVIII.—From a Painting by G. Earl
- XIX.—From a Painting by G. Earl
- XX.—From a Painting by M. Earl
- XXI.—From a Painting by G. Earl
- XXII.—From a Painting by M. Earl

# THE POINTER

## CHAPTER I.
## EARLY HISTORY.

IT is necessary to know something about the pointing and setting-dogs of antiquity—how, when, and where they arose—before attempting to solve the origin of the English pointer. The subject is somewhat complex, embracing, as it does, not only the Laws that dealt with these dogs and the weapons with which they were associated, but also the esteem in which they were held during the centuries: there is, moreover, at the very outset a certain amount of rubbish to be cleared out of their history.

Law Court proof for my theories will not be always available, but in most cases there will be something a great deal more tangible than mere probability. I ask my readers to set out with the feelings of an Alpine party—earnest, patient, and equipped with a coil of sympathetic imagination to keep us in touch. There will be both Statement and Silence—opposites, but almost equally luminous—to irradiate our passage through the mists of antiquity; with Etymology as a torch-light, when the others are obscured.

In the absence of any proof to the contrary, it may be assumed that the pointing and setting dogs originated in Europe; as, though the Bible has a reference to 'hunting a partridge in the mountains'

# THE POINTER

(1 *Samuel* xxvi. 20), and though to the Western mind this may seem rather difficult of accomplishment without a dog, the contempt of the Asiatic for this animal could scarcely have been maintained had they ever been associated in the fellowship of sport. It is noteworthy that in the whole Bible there is not a single mention of a dog used for hunting ; which certainly tends to confirm the view of John P. Robinson that 'they didn't know everythin' down in Judee.' Egypt appears to have left no foreshadowings of a pointing-dog in her records, and the treatise on Venery by Sid Mohammed el Mangali (the tenth century), translated by M. Pharaon (1880), is taken up with hunting and hawking, without even a prophetic hint of the 'partridge-dog'—though this author's range is so wide as to embrace both ants and elephants! M. Pharaon intimates that this treatise is a standard one in Algeria ; and its methods still prevail in Upper Egypt.

As Europe, then, seemed to be the continent where this dog might be said to be indigenous, to its literature did I turn in search of the signs of his birth. In the first place, I thoroughly ransacked the classical writers on sport, both Latin and Greek ; but these writers (see list in the Appendix) told me nothing, absolutely nothing about the sport of hunting partridges or quails with dogs. So when after many a futile quest, one day I came across the following passage in a modern Spanish book, I was naturally somewhat excited by it :—'Already in far antiquity, treating of this subject Pliny and Sallust, Romans, state that their compatriots had taken from Spain, and introduced into France and Italy, the dogs called "*aviarii*," mentioned in the following passage of their works :—" When the sagacious animal approaches the quail or other sluggish bird, he appears to fascinate it

# EARLY HISTORY

by his flashing glance; meanwhile the fowler, now with a kind of cage, now by spreading a net over, gets possession of his prize "' (*Paginas de Caza*, p. 15, by 'Evero,' 1888).

I wrote at once to the author, who published under such an inspiriting pseudonym, to ask for 'chapter and verse' of this remarkable excerpt. His reply was indefinite: he had lost the reference, though he assured me on his honour that his quotation was genuine. I then searched through the works of the two Plinys and Sallust—but in vain. Sallust was a historian of wars and conspiracies, and I could not find even the word *dog* in his writings! The elder Pliny in the eighth book of his natural history gives a bare mention of hounds, but not a sign of a dog for taking birds: the younger Pliny is still more barren of canine lore. Finally, in the *Lexicon Ægidii Forcellini*, that wonderful concordance of the Latin classics, there is no mention of a dog having been ever termed '*aviarius*.' So I dismissed this incident, with the conviction that no mention of pointing or setting-dog had been made by the Ancients, either ·Greek or Roman. I, therefore, left behind the classical times (which, for my purpose,. extended to the end of the fourth century), to glance at the *Origines* (early seventh century) of St. Isidore, Bishop of Seville—in them, however, finding dogs only as guards and for hunting. I read also *Geoponica*, compiled in the tenth century by Emperor Constantine IV., but here again was I disappointed of anything to do with my subject—the dogs mentioned were solely to protect the flocks; and partridges were to be taken by the administration of barley-meal macerated in wine, or by wine and water as a drink (xiv. 21).

Thus working by the process of exhaustion, I decided that the pointing-dog must be a product of the Middle Ages, when owing to the spread of

## THE POINTER

agriculture partridges had become comparatively numerous; so towards the literature I next turned my attention. At this point a statement concerning the *Lex Salica*, in a German book, seemed of the highest promise, as this law of the Salian Franks is computed by Grimm to date in written form from the fifth century.

'From earliest history, dogs were used for catching game. According to the laws the following dogs were distinguished: blood-hounds (*leithunde*), boarhounds (*hatzhunde*), and partridge-dogs (*hünerhunde*). The last referred to as *agutarito* and *hünerhund* in *Lex Salica*, and as *spurihunt* in *Lex Boioar. III.*' (*In Forst und Jagd-wesen*, by H. G. Francken, 1754, p. 270). 'Also in the *Bojoarisch* laws reference is made to dogs for driving (*treibhunde*), used for catching game and also for duck-shooting; also dogs with hawks (*habuchhunt*, i.e., *habicht-hund*); but not before the reign of Friedrich I.' (*id.* page 273). But, alas, Francken's statements would not bear investigation! In the *Lex Salica*, the ten texts with the glosses by J. H. Hessels and H. Kern (1880), a synoptic edition of all the texts, the law about thefts of dogs (Titulus vi.) which is the only one relating to them, contains in Codices 6 and 5 the words '*canem acutarium*,' and Codices 7, 8, and 9 vary the word to '*agutaris*,' while Codex 10 has '*agutarito*.' None of them, however, gives any description of the dog, until the *Lex Emendata* (dating from Charlemagne) promulgates the same law as the other Codices, but with such an important addition that I will quote it: '*Si quis vero canem seusium reliquum, aut veltrem porcarium sive veltrem leporarium, qui et agutarius dicitur, furatus fuerit vel occiderit*,' &c. ('But if from henceforward any one shall have stolen or killed a Segusian hound or a boar-hound or a hare-hound, which is also called *agutarius*,' &c.) Thus the only explanation in *Lex Salica* of the term effectually

# EARLY HISTORY

disposes of Herr Francken's theory that '*agutarito*
meant game-bird dog (*hünerhund*). The only excuse
for such an error must lie in his having misread the
glossarium of Lindebrog of the seventeenth century,
who, although he wrote about the *argutarius* ' this is
a hare-hound' (*veltris leporarius*), quotes a line about
hounds from the poet Gratius, ' which may push up
(*ciat*) the hidden game and point it out by signs (*signis
arguat*)!' This, if Francken had not read the Codices
for himself, might cause him to think that Lindebrog's
'*argutarito*' was derived from *arguere* (to point out)
instead of having its origin in *acutus* (clever). As
regards the '*spurihunt*,' which this author translates
also by '*hünerhund*,' I need only cite, to prove his
absurdity, Lex Baivvariorum, *Titulus xix.*, *Leg. iii.*:
'*Si autem seucem qui in ligamine vestigium tenet, quem
spurihunt dicunt, furaverit*,' &c. ('But if any one
have stolen the hound that is held in a leash, which
they call trail-hound,' &c.)

But if 'Evero' were led astray by carelessness and
Francken by credulity, their sins pale before the conduct of the last of those authors whose misdeeds I am
forced to expose. One M. Castillon (d'Aspet), in 1874,
published a tiny pamphlet with the magniloquent title
of *Los Paramientos de la Caza, ou Règlements sur la
Chasse en général par Don Sancho le Sage, roi de Navarre,
publiés en l'année* 1180. I had heard of this translation
as an important document, and not being able to find it
in England, I had to go to Paris after it. In the dedication it was picturesquely stated to have been 'buried
in the provincial archives of Pamplona since the end
of the twelfth century,' and again 'copied from the
original and translated into French, thus, by my exer-
tions, will it have been published for the first time.'
On reading it I was delighted at finding a mention,
though only an incidental one, of the pointing-dog

# THE POINTER

(p. 48, chap. iii.). This occurred in a protest against coupling together such uncongenial mates as a Navarrese dog and a harbourer, or a hound and a *pointing-dog*, on starting for a day's sport. I was, however, so puzzled as to the word in old Spanish that the translator could render by *chien d'arrêt*, which is very modern French, that I resolved to see for myself the original MS. at Pamplona. But before I left France a friend of mine wrote to the Mayor of Aspet for information of M. Castillon's whereabouts, and learned in reply that our author had disappeared from there many years before. When I, still unsuspicious of fraud, arrived at Madrid, and begged some very kind and influential friends to get me permission to explore the archives at Pamplona, they themselves preferred to make preliminary inquiries from the official custodians of the library there. The result of these was a long letter written by one of these gentlemen; extracts from which, sufficient to show that the *Paramientos* are nothing but clever fakes, I here reproduce.

'Sr. Gutierrez de la Vega, if I remember his name correctly, who had edited certain ancient books on the chase, spoke to me of *Los Paramientos*, and when I returned to Pamplona I searched the archives with the greatest care. My dear friend, Don Juan Iturralde y Suit, Vice-President of the Commission of the Monuments of Navarre, also interested himself in the search. *Los Paramientos*, according to M. Castillon, formed part of a copy of the *Fuero General*. We pressed him with questions in order to verify the references after ascertaining that no known copy of the *Fuero* contained the said *Paramientos*. At first he returned a few evasive answers, but in the end took refuge in absolute silence. If I remember rightly, in speaking of the hunter's dress, "*coinas*" are mentioned. These were not used in Navarre until the beginning of last century,

## EARLY HISTORY

and their use became popular during the first Civil War. Until then the Navarrese wore "*monteras,*" "*zorongos,*" Arragonese hats, &c., according to the various parts of the kingdom. The "*coina*" is of Bearnese origin, and passed from Béarn to Lower Navarre, and from thence its use spread to Higher Navarre. I know a bas-relief of Roncal, the sixteenth century sculptures of which have a kind of "*coina*" on the head, but if they are really such they represent a local fashion. To speak of them in the time of King Sancho the Wise is absurd. The suspicious details of the *Paramientos*, the silence of M. Castillon, and the negative results of the search among the archives of the province of Navarre, are sufficient to allow of the assertion being made, without rashness, that the *Paramientos* are spurious' (Extracts from letter of Arturo Campion, January 17th, 1901).

Having cleared away all this rubbish, I first secured a firm footing in the thirteenth century on the almost synchronous references to partridge-dogs made by two authors of different nationality.

One of these is Brunetto Latini, an Italian and the master of Dante, who, during his exile in France (from 1260 to 1267), wrote *Li livres dou Tresor*. Among its descriptions of dogs, this encyclopædic book contains the following passage :—' Others are brachs (*brachet*) with falling ears, which know of beasts and birds (*des bestes et des oisiaus*) by the scent, therefore they are useful for sporting (*bons à la chace*)' (chap. clxxxxvi., part i., liv. i.).

The other is Albertus Magnus (1193–1280), Bishop of Ratisbon in Germany, who in *De Animalibus* has this interesting account, which is probably the earliest ever written.

'The dogs, however, that are used for birds seem to have these [powers] more from training than from

# THE POINTER

sense of smell, though they derive them from both. They are taught in this manner: they are first led round some caught partridges pretty often, and at length by threats learn to go round and round them; but they get to find the partridge by scent, and thus at the beginning they set (*ponunt*) pretty often at the indications of the captive birds' (book xxii., p. 175).

As we shall see further on the Italian writer was soon supported by Dante and by the pictures of eminent masters. But the German account is isolated, so we must not infer from it that Germany possessed these dogs at that period, especially as Albertus was educated at Padua, and lived for many years after in Italy—in the heart of the pointing-dog district. While on the other hand *Das Buch der Natur*, a fourteenth century book by R. A. von Meyenburg, the earliest German authority on dogs, does not record their being used for sport, but only for guarding; it is three centuries later before we find the Germans employing foreign dogs for small game. 'Spanish dogs, zealous for their masters and of commendable sagacity, are chiefly used for finding partridges and hares. In the quest of bigger game they are not so much approved of, as they for the most part range widely, nor do they keep as near as genuine hunting-dogs' (*Rei Rusticæ Libri Quatuor*, by Conrad Heresbach, 1570, p. 353).

But if as is possible the smooth-haired brach, or pointing-dog, originated in Italy, the unanimity of the nations in procuring long-haired spaniels, or setting-dogs, from Spain seems to fix their birthplace with some certainty. Gaston Phebus, the famous Comte de Foix, who himself owned 'from 1500 to 1600 dogs, brought from all the countries of Europe' (*La Chasse*, p. 368, by M. L. Cimber, 1837), bears witness in 1387 to their introduction into France.

# EARLY HISTORY

'There is a kind of dog that is called falcon-dog (*chien d'oisel*), or spaniel (*espaignolz*) because it comes from Spain, however many there may be of them in other countries. And these dogs have many good qualities, and bad ones also. A handsome falcon-dog should have a massive head, and large well-made body, his coat being white or cinnamon colour (*canele*), because these are the most beautiful and of this colour there are many excellent; they should not be too hairy, and the end of the tail should be tufted (*espiee*). The good qualities of these dogs are that they are very faithful to their masters, and follow them anywhere without being lost. They go also in front of birds willingly, ranging and making play with their tails, and find all birds and all beasts, but their proper business is at the partridge and the quail. For the man who has a good goshawk or falcon, lanner or tassel-hawk, and a good sparrow-hawk, they are very useful, and also when one teaches them to set their game they are good for taking partridges and quail with the net; they are also good, when broken to the river, for a bird that is diving. . . . And as one talks of a greyhound of Britain, the boarhounds and bird-dogs come from Spain' (*Des Deduiz de la Chasse*, chap. xx.).

In 1551, Pierre de Quinqueran de Beaujeu (Bishop of Senès), writing of 'setting-dogs,' says: 'Spain has in common with us another kind of dog of middle size that the other countries have no idea of' (*La nouvelle Agriculture*, cap. xvi., p. 242); and, in the British Museum, an Italian early fourteenth century MS. of book v. of the 'decretals' of Gregory IX. contains an illumination representing a *spaniel* pointing at a hare.

After all these proofs of the estimation in which the Spanish setting-dogs were formerly held, I turned to Spain itself, confident of finding there records of the

## THE POINTER

spaniel at least coeval with the *Deduiz de la Chasse.* But, alas! the early Spaniards must have been a leisurely race, and their sportsmen not addicted to pen or pencil, unless there be inaccessible MSS. mouldering in the recesses of old-world libraries; for until the fifteenth century all is silence, and the only picture I can find of a long-haired setting-dog is in the Madrid Gallery. It is by Ribera (1583–1656), and represents a most typical dog certainly, but—engaged in carrying a piece of bread to San Roque.

Now, to revert to the account of Phebus in which there are several points of high importance! It definitely decides the derivation of the name '*espaignolz*,' whence spring the modern French word '*épagneul*' and the English word 'spaniel.' It establishes the identity in blood of the falcon-dog and the setting-dog, for the falcon was styled 'the bird' by the old writers in all languages. It also shows that this falcon-dog from Spain, with his tufted tail and his moderate feather, was a long-coated dog. Espée de Sélincourt (1683), who makes early use of the generic title gundogs (*chiens de l'arquebuse*), sharply divides the spaniels from the *braques*, though both varieties were evidently being imported then into France from Spain, by defining setting-dogs (*chiens couchans*) as '*braques* that stop at the scent (*arrêtent tout*) and hunt with the nose high; the best are from Spain. The spaniels (*espagnols*) are for the falcons (*oyseaux*), hunting with the nose low and following by the track' (*Table des Chasses*).

Having ascertained that the spaniels passed from Spain to France, and having seen them established there, I shall further trace them to England before attempting the pedigree of the short-haired pointing-dog or brach.

Etymology inclines me to believe that England got

## EARLY HISTORY

her spaniels through France, and not from Spain direct; for it would certainly be a strange coincidence if two nations were independently to invent names so similar: besides, dogs in those days could have been imported with much more ease from France than from Spain. I have found but one pronouncement in favour of the Spain-direct theory, which is that of 'A Quartogenarian' in the *Sporting Magazine* (2nd ser., vol. v., 1832):—'Vespasian introduced dogs (probably spaniels) from Spain into this island to help hawking.' I have in vain tried to find any reference to this in the histories of Tacitus and the biography of Suetonius. So, as there is no evidence that Vespasian ever visited Spain, as the elder Pliny who published his Natural History during this reign never alludes to Spanish dogs, and as British hawking would have been decidedly rudimentary in the first century, I think that this Vespasian idea may be pitched on to the rubbish heap with the other exposed fallacies.

There is another explanation, however, of this hallucination about Vespasian, which may very well be the true one. The Cotton collection of manuscripts was acquired by the British Museum in 1757, and the library in which it had lain, at Dean's Yard, chanced to have its book-cases surmounted by busts of the Roman Emperors. During the removal of the collection, each section was for convenience catalogued after the august head under which it happened to repose. These nicknames were left unaltered at the Museum, and now to demand Nero D. 10, or Galba A. 6, is a matter of course. There is one of these Cottonian MSS., without any title readily visible, which contains a mention of spaniels, and as it happens to be labelled 'Vespasianus B. 12,' a superficial reader might have mistaken the press-mark for the author's name.

And oddly enough, this identical MS., which in-

# THE POINTER

cludes two separate treatises of different date though copied by the same hand, has also caused Blaine, another of the casuals, in his *Encyclopædia of Rural Sports* (1839) to make a mistake, which, if less absurd than the other, is infinitely more misleading.

He makes Twety and Giffarde, 'who were wythe Edward the secunde,' to be the authors of the entire volume, quotes their supposed remarks on spaniels, and thus antedates the mention of this dog by about eighty years; whereas, in reality, they are only responsible for the first nine pages, which are devoted entirely to big game, while the rest, including the index and the passage on 'Saynolfes' (so misspelt), is simply an early transcription of de Langley's *Mayster of the Game.*

But there are many other arguments, besides the etymological clues, to induce the adoption of the through-France alternative. The first mention of a spaniel in English occurs in the *Mayster of the Game,* by Edmund de Langley, Duke of York (1341–1402), or according to modern authorities by Edward—his son—who fell at Agincourt, 1415; and the author frankly enough acknowledges his indebtedness to 'the Erl of Foix Phebus in his booke.' Indeed, so far as his whole description of 'spanyels' is concerned, it is nothing more than a word-for-word rendering of the *Deduiz de la Chasse;* so much so that I was glad to compare my translation with his to be sure of the meaning of certain difficult words. That the Englishman copied slavishly, without having seen a spaniel at all (let alone a setting spaniel), I feel pretty certain, both from the absence of any original matter of his own on the subject and from the silence of other succeeding English writers; for even Dame Juliana Bernes, in her *Mayster of the Game* (1486), beyond mentioning that there were certain dogs called 'spanyels,' leaves the subject severely alone, and the very existence of such

## EARLY HISTORY

dogs had probably been revealed to her also by the perusal of a *Mayster of the Game* earlier than her own.

The story of Robert Dudley, Duke of Northumberland, being the first English trainer of a setting-dog, has probability on its side; as he lived at the period most likely for such an introduction. 'This Robert Dudley, born 1504, Duke of Northumberland, was a compleat Gent. in all suitable employments, an exact seaman, a good navigator, an excellent architect, mathematician, physician, chymist, and what not, and, above all, noted for riding the great horse, for tilting, and for his being the first of all that taught a dog to sit in order to catch partridges' (*Athenæ Oxonienses*, p. 127, vol. ii., by Anthony à Wood, 1721). Robert Dudley was first Earl of Warwick, and was made Duke of Northumberland by Edward VI. in 1551 (Hume's *History of England*, p. 280).

There appears to be a rival claimant in an Earl of Surrey, but he has no better case than the generality of such. 'We are vaguely informed that an Earl of Surrey was the first who taught the dog to stand at game; but which of these noblemen the writer has omitted to state' (*The Shooter's Preceptor*, by T. B. Johnson, p. 3).

In 1551 was published a natural history, *De Differentiis Animalium*, by an Englishman, Edward Wotton; but though he treated fully of dogs of various sorts, he did not know of spaniels, setting or otherwise. In fact, Dr. John Caius of Cambridge was the first to describe them in his *Englische Dogges* (1576). He tells of their method of working, and among the dogs that 'serve for fowling' recounts that 'there is also at this date among us a new kinde of dogge brought out of Fraunce, and they bee speckled all over with white and black, which mingled colours incline to a marble blewe.

# THE POINTER

These are called French dogs, as is above declared already' (p. 15).

Then, later, Louis XIII. sent over to James I. some setting-dogs as a present. For Chamberlain wrote to Carleton (1624): 'A French baron, a good falconer, has brought him [the King] 16 casts of Hawks from the French King, with horses and setting dogs; he made a splendid entry with his train by torch-light, and will stay till he has instructed some of our people in his kind of falconry, though it costs his Majesty 25*l.* or 30*l.* a day' (State Papers of James I., Domestic Series, vol. clviii., p. 149).

So, as our word spaniel is most probably of French origin, and our earliest treatise on setting-spaniels is borrowed in its entirety from the French; as the English author, who was the first to give his own ideas about them, avows that ' marble blewes' [nowadays called blue beltons] came from France; as afterwards all recorded importations were from France; and as there is no shadow of proof that any came from elsewhere, it seems pretty sure that the setting-spaniels, though originating in Spain, were from an early period naturalised in France, and conferred on us by the latter country.

In the preceding pages it has not been my object to trace to its remotest limits the history of the falcon-dogs, although that task would be an interesting one, as before the awakening of their pointing and setting instincts they do not concern the present investigation.

Now to revert to my main theme—the smooth-haired pointing-dog. But before I marshal all my evidence concerning him, I must remark that as regards his pedigree I have come to a conclusion similar to that of Buffon, who, in his *Quadrupèdes* (1777), has declared that the '*braques*' (pointing-dogs) and '*chiens courants*' (hounds) have descended from one and the same stock (p. 23).

# EARLY HISTORY

The first likeness of a pointing-dog that I have found is a pencil sketch of a head (Plate II.) by an Italian, Pisanello (1380–1456), which is supported by a painting (Plate III.) attributed to Titian (1477–1576), and by a picture by Bassano (1510–1592), at Madrid. The scene of this last is laid in the Garden of Eden; and here in a corner is a *bracco* staunchly pointing partridges, which, painted in all seriousness, shows that Bassano (an enthusiastic dog-lover) had never heard of a period without its partridge-dogs!

Spain as well as Italy gives indications of the antiquity of the pointing-dog, as the oldest writers advise crosses between him and the hound *to improve the latter*. From a fifteenth century MS. in the British Museum: 'I also had another dog, bred from a hound and a partridge-bitch (*perdiguera*), excellent on the leash and in following any kind of deer. He worked well in the sun, which I believe he got from the partridge-bitch, for these work hard in the heat, better than other dogs, and have very fine noses, for it takes a fine nose to find a partridge, especially in the woods' (*Tratado de Caza y Otros*, p. 12).

Again, from a sixteenth century MS. at Madrid:—

'*Silvano*. If any time we cannot find very pure-bred hounds, with what dogs can one cross them to have a good breed?

'*Montano*. From a pure-bred hound (*sabueso*) and a pointing-bitch (*perra de muestra*), each the purest of its race, light in body and wiry, and with a good nose' (*Dialogos de Monteria*, p. 472).

From these extracts it is clear that the partridge-dogs of Spain must have been an old-established, separate breed long before the fifteenth century, otherwise they could not have implanted in the hounds their own definite characteristics.

A study of those words that were used to de-

## THE POINTER

note both hounds and pointing-dogs will now be necessary.

The title of '*braque*' (spelt in a dozen different ways in French, '*bracco*' in Italian, '*braco*' in Spanish, and '*brach*' in English) is a word of high antiquity, used in olden times exclusively for hounds, then for both hounds and pointing-dogs, and finally, in those countries where it has survived, to describe the pointing-dog alone. Much the same transitions have also been passed through by the terms '*ventor*,' '*canis sagax*,' '*canis odorus*,' &c.

I find the first occurrence of the word 'brach' in an account of a mission from the Normans to William Rufus of England, by Robert Wace—a Norman poet of the twelfth century.

> 'In England was the King who had many Normans, many English;
> He had called for his hounds (*brachez*) he would go hunting in the woods.'
> (*Roman de Rou*, line 14,908.)

And again in an English romance-poem of the fourteenth century :—

> 'Braches bayed therfore, and breme noyse maked.'
> (*Sir Gawayne and the Green Knight*, line 1142.)

I quote these two instances of this term as the earliest in French and English respectively; but later it is very frequently found in the romances and works on sport of both languages. Shakespeare himself uses it several times in its primitive sense, *e.g.* 'the deep mouth'd brach' (*Taming the Shrew*, Induc.).

But the Italian '*bracco*' can call, besides Brunetto Latini, no less a witness than Dante (thirteenth century), and that in a passage of which the context makes it most probable that he referred to the pointing *bracco*—

## EARLY HISTORY

not to the hound. 'And here you must know that every quality characteristic of anything is admirable in that thing: for instance, in mankind to be well bearded, and in womankind to have the face quite smooth; in the *bracco* to have a good nose, and in the greyhound to run well. As a quality is the more characteristic, so is it the more admirable' ('*Convito*,' in the *Prose di Dante*, edited by G. Boccacci, 1723, p. 72).

England alone did not transform either 'brach or lym' (*King Lear*) into partridge-dogs; because once upon a time she lagged somewhat behind in sporting matters, and when she was ready for them there were the Continental breeds already started for her: thus the terms '*brach*' and '*lym*' faded out of the vernacular when the use of such old-fashioned hounds became obsolete.

Gesner (1516–1587) says of them: 'Some use the common name of brach (*bracchum*) to signify the wise and scenting dog (*canem sagacem et odorem*), others in other manners, as I have stated above, and shall relate further on about the swift dog (*cane veloci*),' &c. (*Historiæ Animalium*, p. 228). 'The kind of dog which in most places to-day is called brach (*braccham*), with long ears, blunt face (*crasso ore*), &c., about which I have written above among the wise and also swift (*sagaces simul ac celeres*), is useful for putting up birds' (*id.* p. 255).

Aldrovandi (1522–1607) is even more explicit as to the confusion caused by this word's general use:—
'Some call him *canis sagax, canis odorus;* Oppianus distinguishes him as *canis agaiæus*. He is commonly called *brachus*, as if from *brochus*, meaning with projecting teeth; because he has a blunt and prominent muzzle. These dogs are of many varieties: as some are for badgers, others for hares, others for birds, and

# THE POINTER

for water-fowl; but all are said to be *sagaces*' (*De Quadrupedibus*, lib. iii., cap. vi., p. 551).

Caterina Sforza (1481) uses the term '*bracco da astore*' (brach for the falcon), and Sforzino da Carcano (1547) writes of '*bracco*' in the same sense, in his book on Falconry (*Gli Uccelli da Rapina*).

Again, Biondo remarks 'concerning the species of the hunting-dog' that 'every dog that pursues wild animals is called a hunting-dog (*venaticus*), either a *sagax* or an *odorus*. But the dog is *odorus* or rather *odorificus*, that follows the scent of wild animals; on the other hand the *canis sagax* is the quester of them and of other animals' (*De Canibus*, p. xxvi.). 'Hunting (*venatio*) differs from fowling, as the latter is concerned with birds, and the former with woodland beasts' (*id.* p. xxv.). But in spite of these precise definitions, 'De Cane Odoro' heads his chapter on the pointing-dog, which is styled throughout by the same title (*id.* p. viii.).

In Spain even, the nomenclature of the sporting-dogs was no clearer, no less confused, than in the other countries. At much the same period wrote Argote de Molina (1532), Lope the poet (1562–1635), Juan Mateos (1634), and Espinar (1644); and yet how differently they define the *Ventor*!

'*Ventor* is the name of the hound of the leash, for finding by the trail. And he, having beaten the wood, finds the roused quarry, the huntsman having gone in by the marks of the track at the same time as the hound; then they loose a number of *ventores*, which follow the game, giving tongue. And another set of *ventores* is placed as a relay to help the first lot that are running the quarry, in order to relieve them. And those that enter afresh follow until they force the stag into the net, or to the spot where the grey-hounds are waiting, or they kill their quarry in the

# EARLY HISTORY

woods' (*Libro de la Monteria*, cap. xv., by Argote de Molina).

'Meeting of Panfilo and Finea.' 'There they stood, the two of them motionless, just like the foolish partridge and the clever *ventor*' (*El peregrino en su patria*, by Lope Felix de Vega Carpio, book v., p. 246).

'Those dogs are called *ventores* that are let loose, before the commencement of the hunt, that they may find the game and make known where it lies, before it is roused' (*Origin y Dignidad de la Caza*, by Juan Mateos, p. 120).

In his *Arte de Ballesteria*, Espinar writes of a 'hound ventor' (*un sabueso ventor*) (vol. ii. p. 152), to be used when hunting the wild boar, while pointing-dogs he also styles *ventores* (vol. iii., p. 242), in agreement with Lope.

Even the word '*navarro*,' applied in modern times only to a partridge-dog of Navarre, was first of all the title of a breed of hound. Espinar says in his book (p. 58):—'There are others [varieties of the dog] that are called hounds, and of them there are two kinds; some of less activity than the others, because they are much heavier. These are called Navarrese or French, because the breed is from France, as it is of the Frisons; they have the head large, the muzzle blunt, the ears very long and broad, and are very heavy everywhere; they are by nature headstrong, and easily tired, although of excellent nose and scenting powers.' He goes on to contrast them with the Spanish hounds, which were much lighter and more active, were very persistent and untiring at their work, and had fair noses. Thus there were two types of hound in Spain, from which apparently sprang two types of pointing-dog. The one the heavy, 'barrel-shaped' Navarrese partridge-dog, painted by Velazquez (Plate IV.), and by Espinosa; the other, as described by Espinar, 'so swift that they seem to fly

## THE POINTER

over the ground,' and, as in *Dialogos de la Monteria,* 'very fast so that they cover much ground.' It was evidently the *navarro* that first found his way to England; and, according to the old accounts, his powers, both for good and evil, were not impaired by the journey.

I have now sufficiently exemplified how in the days of their infancy the pointing-dogs were spoken of everywhere by the name of some hound or other, and how the same author would frequently call hounds and pointing-dogs by the same title—almost on the same page. It remains to show how little would have been required to change the French '*limier,*' which in English would be called 'lymer' or 'leash-hound,' into a pointing-dog. To avoid prolixity, I will take the French descriptions as typical: they are perhaps the clearest, but similar definitions occur also in the books of other languages.

'*Limiers* — dogs that are mute' (*La Vénerie,* by Jacques du Fouilloux, 1561, '*Recueil des Mots*' in the edition of 1888). 'It is better that he carry his head high than low, because he will judge his wolf more correctly' (*id.* p. 91).

Jean de Clamorgan (1570) confirms Du Fouilloux's pronouncements, almost word for word.

'The *limier* is a questing dog (*querant ou quêtant*)' (*Traitté fort curieux de la Venérie,* by Antoine Pomey, 1676, p. 30).

'The *limier* must work to the hand, and must be perfectly mute' (*Traité de Vénerie et de Chasse,* by M. d'Yanville, 1788, p. 213).

From this catalogue of the lymer's qualities it would seem almost a matter of indifference whether he were broken for the wolf, the stag, or the partridge!

Now having sufficiently treated the etymological side of the subject to show the filial relationship of the

# EARLY HISTORY

pointing-dog to the hound, we will leave it to du Fouilloux picturesquely to taper off their ancestry into those far-away times when prose blends with poetry, and reality pales into romance. He cites, from *Joannes Monumentensis*, that Æneas after the destruction of Troy wandered to Italy with his son Ascanius, who begot Silvius, who begot Brutus, who killed his father out hunting and had to fly to Greece. Thence with companions and a great number of hounds and greyhounds (*chiens courants et lévriers*) he sailed away through the straits of Gibraltar, and landed at the Isles Armoriques, to-day called Brittany; and here Brutus and his son Turnus, after seizing the country without resistance, hunted in the great forests that extended from Tiffauge to Poictiers: from Turnus did the town of Tours derive its name. Our author continues:—' I have been anxious to tell this story that it may be understood for how long a time hounds have been used in Brittany, and I positively believe that these Trojans were the first to bring the breed of them into this country, because I do not find any history that pretends to an earlier knowledge of them. And it is a thing assured that most of the hounds that are in France and the surrounding countries are derived from Brittany, excepting the white dogs (*chiens blancs*), the ancestors of which I fancy came from Barbary; Phébus agrees with this opinion' (*La Vénerie*, p. 1). Ah, well! Æneas—Troy! 'Tis far enough! So now, having firmly rooted him in antiquity, the after-career of the pointing-dog as he drew nearer England must be studied, until his subsequent evolution into the POINTER.

In the fifteenth century the Italian pointing-dogs were not only highly esteemed in their own country, but were also famous abroad.

Caterina Sforza, writing on August 16th, 1481, to

# THE POINTER

the Duchess of Ferrara a letter entirely taken up with sporting-dogs, specimens of which she craved as a present, desired among others 'a pair of good hounds (*segusi*), and a pair of good brachs for the falcon (*bracchi da astore*).'—*Modena, Archivio di Stato*. And about the same time the French were importing *braques* from Italy, as we find in the *Traité de Vénerie* (1783) by M. d'Yanville, that 'Louis XII. had an Italian brach bitch covered by one of these latter [white dogs of St. Hubert]; these newly invented dogs were called *chiens greffiers* (clerks' dogs), because the bitch belonged to one of the secretaries of the King, who then were called *greffiers*' (p. 205). Evidently the same bitch is referred to more explicitly in the following passage :—' The earliest mention of this race [the *braque*] that we find is that of the Italian bitch, Baude; which about 1480 was crossed with a white St. Hubert Dog' (*Traité pratique du Chien*, by A. Gobin, 1867, p. 96). 'The *braque* of Italy was white—Baude was of this colour' (*ib.*). I have heard too that after his captivity François I. took back with him from Lombardy eighty sporting-dogs; but as I have not been lucky enough to verify this, I only give it as rumour.

About this time, moreover, even Spain herself did not disdain to borrow from Italy, as witness the following concerning the renowned partridge-dogs of Gorga :—

'In this part of Spain (Valencia) there are no pure-bred sporting native dogs of any kind. The famous breed that existed here for three centuries—the *Gorgas* —so called from the little coast town of that name near Denia, where they were raised—are now extinct or so crossed by inferior breeds as to be indistinguishable. They were nearly pure white, and much lighter than the old cylindrical Navarrese dog. They were noted for their gentleness, and fineness of nose, but

# EARLY HISTORY

were wanting in backbone for rough work. Tradition says they were of foreign origin, the first pair being presented by an Italian prince, a Count of Gorga. The fact that they first came into notice in an unimportant coast town gives colour to the tradition that they were not of Spanish origin' (Extract from letter of J. L. Byrne, U.S.A. Vice-Consul at Valencia, October 28th, 1900).

But doubtless the French were the chief admirers of the Italian *braque*, called in the sixteenth century *cane da rete*, dog of the net (*I quattro libri della Caccia*, by Giovanni Scandianese, 1556, p. 69), and his popularity with them is evidenced by their having adopted his name, which was easily recast and converted into their idiom as *chien d'arrêt* (literally, stop-dog), which term assuredly did not exist in France before the seventeenth century. And after a time, though the heavier type of their own and the Navarrese brach still survived, it was quite eclipsed by the beautiful and racing-like Italian dogs with which Louis XIV. and Louis XV. filled their kennels, and that Desportes and Oudry vied with each other in painting with such truth and skill. 'The *braques* that Desportes and Oudry have handed down to posterity in their paintings, and that belonged to the Kings of France, were probably descended from the fawn-and-white brach of Italy' (*Les chiens d'arrêt français et anglais*, by MM. De la Rue and De Cherville, 1881, p. 15). The old French *braque* of native origin did not achieve popularity till considerably later; for I gather from *Les Races de Chiens*, by M. Megnin, that this dog is called the *Braque* of Charles X.; and I have no evidence to show that he had any ancestral share in producing the English pointer.

Of the pictures by Desportes and Oudry in the Louvre I had to limit my selection to two, one by each

# THE POINTER

artist (Plates V. and VI.), which, where so many were typical, was an ungrateful task. Among those I especially regret is a portrait of Tane, a practically white bitch, black-nosed—and of the highest quality. But Plate V. has an interest quite apart from its external charm, because it is dated 1720, according to the Louvre Official Catalogue. Now this is just five years before the date on the Thoresby picture by Tillemans (see Redgrave's *Dictionary of Artists*). This last (Frontispiece) is of the Duke of Kingston and his pointers, and is, I believe, the earliest record of the Race that has ever existed in England. All of these pointers are pronouncedly of the elegant Franco-Italian type, which is not remarkable considering the Duke was constantly in France, lived with a French mistress, and had for his intimate friend the Comte de Buffon, the eminent naturalist. But it must not be assumed that the first importation of pointing-dogs into England was from France, for etymology cries aloud against this. It reveals that the word pointer is a corruption of the Spanish *de punta*, and that our new word was to us as easy and appropriate as even their witty *chien d'arrêt* to our neighbours. It also insists that the Spanish partridge-dog, unlike the spaniel, was not introduced to us *viâ* France, because the name *pointer* belongs only to Spain and England. And there is additional proof of this successful 'Spanish Invasion' in the favourite old names of English dogs—in the numberless Dons, Sanchos, &c., and more especially in Pero, an evident derivative from *Perro*, the Spanish for dog.

Again, at first the Pointer was called in England the *Spanish Pointer;* for instance, in the earliest notice of him that I have found :—

'The Spanish Pointer is esteemed the incomparable, and even without teaching will point naturally at a

# EARLY HISTORY

partridge ; and, as he is large, will range well and stand high enough to appear above any high stubble ; and yet one may breed him to stand till a net be drawn over him ; but 'tis hard to do. However, when he points, you may be sure of birds within gun-shot' (*The Gentleman Farrier*, 1732, p. 105).

The above is the only sentence in the book relating to the pointer; and I think it shows, from its scantiness and caution, how new and unfamiliar the dog was to the writer. But it is not on style I shall rely to show the date of the pointer's introduction, so much as on hard facts. And first I will cite some apposite statements :—

'The pointer was not known until after the introduction of shooting flying, somewhere about the beginning of the last century. They first began to be generally known in England about the period of the celebrated Mordaunt Earl of Peterborough's campaigns in Spain. This is certain' (*Sporting Magazine*, second series, vol. v., 1832). These campaigns continued from 1705 to 1707, but not till the Peace of Utrecht, in 1713, was the war brought to a termination.

'The Spanish pointer was introduced into this country by a Portugal merchant at a very modern period, and was first used by an old reduced baron of the name of Bichell, who lived in Norfolk and could shoot flying ; indeed, he seems to have lived by his gun, as the game he killed was sold in the London market. This valuable acquisition from the Continent was wholly unknown to our ancestors, together with the art of shooting flying' (*Cynographia Britannica*, by Sydenham Edwards, 1800, p. 1). It is noteworthy that Mr. Edwards connects the introduction of the pointer with that of shooting flying.

'Pointers.—As nothing has yet been published on these dogs (at least that I have met with), I am inclined

## THE POINTER

to think that they were originally brought from other countries, though now very common in England. Their great utility and excellence in shooting partridges, moor or heath-game, which make them worthy of our regard, are well known' (*The Art of Shooting Flying*, by T. Page, 1767, p. 80). Mr. Page was a very well-known gunmaker, and his statement, made when the middle of the century was long past, that he had not met with any work dealing with pointers, is interesting as evidence of the barrenness of the eighteenth century as regards books on this kind of sport.

'The Pointer.—This kind of dog was introduced here in the beginning of the present century; and is acknowledged to be a native of Spain or Portugal; as many were, and yet are, brought to us from both kingdoms. The first I remember to have seen was about forty years back' (*A Treatise on Field Diversions*, by H. Symonds, 1776, p. 14). This is the direct statement of an educated gentleman and noted sportsman; and so it is of great value, when taken in connection with the other proofs.

Thomas Pennant, the naturalist, writing in 1766, was evidently himself unfamiliar with the Spaniard, as he sums him up in the following fourteen words:—
'The Pointer, which is a dog of foreign extraction, was unknown to our ancestors' (*British Zoology*, p. 26).

I will give one more quotation on this theme, because in spite of its vagueness and pessimism it contains a slightly divergent view.

'No traces remain of the date of such importation from Spain, or of how long pointing-dogs, as distinguished from setters, have been used by English gunners. Two centuries have been nominated as this period, the accuracy of which we much doubt, having been informed, or having read somewhere, that the pointer cannot be traced in England beyond the Revo-

# EARLY HISTORY

lution in 1688. Perhaps Spanish pointers may have formerly been imported into this country, although no man, nor any book, can furnish us with the *how*, the *when*, or the *where*' (*The Sportsman's Repository*, by R. Lawrence, V. S., 1820, p. 115).

Now, the *School of Recreation*, by Robert Howlitt (1684); *The Gentleman's Recreation*, by Nicholas Cox (1686); *Gentleman's Recreation*, by Richard Blome (1686); *Synopsis Animalium*, by John Ray (1693); and *The Compleat Sportsman*, by Giles Jacob (1718)—are all silent about the pointer, though many of them treat exhaustively of the other sporting dogs, and shooting. And it is a remarkable fact that *The Sportsman's Dictionary* (1735), which Osbaldiston, years afterwards, thought worthy to crib from, does not mention the pointer, though a dictionary most full in its definitions of all other sporting dogs. It gives a plate of a setter setting some partridges, and two sportsmen about to have a shot at them on the ground; but it does not in the letterpress name such a sport as shooting partridges *over* a dog, although there are elaborate instructions as to netting these birds with a setter, and shooting wild-duck with guns. So I judge that the plates must have been introduced after the book was written; and in that case, they only testify to a desire on the part of an energetic publisher to keep up-to-date.

I have now stated all my evidence about the advent of the pointer, and will proceed to sum it up. The entire silence of all authors up to the close of the seventeenth century would alone be enough to justify the hypothesis that the pointer was unknown in England before the eighteenth century, but when this silence is corroborated by the opinion of eighteenth century sporting writers in general, by Mr. Symonds' direct statement in particular, and by the inherent

# THE POINTER

testimony of the *Sportsman's Dictionary* that even in 1735 this dog was not widely known, supposition hardens into certainty. The assertion, therefore, seems justified that 1700 is the earliest possible date for the introduction into England of the pointing-dog ; while 1725, the date of the Duke of Kingston's picture of French pointing-dogs, of course determines the latest : there is also etymological proof that the pointers were not imported first from France, so that epoch clearly lies between 1725 and 1700. A lucky clue is Quartogenarian's ' certain ' declaration that pointer-dogs were heard of first in England about the time of Lord Peterborough's campaigns in Spain. The English commenced the War of the Spanish Succession in 1704, but Lord Peterborough was recalled in 1706. It is not likely that he himself took any dogs back with him, because he was not a sportsman, because he went home by way of Italy, Austria, and Germany, taking a year over the journey, and because he left in disgrace. But by the Peace of Utrecht the war was terminated in 1713, and the British army returned to England. Now, nothing could be more natural than for the British officers to carry away with them specimens of the wonderful pointing-dogs from the country in which they had spent nearly nine years. It is also intelligible enough how this importation should have escaped the notice of the chroniclers, amid the stir and bustle caused by the return of an entire army.

If they carefully consider the evidence, I believe my readers will be of one opinion with me as to the pointing-dog having first arrived in England with the returning soldiers after the Peace of Utrecht ; for, though many of the arguments are inductive, and much of the evidence is circumstantial, they are none the less irresistible, so neatly do the parts of the puzzle dovetail into one another.

# EARLY HISTORY

By the establishment of the setting-dogs and pointing-dogs in the British Isles, after their slow drift thither, much has been accomplished; but before the present chapter can be deemed in any way exhaustive, the salient points concerning the sport with which these dogs were associated, their characteristics, and their status in their native countries before this event must have been at least indicated.

I have found in many languages treatises on the working of pointing-dogs, all interesting, some excellent; space alone forbids me from transcribing them all. But in Spain there are two masterpieces of fowling lore, aglow with the eternal youth of genius, as fresh and instructive to-day as on the day they were written: these I make no apology for presenting at fullest length in this book. I found them quite easy to translate literally, as in the majority of cases the old Spanish sporting idioms are identical with our own; but it must be borne in mind that the cross-bow was the weapon employed, so that the partridge had not only to be seen on the ground, but also shot there.

*Dialogos de la Monteria*, anonymous MS., sixteenth century:—

'The most noble way, and the best sport that exists, is to kill them [partridges] over pointing-dogs (*perros de muestra*), which is done in the following manner:—As the partridges have to be found by the powers of the dog, which cannot come across them so well by sight or hearing as by smelling, the first thing the sportsman must do, on reaching the shooting-ground, is to note the direction of the wind, and, having got it in his face, seek the birds thus from haunt to haunt. On reaching the first haunt he should look for the highest point, and may make a start there, holding up the dog and making him keep on crossing the wind; and the common terms for telling him what

## THE POINTER

he has to do are—try here! back here! go there! try up! try down! calling him by his name. After having beaten that haunt, he must move on to another, always seizing on the highest point, so that he will be better able to see the partridges drop, or fold the wing in settling. He should hunt his dog by whistling to him whenever he is among game, rather than by calling to him, and so avoid the noise that always disturbs it much. When the dog comes upon the partridges on the feed, that is before they have been flushed, as soon as the dog finds them and is on the point the sportsman must walk quickly to make his round of scrutiny, with the curve rather wide at its commencement, but gradually narrowing until he reaches the "circle" or point (*vuelta ó punta*) of the dog; that is to say, the sportsman must get directly opposite the place to which the head of the dog is turned in pointing, for this is where the game generally is found, and in this manner he will lull the game so that he could shoot at it many times if he wanted to; and going on he will all the while diminish his circles, watching the spot to which the dog's head is turned, ready to get a shot at the game, for there it will most likely be. And always when rounding them on the feed, the closer he keeps to where the dog is standing the less likely he will be to stumble upon a bird that has separated from the rest; and, if such a one flies away, the rest are wont to follow. So to have no fear of this mishap, it will be necessary for him to light upon them within shot of the spot where he faces the point of the dog, as if he go on further he will probably flush the covey. Finally, let him by all means make his shot before he completes the whole circle, for on the feed before being flushed they lie badly.

'*Sil:* How is one to know, after having killed the partridge, if it be a single bird?

# EARLY HISTORY

'*Mon:* By the way in which the dog holds his head—if drawn in and sharply inclined, his partridge is close by, but if outstretched, the contrary. If this is a chance point, by which is meant that the dog stops himself suddenly when he is going fast and hunting freely without having a notion of a partridge nor of its scent, but all carelessly as he is going gets a whiff and becomes rigid, the sportsman must not only scrutinise that place at which the dog is pointing, but also all round about him, if he does not see the partridge where the dog first points. The usual reason for the dog pointing with so little certainty is that he stops at the warmth of the partridge, by which is meant the scent that reaches him from the place where the partridge was sitting, and, as it has shifted though it may still be near by, he does not point where it now is, but where it was at first,—and this is why he does not point with certainty, why it is so difficult for the sportsman to see the bird. Note also that if the day be still and fine the birds will usually be in the shade of thick cover, thinking to be better hidden; and if the ground be wet, especially if the day be threatening, they are usually to be found in very thin cover half-squatting, neither nestling down nor quite standing, to avoid the cold of the damp ground. If it rain ever so little, they seek open ground, but near some cover; and very often though they may be on foot, on that account they will wait longer on such days, although they are easy to see.

'*Sil:* And when they are flushed, what should the sportsman do?

'*Mon:* The first thing is to count them mentally as they fly, for they seldom go so fast or so close together that this cannot be done; and, as they fly, if the ground be not open enough to see them settle, he must watch and carefully notice the direction of their

## THE POINTER

flight, and then he will see them fold up the wing on one side of their line of flight, where they intend to settle. By this sign, and the distance of the place from where they rose to where they folded the wing, and the lie of the country, he will easily perceive where they have dropped within fifty paces more or less, taking into consideration whether they are young, when they fly but little, or old, when they fly a long way. When he starts to find them, he should always hunt the dog up wind, making him quarter to the leeward of them; and if, as may happen, the wind blow unfortunately for where the birds flew, let him go round on one side, so that when he enters the place where they dropped, it may be nose towards the wind. Then let him stand quiet at the spot where he can best see to shoot, until it have been well tried and every bird accounted for according to the number he counted when they rose. If he have a comrade, it is very important to place him to mark where the partridges fly and drop, for it will make it much easier for him to find them, and he will bag much more game. If ever the dog disappear and do not return quickly at call, let the sportsman follow in the track of the dog so as not to stumble on the partridges and flush them, and let him not take one step in the place where they dropped, unless the dog have first been over it. And if the game be not lying well, it is the proper thing not to speak to the dog, but only to give him a whistle, at which he will turn his head and look to see what is wanted, and let the sportsman sign with his hand to that part he wants beaten, and if the dog be what he ought, with that he will obey him. Again, when the dog is pointing partridges already flushed, which are those that lie best though they are the most difficult to see, it is necessary, in order to see them sooner and to have a better hope of them, not to wait to make the first

# EARLY HISTORY

half-circle broad, as we enjoined in rounding them on the feed, but to come straight up to that place where the dog is standing. But it goes without saying that one must find the partridge according to the nature of the cover in which the dog stands at point; and as he generally points in such thick stuff that the partridge cannot be seen except through some tiny hole, it is well, before getting alongside of him, to take short steps, because the sportsman may not happen to see the bird before he already approaches the end of the path (*rencera*) where he ought to have discovered and shot at it. As this cannot sometimes be avoided, let him not turn back, for this repetition would put up the partridge; but let him go forward and complete his round, returning quickly, and before he comes to the opening where he saw the bird, let him have his crossbow ready (*vuelva emballestando*) and shoot at it; and, when he may have to stop to shoot it, let him take short, quiet steps, for if he go fast the noise that he is making will flush the partridge when he stops to shoot at it.

'*Sil*: If in thin cover he see the game disturbed and about to rise, what must the sportsman do to quiet it down?

'*Mon*: He must disguise his head in some sort with a piece of the cover itself that the partridge may not see him making ready the crossbow and stopping to shoot it; for with this precaution he will be able with certainty to get a shot, and it will not rise, because it thinks he is continuing his walk and does not wish to molest it.

'*Sil*: And if he be in some leafless (*tamarosa*) place, where he can find nothing to cover his head with?

'*Mon*: Let him make his round well away from the part towards which the bird is facing, and approach in

## THE POINTER

the direction of its tail until he finds himself within range, and thus the partridge will lie for him.

'*Sil:* What must the sportsman do to see the game more easily, as well on open ground as in woodland?

'*Mon:* He must take care when he makes his round in search, not to spoil his sight by spreading it over the whole of the cover, but to keep it always concentrated and fixed upon one spot, for so his sight will have more strength; and when he has scrutinised that spot let him pass on to another, and so on as he makes his round, and in this way he will see the game more certainly and quickly; for there are two drawbacks in glancing here and there:—one is that he will often see the game without recognising it, and the other is that his eyes will fill with water, what with the wind, and his anxiety, and the annoyance at not seeing the game quickly enough.

'*Sil:* If the point be made on a rather steep hillside, what must be done that the game may lie better?

'*Mon:* Carefully avoid facing the dog at the highest point on your round; because, as you approach, the bird will rise to a certainty, as it greatly dreads any one being on higher ground, although from below it may be approached quite near enough to see and shoot it.

'*Sil:* All this that you have said seems to be concerning the dog that points (*perro de punta*). But if it be the sign (*muestra*) of the dog that circles (*perro de vuelta*), what method should we follow to perceive it at once? For it is usually very difficult to see, and I should like to know the reason why.

'*Mon:* The reason of it is that, as you have heard, the dog generally points with his nose to the wind, and, if he be a "circler," when his nose tells him that the bird is disturbed, he fears that it will run up-wind to escape from him, so he leaves his point and makes a

## EARLY HISTORY

detour, and when he gets to windward he points it again to baulk it of the tendency it had shown of escaping in that direction; and as he stands pointing down-wind at the partridge, he does it with great difficulty and uncertainty because he is without the sense of smell, which he has need of to point with certainty. Therefore, in order to see the bird quickly, one should not take heed of the direction in which the dog at first pointed, unless, when he goes rounding it and is right for the scent of the partridge, he indicates it with his eye, and continues his round; and then the sportsman must note the spot at which the dog glanced, for there without doubt will it be. And if this be a district where partridges are hawked, you should put on the dog a little bell which will sound like that of the hawks, for, fearing that it may be one, the game will as a rule lie better; and if it be not such, but a land of herds, a small bell, such as the cattle wear, is better.

'*Sil:* Is there anything further to say concerning this kind of sport?

'*Mon:* Nothing, except that you may know that if the partridges or other game be very wild and the day very boisterous, with rain and a south-west wind blowing, no hawk-bell or cattle-bell should be put on the dog; nor can you do more than hunt with all possible silence, whistling, and beckoning, and thinking, if you possess mind enough, of every stratagem' (p. 366, *et seq.*).

'*Mon:* He [the pointing-dog] must be so keen-scented that he can make many points with little trouble to himself and the sportsman; for, if his nose be short, he will make but few, and of those he does make most will be face to face, and therefore the game will lie badly—a great drawback, especially during summer, when the scent of the partridge is less, because

## THE POINTER

those three months the various odours of the woods are so penetrating that they overwhelm it. He must be very fast, so that with little trouble to the sportsman he may get over much ground, and find the game that he would not have found had he been slow, as then the sportsman would have had double labour, for he would have been obliged to accompany the dog in his casts up and down. But if the dog be such as I have approved, all this will be avoided, for the sportsman may stand still and hold up the dog, who will range over much ground. He must be well broken for this purpose, as otherwise he will not properly understand the ground, nor will he find much game; and what he does find will not lie, for the sportsman will be obliged to shout to him so often to make him beat the haunts that it will frighten and disturb the game. He must be a "circler" (*de vuelta*) if the ground be open, so that his going round may make the game lie better, but if it be wooded he should be a pointer (*perro de punta*). For there are two drawbacks to his being a circler : one is that it is very difficult to see the game, the dog's point being so uncertain, and the other is that very often in going round one bird he stumbles over others, especially if they are in coveys. He must have hard feet, that he may not get footsore, and he must be very wise in making out (*sacar*) the partridge after coming upon the line of one.

'*Sil:* What do you mean by making out the partridge?

'*Mon:* The dogs do this in three different ways. One is by never raising their noses from the foot-scent until they find the bird, and it is pretty sure to be flushed by this manner of making it out, especially if it has run down-wind, for then the dog, having to follow it with the wind at his back, cannot go with certainty, and runs it up. Another way of making out the

## EARLY HISTORY

partridge is sometimes to follow the foot-scent and sometimes to raise the nose, and this is a better and safer way of finding it with certainty. The last of the three ways is for the dog, as soon as he touches on the foot-scent, to go right away and make a wide circle, breaking away from foot-scents, until he gets round the partridge; then he goes in, with his nose to the wind, until he finds and points it, and this is the best and surest way of all. He must be also an insatiable glutton for work, for if he be lacking in this he lacks everything, as a good one is of all sporting dogs the hardest worker, so much so that he will sometimes pass blood. He must be in good condition to endure hard work, because he never says "no," however tired he may be, but the sportsman must not for that reason be sparing of punishment, so that he may not disobey. He must likewise carry his head high and freely, that he may the more be lord of the air, and the less a flusher of game. He must be light and sinewy in order to feel the heat less, and have strong bone to stand the work. His feet should be greyhound-like (*galgarenas*) and sinewy, so that he will not get footsore. If she be a female, the nose will last longer in good order, for in littering she will be purged and cleared of all bad humours; but for the males, who lack this remedy, we use an artificial purge that serves for all sporting-dogs alike. . . .

'*Sil:* In what kind of dogs will be found those points that you say they must have?

'*Mon:* In dogs of medium size, for the large ones are lazy and the small ones weak; and they are difficult to see in the fields unless they are white, which is the useful colour; moreover, the dogs of Gothic blood (*agoscados*) have more genius (*instinto*) than those of Navarre (*navarros*), but they have more vices and are more ill-conditioned, though they do more work, but

# THE POINTER

the *navarros* have the better noses and better tempers. If a *navarro* dog be put to an *agozcada* bitch, a wonderfully good breed of dogs is the result, for they have the good qualities of both parents. But you must not put your dog to a bitch of a bad stock on either side, nor brother to sister, nor mother to son. These dogs are reared tractable, domesticated, and obedient from pups, and the owner or sportsman must not correct their faults, but some other members of the household, so that they may love and obey him. From the time they are six months old they are taught to find bread, and that they may learn better they are to be turned out of the house, and, when not being taught, kept chained up, that they may be more eager to go out; and let them be rather hungry, that necessity may urge them to find the bread. Throw the bread without letting the dog see where, then set him with his nose up-wind, talking to him and teaching him to understand by: Come here! try again! go there! cast about! come and seek and take! The first day let him eat the bread without punishing him, and afterwards repeat to him the aforesaid words, and if he go into the bread let the punishment be very slight, for if it be severe he will be so frightened that he will never obey afterwards. In this way you may teach him to point, and in accustoming him to that, make him take a circle as he must do later for the partridge, then stop him and snap your fingers, at which sign let him go in and take the bread. When the dog is nine months old and upwards, take him into the field and try him at partridges in the same manner as at the bread; and if he be so unruly that, in spite of punishment, he flushes the partridge without pointing, then fasten a long cord round his neck, and try him with a tame partridge, first tying it in a thicket where he cannot see it. Then give him the wind, and let him go, warning him in the words aforesaid until you have made him point it. But this partridge must be kept in a cage, and placed by itself in the dew at night, that the freshness may remove any scent of the sportsman having approached it; and afterwards, when you tie it in the thicket, do not touch it with your hands, for if you handle it the dog will not care about going near it, or take any notice of it till you make him point it. Give him the intestines of the bird, and for any faults he may commit do not flog him to excess, especially about the ears, for it sometimes makes them grow deaf, and instruct him by this method until he understands. If you wish him to be a circler, in teaching him when young with the bread, you should tie round his neck a cord two lines in length, fastening the other end to a stake, then place the bread where he cannot reach it though it is near, then speak to him, saying Go seek! and he will go round and round in a wide circle, and will get the habit of doing so, and will do it in the case of partridges. If when you make him find the bread you place it in the niches of the walls, about half way up, he will get the habit of raising his head more freely at work later on, and if you break him on young partridges you will train him sooner, because they lie better; but do not break him on quails, for that will teach him to point very near. When the partridge-dog is hunting for partridges he is wont to keep on always wagging his tail with the pleasure and gladness that he feels, and if he has not got a tail he makes this movement with his haunches, and thus becomes sooner tired. To avoid this, therefore, it is well to leave it long enough for him not to lack means of showing his content' (*id.* p. 467, *et seq.*).

And of an importance equal to the foregoing *Dialogos* is the *Arte de Ballesteria y Monteria*, by Alonzo Martinez de Espinar, 1644:—

'They [partridges] are shot on the wing with an

# THE POINTER

arquebuse, and for that reason they do not exist in such numbers as formerly, nor are there any longer such pointing-dogs (*perros de muestra*) to find them and point them with cleverness so great that large quantities of them could be killed with a crossbow. In those days the sportsmen were most dexterous, now such are wanting; for, as the game is killed more easily, nobody wishes to waste his time in training dogs, as the man has not to shoot the partridges on the ground; and the only use he has for dogs is to flush the game, and that takes no training, as the dog does it naturally. However, that this sport, which was so much practised in old times, may not be altogether forgotten, and as it has some excellencies that the curious will take pleasure in knowing, the following chapter will treat of it.

'Among the numerous methods for killing partridges, that which seems as a rule most congenial to the sportsman is to watch the efforts of a dog to find them, for this animal is the hardest of workers, and so good are his wind and activity that from morning to night he will not cease galloping, and there are some so swift that they seem to fly over the ground: and when the dog is lucky in coming across the scent of these birds, he redoubles his efforts till he points them, which is what his master desires. Of old it was by the instrumentality of the pointing-dog that most of the partridges were killed: in those days the sport was practised with the address that it demands, which cannot be acquired thoroughly without continual practice, but, without that trouble, the information in this chapter will be of advantage to any one interested. One cannot be too attentive to the education of pointing-dogs from the beginning of their breaking, because, as they have to work independently, it is necessary to train them while they are young.

'The first thing that they must be taught, is to be

# EARLY HISTORY

under such command that they will come as readily to their master for punishment as for caresses, for when they have learned obedience any faults they may have can be easily corrected; and much will depend on a knowledge of their natural dispositions, as some will obey with only chiding them, while others not even punishment will improve; and, therefore, it is necessary to know how it has to be given, much or little, and at what time. This groundwork should be taught them before taking them out to the field; and at home do not punish the dog severely for a trifling fault, for fear of cowing him for the future; and, granted the necessity, it must be first tried if he will obey orders by scolding him, but if that be not enough, he must be chastised into obedience.

'On taking them to the field, one gets to know what they are, and whether they tend to seek the partridges by the foot-scent or by the body-scent (*por el rastro, ó por el viento*). I do not recommend taking the trouble to teach those that have little pace and nose; because, even if the sportsman be very clever, he will not get much good from a dog that fails in these two important qualities. Above all it must be insisted that they quest the partridges more by the body-scent than by the foot-scent, hunting them at first up-wind (*pico á viento*) that they may become body-scenters (*ventores*) and not trackers (*rastreros*): for there is a great difference between these two ways of seeking the birds.

'The slow dog with a bad nose can only hunt by the track, and when he loses the track he has not nose enough to find the game in the other way, and, again, his usefulness is much lessened by his want of speed. The dogs that have these so necessary and excellent qualities work much better in every way; if they chance on the line of a partridge down-wind (*rabo á viento*),

## THE POINTER

they leave it at once, and, beating for the wind (*abarcando*) and circling up and down in all directions, try from different places if the trail goes on or stops, until they succeed in finding what they seek. But for this a good sportsman is necessary, as young dogs are always more inclined for foot than body-scent, and if they were allowed they would follow that inclination. But if, when the sportsman sees that the dog is touching on a line down-wind and is following it, he order him to leave it and come away, on four successive occasions, and the dog recognise that he can find by the body-scent the partridge that he was tracking, he will make use of that power for the future without his master's command, and will evermore remain with that method of questing : but if there be no one to teach him, up-wind and down-wind alike he will follow the partridge by the foot-scent.

'The sportsman should also know when the dog makes a fault, when he must be punished, and of what degree this punishment must be, so as not to punish him in the same degree for all his errors ; as on one occasion he deserves much for flushing the partridge ; and at others, though having flushed it, one must not punish him with full severity. When the dog, going up-wind, does not attack the partridge, but it rises because it will not lie to him, the dog may be to blame for getting too near it ; for this he must be corrected, but it is enough to pull him by the ears, saying to him : Have a care ! for the dog's intention was to point the partridge, but by inclining to go too close, he flushed it ; still, in order that another time he may not approach too close, he must be corrected. But when the dog, going up-wind and knowing where the game is, unceremoniously springs it by running it up, he must be severely punished, as that is the worst fault he can be guilty of, and proportionate must be the

# EARLY HISTORY

punishment. But if the sportsman do not know how or when to administer it judiciously there will result a thousand vices, for which he himself will be to blame; and there are some so wanting in intelligence that when the dog is going down-wind, and, without having the scent of the partridge, suddenly comes across and flushes the bird, they will almost beat him to death, though it was not the fault of the dog; and as this injustice is done to him and he does not know why, he will have no confidence in hunting either up-wind or down, not knowing the wrong from the right, often running away from his master, being unwilling to range when he is told, and only doing so when he chooses; and having arrived at pointing the partridges, when he sees the shooting approaching, he comes to heel from fear, leaving his point, which is as if it had never been made. That these animals may not contract this vice, the sportsman has need of wisdom in punishing his dogs according to their dispositions rather than according to the fault they committed, and in the beginning he must always be sparing of punishment; as it is well to accustom them beforehand to kindness, not severity, that they may not behave as I have described. For it is much better in ridding the dog of a fault to correct him thrice than to frighten him once.

'Partridges lie much better to the dog that finds them not by foot-scent but by body-scent, and measures his distance by their tameness or wildness, for he can tell by the body-scent if they are restless or tranquil, and even if he get among them, they are not sure that he is after them. When, however, he goes by foot-scent, what terrifies them is to see the dog following the track by which they have gone to hide, and if he do this down-wind, very probably he will stumble on them. And even if sometimes he point the partridges, there is no certainty in it; because the dog, not working

## THE POINTER

up-wind, is forced to point where he is sure of the scent, and as a rule that is very close, and therefore they do not wait for him.

'Formerly when this sport was practised, the dogs were very clever and the men very scientific about it, and he who prided himself on being a sportsman shot over a dog so well trained that, as the saying is, he could do everything but speak ; and those that kept their dogs in food by the crossbow were always the most eminent, as the skill of the sportsman and his dog had to make up for the deficiencies of the weapon. For in order to shoot the partridge when pointed, it had to be in a place where it could be seen and no rough stuff interfered with the aim : so, when the dog pointed where there were not these advantages, if skill in any way could help the attainment of his wish, it was certain that the sportsman would not fail, but he who was not skilful would be unsuccessful. Three requisites there were, all being essential and of the highest utility : a good sight ; when the dog was pointing game, a quiet foot to steal round it ; and knowledge from the surroundings how to stalk it successfully. These things smoothed the difficulties that presented themselves in this sport ; and those who went out shooting and ignored them, would return home with more hunger than partridges. Good sportsmen observed carefully the habits of these birds, which is very necessary, as on knowledge of them depends the killing or not of your bird.

'To-day, when one has no longer to shoot with a crossbow, no one remembers the craft the sportsman formerly possessed. He had to consider, when he saw the dog on point, before going up to find the partridge, where its haunt was and whither it would probably fly ; then the first thing to be done was to close that exit, because, if left free and the approach made from the other side, the bird would not wait. Experience in this sport taught a man that by such-like knowledge was the game killed, and that he must try to get his shot on the half round that faces the haunt, as without this precaution the birds very rarely waited; if, therefore, it were not possible to sight from that direction, he must gradually withdraw, so that the bird seeing him go away might stop there itself. But when he returned again, knowing the position of the haunt, he went much nearer than before, until he succeeded in his purpose; for as this could not be done by force he had recourse to cunning, knowing the danger that there was in going far round the game.

'The dogs trained for this sport understood their master's wishes without a word, going where he wanted at a low whistle and a sign of the hand, and so clever were they in these things that, after a covey of partridges had taken a flight, there were dogs which would make ten points at them, a bird at a time. Before attaining to this the training of these animals cost the man labour, but once got to that condition they developed wiliness as game was shot to them, and each day by working became more clever.

'Once the dog has pointed the partridge he has done his work, and there remains that of the sportsman, which is to kill it; and to accomplish this he must do as he has been advised above, and that is not difficult, for the very birds teach him by hardly ever flying to any place but their home, with the idea of taking refuge there. In order to sight the birds that your dog is pointing, you must observe his posture as to how he is holding his head—high or low; if high, he has them far off; if low, they are near to him. Besides the axiom as to watching the haunt, when you are making your round you must go very quietly, taking care, by looking where you place them and walking very slowly,

## THE POINTER

not to make a noise with your feet, for when you are making your round of the game, the snapping of a twig, or the trampling of a thistle, is all that is needed to flush it; and you must go slowly the better to examine the tussocks, as the partridge is a bird that hides itself well and requires some finding, and by walking at full speed that will rarely be accomplished. At the same time when you are making your round, you must not stand still, nor take a step backwards, nor move your head from side to side, as all these things hinder the game from lying.

'Furthermore, the sportsman must understand that the partridge is not always in front of the dog's nose when he points; for when he is going down-wind he points not at the partridge but at its scent blown about, as he being to windward cannot of course smell the bird. The cause of this is that, over uneven ground, the wind does not blow evenly, and sometimes the scent of the partridge is caught up by it, and carried now in one direction, now in another, but the dog, wherever he chance on it, stops on point. If the sportsman lack experience, he will see nothing out of the common in the attitude of the dog, and will expect to find the partridge by looking in the place towards which the dog is facing; but he will not be successful, because it is not there. He must look where the blow-back (*revoco*) is likely to come from, and there he will see the partridge. There is a chapter in this book that treats solely of the blow-backs of the wind, though as applied to hunting and the larger game; the same, however, applies to the pointing-dog and smaller game.

'Dogs have three methods of pointing: some simply point, others only circle the game, and others again do both. The dog that points (*de punta*), on finding the partridges, stands stiff in that direction whence he

# EARLY HISTORY

obtains their scent; and as a rule they do not lie to him very well, as they are frightened at the sight of him pointing so near them, and therefore take flight. The dog that circles (*de vuelta*) is much more certain, for two reasons : because, as he knows how to move from where he is, if he find out from the scent that the partridge is very close to him, he draws away as far as he thinks necessary not to disturb it ; and, again, as he circles it, it crouches closer, thinking that he does not know where it is ; and these dogs are not deceived by the blow-back (*revoco*) as are the dogs that point, for as they go round they come across both the scent of the partridge and of the blow-back. Among these circling dogs there are two ways of showing the game : one by going round it and never standing on point, but, when they come to where they can smell the partridge, turning their heads towards it as a signal where it is without ever stopping ; and some do this with such subtlety that, if the sportsman do not understand them, it will be a marvel if he see the game, where there is any scrub or rough ground in which it can conceal itself. There are others that go round and then point with the wind, indicating the game, and these are the best, as they plainly show the sportsman where the game is. Others again there are that make half the circle and point without the wind, but these generally do not know what they are about, and if they attempt the whole circle, lose themselves, and stumble on the partridges, and run them up.

'In all these ways do dogs hunt : but the best are those that point and circle as well, and those that simply circle. Where all are imperfect, the best is the dog that points; because, when he does get a point, he is quiet, and does not disturb the game ; but where all are good, the dog that both circles and points is worth far more than the others. The qualities that a good

## THE POINTER

dog should have are nose and speed to excess, obedience, and a good colour. To the white and wax-coloured dogs the partridges as a rule lie much better, for there is no white animal resembling the wolf, the fox, or the wild cat, of which they are afraid ; while the dark-coloured dogs are frequently lost sight of by their masters in woody ground, and often much time is wasted in seeking for them' (p. 240, *et seq.*).

That poaching was not unknown to the Spaniards at a very early date is proved by a sentence from the Laws and Ordinances of Navarre (*Fueros y Observancias de Navarra*) in 1556.

'For it has been and is proved by experience that many persons of this said kingdom, both noblemen and peasants, in their unrestrained ardour, busy themselves in killing partridges and hares with snares, nets, and the stalking-ox by day, and with lights at night, and decoy-birds, and pointing-dogs, and by many other contrivances during the breeding season as well as at any other time' (*De la Caza y Pesca*, ley i., tit. vii.).

And the following passage, which I found in a manuscript at the Madrid National Library, tends to show that 'faking' is not necessarily begotten of 'the Fancy' of to-day.

'If you wish the dog to have a long tail, leave it so ; and if you wish it to be short, like that of a pointing-dog (*perro de muestra*), cut it to what length you please. If you wish him to have long ears, prick the tips thereof with a pin until blood be drawn, and work them well with the fingers until no blood be left in them, and this will make them grow very long. You may also hang small weights to the ears, for, in truth, these partridge-dogs look much handsomer when their ears hang very much' (*Tratado de Monteria y Cetreria*, by Mossen Juan Valles, 1556, cap. xxvi.).

# EARLY HISTORY

To counterbalance the last two quotations, I will add two more that bear pleasant testimony to the high esteem in which these pointing-dogs were held, and the scientific care that was lavished in picking the pups. The first is from a seventeenth century manuscript formerly belonging to the Duke of Osuna, but now in the National Library at Madrid.

'The points by which they should be chosen at birth are as follows :—

'The dog when born should have the following points, which are desirable. In the first place, the head should be large, and the nose large, with very open nostrils, wide and blunt ; the ears long, broad, and very soft ; the forelegs short, and the paws broad ; the coat white, or with very few markings, and these in the right place, such as on the ears or back. It is important that he have a few small spots on the forelegs, and between the nails, which is best, and also that the nails be black. The reason is that when they have these points they are not so often headstrong, and those that have white paws are more tractable, and are employed more easily. It is also well that the body should be small, as they are more industrious, more obedient, and have more endurance. The reason is plain : a bigger dog has more trouble in moving, is very slow, feels hard work very much, generally has some vice, and is always tardy in obeying. Therefore, I say, let them be white, for they are seen more plainly in the field and are more clever. They are handsomer and always look better, and the points that they make are more beautiful. On the other hand, a dark dog is not seen and, though he may do wonders, does not look so well ; and they are hotter, more impatient, and not so easily handled as the white ones and are behind them in all good qualities' (*De las Propriedades del Perro Perdiguero*, cap. i.).

## THE POINTER

The following passage, though of a comparatively recent date, I cannot help reproducing :—

'A lover of them [pointing-dogs] will know the best dogs he has, those that quest with the heads high, both dog and bitch, and will be careful in mating, so that the bitch pup to a good sire, and will endeavour that both be excellent of their kind. The pups must have great heads, with good occipital-bone, ears large and soft, a square muzzle with much lip, a fine coat, strength in the fore feet, nails black, a very thin tail, and, if possible, let them be white. If, on lifting them by the ears and swinging them round twice or thrice, they do not yelp and cry out, it is a good sign, as by that you can be sure of them. The black nail is a sign of vigour—no skulking or becoming lame. The being white is to be seen from afar when out shooting. The lifting by the ears is to prove their courage. The occipital-bone well developed denotes excellent scenting powers. The large head, the ample ear, the squareness of muzzle with much lip, the fine coat, the thin tail, are the signs of high birth' (*Arte de Cazar*, by Juan Manuel de Arelanno, 1745, p. 96).

The most noteworthy facts in the books of the old Italian sporting writers seem to be the descriptions of the characteristics of the pointing-dog, though their scrupulous care of their kennels and minute instructions as to breaking must evoke our admiration. I append some typical examples of the former :—

'About the scenting-dog (*de cane odoro*). Some declare that this dog is the most eminent of all. Briefly, we prefer him with a muzzle rather turned up than down (*simo potiusquam adunco rostro*), and a pleasing head. Let not the forepart of his body seem greater than, but in exact proportion with, his hind legs, nor his breast too large for his belly, and his back and croup lengthy and level even to the tail. Restlessness (*agilitas*),

# EARLY HISTORY

with repeated movements of the eye, a pricking of the pendant ears, and a frequent wagging of the shortened tail, are faults in the scenting-dog. The one that seeks his game by sniffing a long time at the brambles and thorn-thickets is a good dog, it is said; but the one which stops for his master as soon as he may have found game, is the most excellent scenting-dog. Concerning colours, a parti-coloured one is preferred, very like the spotted lynx; still, a black dog is not to be despised. White, also, and a tawny colour look well on this dog' (*De Canibus*, by Biondo, 1544, p. 8).

'The more the scenting-dog is necessary for the finding of game, the more is valued one that keeps his find undisturbed till his master comes up' (*id.* p. 12).

'When the *canis sagax* that is trained for the taking of quails, partridges, and pheasants, in ranging over the fields sees the above-mentioned birds, he looks back at the fowler and moves his tail. By which the fowler knows that there are birds near the dog, and so covers over both dog and birds with his net. Therefore the Italians call these dogs net-dogs (*retiarios*), as they are used with the nets and allow themselves to be enveloped in them' (*De Quadrupedibus*, by Aldrovandi, 1522–1607, lib. iii., cap vi., p. 552).

'For this sport two things are necessary, the dog and the nets. The dog is called by many the brach of the net (*bracco da rete*), by others stopping-dog (*can da fermo*), because on seeing the game he stops, and thereby causes it to stop. The indications of the best are that they have a large head; a large, broad, moderately thick, and dropping ear; the nostrils well opened and always moist; the mouth chopped, and spotted within on the palate with black; a capacious chest, which is covered with hair thick and harsh on the breast-bone, and the same under the belly; legs rather thick than otherwise; a large foot, with pads well formed, and

## THE POINTER

lean rather than fleshy; the coat on the rest of the body fine and glossy, ticked or dappled with tawny (*lionato*) or other colours. You must never let him hunt when it is cold, especially after medicine, nor until the sun has dried up the dew, because otherwise he loses the scent and hurts his feet. You must also take care, when you have arrived at the place you are to hunt, to commence to leeward, so that the brach will get the wind of the game' (*Ucceliera*, by Olina, 1622, p. 51).

'How the sportsman should break his brach for shooting flying, and what the qualities of the said brach should be:—

'Endeavour to obtain a quite young brach of about four months old that comes of a good breed. This puppy should have a large square head, the muzzle large and sense of smelling keen, the chest capacious, the body short, the paws large, with sharp claws to the feet. And let him be white and dappled with chestnut, more inclining to the white than the red. The best breed of all is that of the Marchese Fortunato Rongoni, of which I have had one called Pastizzo, who did everything a dog could do, both in roading up and finding birds alive or dead, and in catching them in the water very quickly with wonderful dash and spirit; and at the present time I have another of them called Falcone, which is not at all inferior to him. A breed of these same is now established at Bologna, where many gentlemen who have had them, have bred them up to the same type. They are excellent for the stubbles in the open, but they are also excellent in cover and in marshy places' (*La Caccia dell' Arcobugio*, by Bonfadini, 1652, p. 73).

The preceding quotation marks the commencement of the era of shooting-flying with the arquebuse in Italy, and the following shows a slight development of method.

# EARLY HISTORY

'The brachs that point (*bracchi da ferma*) should be spotted and dappled with bright tawny, and have large ears, long muzzle, black nose, feet spurred (*spronati*), hind legs well bent, and tail fine. To make use of them with the gun, it is necessary that these dogs be steady on point, nor ever flush the game that they have found ; so that the sportsman, by carefully circling round his dog with the arquebuse before the game is sprung, may obtain a shot' (*La Caccia dello Schioppo*, by Spadoni, 1673, p. 75).

Dogs have always been held in high esteem in France, and from the days of Gaston Phébus setting-dogs have been prized. Their value in 1492 is emphasised quaintly by Tardif, who seriously makes this suggestion :—

'To relieve great thirst in a dog working, when there is no water, break two or three eggs, and put them into his mouth, which will assuage great thirst' (*Des Chiens de Chasse*, p. 17). A sentence precursory of the question of the Duchesse de Polignac, during the bread riots in 1789, as to why the people clamoured for bread when they could buy such nice cakes!

One of the earliest contributions to our knowledge of shooting with dogs is from the pen of the Bishop of Senès, who writes as follows of '*chiens couchans*.'

'Having by ranging found the game, partridges, quails, woodcocks, hares, rabbits, and the like, which is indeed their nature, they stop quite short, and bowing their knee, bend (*bandent*) their nose ; and by their gestures, substitutes for words, point out the game. Others, glued to the ground, await the hunter, who, putting into position (*couchant au joue*) his crossbow or harquebuse, ranges (*raude*) three or four times round his dog, not daring to stop walking nor measure his shot, until he can spy his quarry cowering under a tuft, that so he may get an open shot at it with his arrow or

## THE POINTER

bullet, and hitting with the premeditated shot, may rejoice and be happy over it' (*La Nouvelle Agriculture*, by Beaujeu, 1551, cap. xvi., p. 241). With the gradual improvement of the arquebuse, and its more general use, the setting-dog became more and more important among sportsmen. Jean de Clamorgan (1576), in the middle of his wolf-hunting, mentions rather gratuitously that there are spaniels for springing and finding partridges and quails, called setting-dogs (*chiens couchans*) (*Chasse du Loup*, chap. viii.); and D'Arcussia (1605), an enthusiastic falconer, to prevent boredom when the falcons are in moult and the corn puts a stop to hawking, recommends, among other diversions, ' shooting over the setting-dog with the arquebuse' (*La Fauconnerie*, p. 19). He also describes '*braques*,' but by no means favourably, as ' soft, sensitive to cold, timid, gluttons, eaters of game, and robbers of the falcon.' I presume he referred to the native *braque*.

D'Aubigné, in 1573, relates how a setting-dog was indirectly instrumental in capturing the town of Menerbe for the Protestants. For the Catholic 'Curate of Vous (who had for long wished to change his religion; and had access to the place on account of a setting-dog that was the cause of many a dinner of partridge to the Governor)' was the inventor of a stratagem that resulted in a party of Vaudois breaking open a gate, forcing an entrance, and surprising the town. ' I will only add,' grimly remarks the historian, ' that the *curé*, being captured in some fight, drowned himself in the Darance as they were taking him to Avignon' (*Histoire Universelle*, tom. ii., p. 144).

After a lapse of about seventy years, our subject may be found filling the position of exemplar to man himself in the work of the moralist, Descartes. ' When a dog sees a partridge, he is naturally inclined to run after it, and when he hears a gun fired, the noise naturally

# EARLY HISTORY

inclines him to escape; but, nevertheless, setting-dogs are commonly trained in such a way that the sight of a partridge makes them stop still, and the noise that they hear afterwards, when they are shot over, makes them approach.' He deduces from the above the possibility of 'changing the movements of the brain,' and an encouragement for men desirous of gaining an 'absolute empire over all their passions' (*Passions de l'Ame*, 1649, tom. i., p. 50).

The pointing and setting-dogs are very interesting as Court favourites under Louis XIV., but the strange glimpses that we get of them now and then, only whet our appetite. From the *Mémoires* of the Duc de St. Simon we gain most of our scanty knowledge.

'The King amused himself by feeding his setting-dogs, then asked for his wardrobe,' &c. (*Oeuvres complettes de Louis de St. Simon*, p. 171).

'The King, wishing to go to bed, went to feed his dogs, then said good-night,' &c. (*id.* p. 176).

'He (Louis XIV.) wished to have his setting-bitches excellent. He always had seven or eight of them in his apartments, and found pleasure in feeding them himself, to make them know him' (*Mémoires de M. le Duc de Saint Simon*, tom. i., p. 126, 1778 Edition).

Here is another basket-full, collected by M. Dunoyer de Noirmont!

'Louis XIII. slept with his dogs. The Duc de Vendôme, the conqueror of Villa Viciosa, pushed still further his toleration for them. A crowd of dogs slept in his bed, his bitches littered there, says St. Simon. His brother, the Grand Prior, had the same customs. When M. de Contades was made Major of the regiment of Guards, it was said that he owed his advancement to the present of some very well-broken setting-bitches which his father had sent to the King' (*Histoire de la Chasse*, tom. ii., p. 286).

# THE POINTER

'Louis XIV. did not allow himself this excess of "*cynisme*," but he was very fond of dogs. He was particularly fond of his spaniels, among which he was pleased to distribute every day with his own royal hand seven biscuits, which the court-baker was expected to make for them ' (*ib.*).

But it is instructive to contrast the public Acts of these Kings with their private demonstrations of affection; and for this the *Code des Chasses*, by M. Saugrain, 1765, is very useful, as it contains all their Sporting Ordinances, from which I will cull a few extracts.

Henri III. (1578), Art. II.—'And as there are several nobles and others who have setting-dogs, which are the destruction of all the game, we wish to make it forbidden to all persons of whatever rank and condition, either to own or make use of setting-dogs, under penalty of, for the non-nobles corporal punishment, and for the aforesaid nobles of displeasing us and incurring our anger,' &c. (tom. i., p. 171).

Henri III., Art. II.—'And in order to make the keepers of our forests and warrens, archers, &c., more careful about doing their duty in this respect, chiefly for the prohibition of the aforesaid setting-dogs, we promise to give and accord to the aforesaid archers, for each of these setting-dogs that they will take and bring to us, four crowns, that we wish to be paid to them promptly by our treasurer, whom we command to do so without question ' (*ib.*).

Henri IV. (1596), Art. III.—'We forbid very expressly the use of setting-dogs, which are very destructive, under the penalties carried by our aforesaid ordinances, and, besides these, a fine of a hundred pounds (*cent livres*) for the first time, and to be kept in prison till its payment in full; for the second time to be flogged, and banished for three years from the province where the destruction has been done; and for

# EARLY HISTORY

the third time, to find no mercy in Us' (tom. i., p. 191).

Henri IV. (1600), Art. XX.—' Those who sport with setting-dogs and the arquebuse, otherwise than we have declared above, and are caught in the act, will be fined thirty-three crowns, a third of the penalty, twice as much for the second offence, and thrice for the third, if they have the money; and in default to be, the first time beaten with rods in private, the second time in a public place, and the third time banished for life from their home; and in each of the aforesaid cases the dogs will be hamstrung, and the arquebuses confiscated' (tom. i., p. 203).

Henri IV. (1607), Art. VI.—' And inasmuch as the use of setting-dogs is the cause that hardly any partridges and quails are to be found, we have, conformably with the former ordinances of the Kings Our Predecessors and of Ourselves, totally forbidden this same usage to all men, of whatever rank or condition they may be, either to keep, or to feed, or to educate setting-dogs, &c.' (tom. i., p. 267).

Louis XIV. (1669), Art. XVI.—' The use of setting-dogs is strictly forbidden by all the ordinances following, because it is a pot-hunting sport (*chasse cuisinière*). But because it gives much pleasure, it produces also many law-breakers, who are to be punished with the penalties contained in the present and following sections. We have forbidden and do now forbid our officials and others, whoever they may be, to take to our said forests, plantations, and warrens, any dogs, unless they have them tied, and lead them; and if it be found that it be done otherwise, for the first offence, the dogs shall be hamstrung; for the second, they shall be destroyed; for the third, those with them shall be punished by a penalty dependent on Our Will' (tom. i., p. 384).

# THE POINTER

In the face of ferocious edicts like these, aggravated, in the case of Louis XIV., by their transparent hypocrisy, it is not wonderful that witty Elzéar Blaze retaliates with sarcasms on the sport of Kings:—

'Charles X. was a great sportsman, he killed from seven to eight hundred head a day; in front of him passed unendingly partridges and rabbits, hares and pheasants; there was only the trouble of choice. In my opinion it was a very dull amusement. The pleasure of the true sportsman commences when his dog meets him; Kings have no dogs, or rather no pointing-dogs, and if they have, they don't use them—two hundred beaters take their place. The pleasure increases when the animal makes a good point; Kings have never seen a dog on point,—an unceasing stream of game flows before them. The sportsman delights in gathering his bird, in handling it, &c.; Kings do not see the dead game nearer than twenty paces,—touch it never. Their business is to fire a thousand shots; a steam engine could do it as well' (*Le Chasseur au chien d'arrêt*, 1846, p. 256).

'You must search for the game! If it come to you, the pleasure is diminished. A pretty woman who offers herself, loses three-quarters of her attractions. What do I say? She loses them all' (*id.* p. 258).

'I put the sport over pointing-dogs before other sport' (*ib.*)

Besides the two foregoing aphorisms, which I feel bound to include, I will quote his perfect summing-up of the English pointer: only two or three words, and —Hey, Presto—behold the genuine article!

'The best are commonly whites and blacks, high on the leg, with long narrow feet, the coat so short and smooth that one sees their muscles as in thoroughbred horses. Their eye is prominent and lively' (*id.* p. 282).

# EARLY HISTORY

I must now devote a little space to the development of the arquebuse and the art of shooting flying, as, from their influence on the evolution of the pointing and setting-dogs, such study is necessary for the proper comprehension of the ancestry of the gundogs.

In epitomising this interesting subject I am fortunate in having the help of three authors, all of the first magnitude, MM. Magné de Marolles, Baudrillart, and Blaze.

' It was in the opening years of the sixteenth century, a little before the accession of François I., who became King in 1515, that small arms mounted on a stock (and adapted for taking aim with) called then *hacquebutes*, and later *harquebuses* and *arquebuses*, began to come into use' (*La Chasse au fusil*, by Magné de Marolles, 1788, p. 38).

' The Hunting Ordinances of François I., in the year 1515, already makes mention of *hacquebutes* and *echoppettes*, as sporting weapons. This is the earliest mention of them ' (*id.* p. 48).

' I have found in a little book entitled *Eccelenza della caccia de Cesare Solatio Romano*, printed at Rome in 1669, that at the time when the author wrote the method of shooting flying had been known at Rome about eighty years. In Italy therefore they commenced to shoot flying about 1590; and it is reasonable to suppose that at the same epoch this method became pretty general in the other countries of Europe. I think then I can state that until 1580 they never shot flying. I rely also on the sporting plates of Stradanus, who lived at this period, as among them is not to be seen one single gunner who shot flying or even running; and in the poem entitled *Le Plaisir des Champs*, by Claud Gauchet, first printed in 1583, although the author, a thorough sportsman, describes several forms of sport with the arquebuse, and recounts his exploits

## THE POINTER

and those of some brother sportsmen with it, he does not make any mention of shooting flying' (*id.* p. 50).

'*Arquebuse*—this firearm, which is now obsolete, was first used in the early years of the sixteenth century, a little before François I. came to the throne in 1515. It was then fitted with a stock, and meant to be put to the cheek, and was called at first *hacquebute*, afterwards *harquebuse* or *arquebuse*. Of this hand-arquebuse, there were two kinds; one called the match-lock (*l'arquebuse à mèche*), the other the wheel-lock (*l'arquebuse à rouet*)' (*Traité des eaux et forêts*, by Baudrillart, 1821, part iii., *Dictionnaire des Chasses*, p. 126).

'It appears that the flint-lock (*platine à rouet*) was invented in Germany about the year 1540. For a long time the match, the wheel, and the flint-lock as it is to-day, were used concurrently for game-shooting; but, finally, the last being most simple and expeditious, has banished the others. The cross-bow was not disused for sport, till the handling of the arquebuse was sufficiently perfected to admit of shooting flying; this was about 1590' (*id.* p. 127).

'Before the invention of the flint-lock, it is certain that one could not shoot but from a rest' (*Le Chasseur au chien d'arrêt*, Blaze, 1846, p. 24).

'The gun was not a convenient weapon, and easy to handle, till about the year 1620. It was not till 1750 that the first double guns, with two barrels parallel, appeared' (*id.* p. 25).

'This prince (Louis XIII.) was a very good shot; among his titles to distinction can be counted that of having been the first to shoot flying' (*id.* p. 255).

But it is evident from the computation of De Marolles that Louis XIII., as he was not born till 1601, could not be the inventor of shooting flying; though he may have been the first to introduce it into France,—and this, a parallel story to our own Robert

# EARLY HISTORY

Dudley and the setting-dog. Be that as it may, he was undoubtedly a keen good shot, and so was his son, Louis XIV., as the following extract from the *Journal* of the Marquis de Dangeau tends to prove :—

'Fontainebleau.—The King on rising from his meal went out to shoot flying (*tirer en volant*) ; he found on his beat, while seeking partridges, a large wild boar. He put a ball into his gun, and killed him' (October 30th, 1686).

It appears that on the Continent in 1789 some modern methods of shooting were practised, as De Marolles accurately treats of shooting in line, adding that dogs were almost unnecessary in this sport—at least, that only one, on a lead, should be used for wounded game. Posting the guns round a cover, he describes also, with the dry comment :—' This method is much practised in Italy ; it is in general a very murderous sport' (*La Chasse au fusil*, p. 174).

In like manner the old sporting literature of Germany is very interesting, but the greater part of it lies beyond the boundaries of this book ; as the German pointing-dogs, though probably off-shoots from the same tree, were in no way concerned in the birth of the pointer. I shall quote, however, a few passages mainly connected with methods of work, which distinctly assist my history of sport. An early specimen of these is found, in a curious rhythmical form, on the title-page of *Ein neuw Thierbuch*, published anonymously in 1569 :—

'When he perceives game,
He holds himself still before approaching it,
And indicates its presence with his tail
To the hunter, who follows carefully
Whither the scenting-dog (*spurhund*) guides,
To where the game sits in secure comfort.'

# THE POINTER

And Gesner wrote about 1551 : ' We Germans and the French call these dogs quail-dogs (*coturnicos*), because their work is principally concerned with this class of bird. The Italians call them net-dogs (*canes retis*), for they help them with the nets, in which they will even allow themselves to be enveloped, whence they derive another name with us, *vorstehhund*' (*Historiæ Animalium*, 1620 Ed., lib. i., p. 255).

The following are the remarks of J. C. Aitinger (1653), an enthusiastic netter :—

' Shooting is a very vulgar method ' (*Vogelstellen*, p. 17).

' When the pointing-dog gives signs [of game] he should be called back and tied up, and the place marked for netting ' (*id.* p. 20).

' To catch partridges by the aid of the " cow " is the most artistic method of all. When the dog points, lay the draw-net swiftly as is proper, and so that the birds run up wind and do not get their tails disturbed by it [the wind]. Then make a wide flanking movement, get behind a mound so that the birds do not see you, then pull on the " cow," and go slowly up to the place where the dog is pointing ' (*id.* p. 23).

' In France they use the draw-nets so large that they must be carried between two riders on horseback. In England this form of sport is considered vulgar and the worst taste, and they use hawks or falcons. When the dog points, they let the bird fly ' (*id.* p. 32).

' The best way to take partridges, as is done by princes and nobles, is to shoot the birds neatly, with a pointing-dog ; or to take them by means of a pointing-dog and nets. Before I continue, it is necessary to describe the pointing-dog, which is used with the hawk, for shooting or hawking. This sort of dog is usually white and brown marked, or white and speckled, or brown spotted, and the taller and stronger the better the

## EARLY HISTORY

dog, so that he can take the scent high: for pointing-dogs should always hunt with noses high in the air' (*Der Dianen Hohe und Niedere Jagd-geheimnisse*, by Täntzer, 1734, p. 96).

'When the dog points he should not be called to, but encouraged with "gently!" so that he may stand still, until such time as the fowling-net can be got ready. Then run rapidly on to the game and the dog, so that the net cover both, and having strangled the birds give the dog some bread. At first the dog will hate the net, but must be well trained to endure it patiently, and as it is rare to find a dog combine both qualities (pointing, and standing to the net), it is wise for the sportsman to have two dogs, one for each purpose. And as the partridges will not often stay quiet a conveniently long time before the dog, not to mention the net, but scatter themselves away, the hunter must have with him his hawk, which the game will recognise as their enemy, and will crouch upon the ground and hide from it, lying motionless before the pointing-dog until the net covers both them and him' (*id.* p. 98).

'Take a pointing-dog, a hooded hawk, and a living pigeon on a long string in the game-bag, and start early. When the dog finds and points, hastily unhood the hawk, call warningly to the dog, and as soon as conveniently near to him (holding the hawk with its breast to the partridges and the dog), call out to him: "Berr!" On which, the dog springs into the middle of the partridges. They scatter off like dust, and the hawk after them. Then the hunter rides till the hawk strikes, and falls with his quarry to the ground' (*id.* p. 103).

'The greater number of sportsmen, or bird-netters, accustom themselves diligently to speak French to their dogs, such as "Allons chercher, mon Amy!" "Garde bien!" "Venés icy!" or "Retirés vous!" and such foreign phrases, in order that the dog, if lost, shall not

## THE POINTER

be so easily made use of, as if addressed in the Muscovite or Polish speech' (*Der Volkommene Teutshe Jäger*, by L. F. von Fleming, 1749, p. 178).

'These "*barbets*," as the French call them, are also to be accustomed to the French language, and a sportsman will find them useful to work with the partridge-dog upon all conceivable occasions' (*id.* p. 181).

The above extracts shows the workings of the Teutonic mind on the problems of dog-breaking, and Herr Täntzer's grip of the subject seems remarkable, while Herr von Fleming is the first, I believe, to recommend working a spaniel with a pointing-dog.

In Great Britain the history of the work of setting-dogs begins with Dr. Caius's racy account of them.

These [setters] attend diligently upon theyre Master and frame their condition to such beckes, motions, and gestures as it shall please him to exhibit and make, either going forward, drawing backwarde, inclining to the right hand, or yealding towards the left, (In making mencion of fowles my meaning is of the Partridge and the Quaile). When he hath found the byrde, he keepeth sure and fast silence, he stayeth his steppes and wil proceede no further, and with a close, covert, watching, eye, layeth his belly to the grounde, and so creepeth forwarde like a worme. When he approacheth neare to the place where the birde is, he layes him downe, and with a marcke of his pawes, betrayeth the place of the byrde's last abode, whereby it is supposed that this kinde of dogge is called Index, Setter, being in deede a name most consonant and agreable to his quality. The place being knowne by the meanes of the dogge, the fowler immediatly openeth and spreedeth his net, intending to take them, which being done the dogge, at the accustomed becke or usuall signe of his Master, ryseth up by and by, and draweth nearer to the fowle that by his presence they might be the

## EARLY HISTORY

authors of their own insnaring, and be ready intangled in the prepared net' (*Of Englishe Dogges*, 1576, p. 16).

Now about forty years before the publication of *Englishe Dogges* there had been issued, the first of its kind, a Statute of Henry VIII., an act against 'Crosbowes and Handguns,' which regulated the length of guns, and forbade one to order his servant to shoot at 'any deare, fowle, or other thinge except it be only at a Butt or Banck of earth in place convenient, or in defence of person or house.' Licenses also were authorized to be granted and sold, but the buyer had to particularize the kinds of 'beasts, fowles, or other thinges' he desired to kill. In fact it was the dawn of small game preserving (23 Hen. VIII., c. 17).

Another Statute, of Edward VI., on the same subject, is so interesting that I am printing the full text: it is entitled 'An Acte againste the shootinge of Hayle shott.'

'Whereas an Acte was made in the XXIIIth yere of the late Kinge of famous memorie Henrie the Eighte, for some libertye to shoote in Handegonnes hakes and hacquebutes, by which Acte nevertheles it was pvided that noe psone shoulde shote in anye of the abovesaide peeces but at a banke of earthe, and not to any deare or fowle, unless the partie might dispende one hundreth poundes by the yere: Foreasmuche as the saide Acte havinge byne devised as it was then thought for necessarie excise tending to the defence of the Realme, ys growen sythen to the mayntenance of muche ydleness and to such a libertye as not onelye dwellinge houses dovecotes and Churches daylye damaged by the abuse thereof by men of light conversacion, but that also there ys growen a customable manner of shotinge of hayleshott, wherby an infynite sort of fowle ys killed, and muche Game therby destroyed to the benefytt of no man, wherby also the meaninge of the saide Statute ys

## THE POINTER

defrauded, for that the saide use of hayleshott utterly destroyeth the certentye of shotinge, whiche in Warres is much requisite ; Be it therefore enacted that no pson under the degree of a Lorde of the Parliament shall from hensforthe shote in anye handegonne within anye Cittie or Towne at any fowle or other marke, upon any Churche house or dovecote ; neither that any pson shall shote in anye place any hayleshott or any more Pellottes then one at one tyme, upon payne to forfayte, for everie tyme that he or they shall soe offende contrarye to this Acte, tenne poundes and emprisonement of his bodye during three monethes. Provided alwayes, and be it enacted by thauctoritie aforesaide, that this Acte, nor anye thinge therein conteyned, shall extend or be prejudicyall to any pson or psons auctorized by value of lande to shote in any handegonne or crosbowe, but that they maye so doe in suche fourme and order as they sholde do and myght have done, before the makinge of this Acte, (hayleshott excepted as indeede that kynde of shott in the saide Acte was not ment),' &c. (2 & 3 Edward VI., c. 14).

This Statute passed in 1548. The mention of 'hayleshott, wherby an infynite sorte of fowle ys killed' at so early a date on such good authority makes one wonder if the English, instead of the Italians, were not, after all, the inventors of small shot.

In 1603, James I. made the first statutory mention of the setting-dog as follows :—

'That all and everie person and persons which from and after the first day of Auguste next following, shall shoote or destroy or kill with any Gunne Crossebow Stonebow or Longbow any Phesant Partridge House Dove or Pigeon Hearne Mallarde Duck Teale Wigeon Grouse Heathcocke Moregame or any such Fowle, or any Hare ; or after the saide firste day of Auguste shall take kill or destroy any Phesant Partridge House Dove

## EARLY HISTORY

or Pigeon, with settinge Dogges or Nets, or with any manner of Nettes Snares Engines or Instruments whatsoever, shall be committed to the Common Goale, there to remaine for Three Moneths,' &c. (1603-4, 1 Jac. I., c. 27).

Unlike the French Kings, however, James was sincere in his dislike for setting-dogs. 'We have from that Monarch's own hand, without presuming to make any alteration in the diction of the royal author : " I cannot omit here the hunting, namely, with running houndes, which is the most honourable and noblest sort thereof ; for it is a theivish forme of hunting to shoote with gunnes and bowes "' (*Sports and Pastimes*, by Joseph Strutt, 1801, p. xiv.).

Robert Burton mentions fowling as a sport carried on with 'guns, nets, and setting-dogs,' and adds inimitably that 'Fowling is more troublesome [than hawking], but all out as delightsome' (*Anatomy of Melancholy*, 1621, part 2, sect. 2, mem. 4, p. 339).

Oddly enough, Gervase Markham, who the same year (1621) published 'Hunger's Prevention; containing the whole Art of Fowling by Water and Land,' evidently knew nothing of shooting birds, as he expressly states that 'the art of taking fowle' must be 'applyed or used two several wayes, that is to say, either by enchantment or enticement, by winning or wooing the Fowles unto you with Pipe, Whistle, or Call ; or else by Engine, which unawares surpriseth and entangleth them.'

Robert Howlitt and Nicholas Cox, writers at the end of the seventeenth century, had never heard of shooting flying, but Richard Blome in *The Gentleman's Recreation* (1686) has (p. 125) a plate, entitled 'Shooting Flying,' of two sportsmen firing from horseback at some partridges flying past them, with several spaniels rushing about and yelping excitedly. In the

## THE POINTER

directions for practising this art you are advised, 'whether the Game be flying or on the ground,' not to shoot 'at a single Fowl, if you can compass more within your level' (*ib.*). This book, however, deals almost exclusively with netting, and apparently the union of gun with setting-dog had not yet taken place : another of its plates represents a setter on game, but having a net drawn over him. Although it seems incredible that new ideas should have spread so slowly, it took over thirty years after the publication of Blome's book for others to follow up his discovery. In 1718, Giles Jacob, in *The Compleat Sportsman*, certainly mentions shooting wild ducks flying—but not a word of thus killing partridges. Then later still, in 1732, *The Gentleman Farrier*, who first mentions the pointer, detailing the business of a setting-dog in the taking of partridges, only gives instructions how to ' learn him to let a net be drawn over him without stirring ' (p. 104) ; while the *Sportsman's Dictionary* (1735) ignores shooting on the wing any birds but water-fowl.

Thomas Oakleigh gives an instructive epitome of sport of the eighteenth century in England :—

' Falconry fell into desuetude in the days of the Georges. As falconry fell into disuse another kind of sport, which is now considered as disreputable, and practised only by poachers, was pursued by the country gentlemen ; the capturing of birds of the game species by means of nets and setting-dogs. Netting was considered as a fair mode of taking game, until the fowling-piece came into general use ' (*The Shooter's Handbook*, 1842, p. 21).

' At the time of the accession of the House of Hanover, falconry, netting, and shooting were contemporary amusements. The number of shooters were very limited, the inferiority of the guns, and ammunition, being such as not to induce their general adoption ;

# EARLY HISTORY

hawking was going out of favour, and, of the three sports, netting was the most commonly practised, until the beginning of the reign of George III., after which it was no longer deemed the sport of gentlemen. At what time the fowling-piece first came into use is uncertain. We learn from Pope that pheasant-shooting was in vogue in Windsor Forest, during the reign of Anne :—

> 'See from the brake the whirring pheasant springs,
> And mounts exulting on triumphant wings;
> Short in his joy, he feels the fiery wound,
> Flutters in blood, and panting beats the ground!'
> (*id.* p. 22).

The German writer, Aitinger (1653), states that the English at that time used the falcon in connection with the setting-dog, but I have been unable to find any evidence of this. In fact, the following is the only instance, except at the present day, that I have met with :—

'The subject of the plate (No. XXX.) is taken at the most interesting time, when the dogs are setting, and the falconer is unhooding the birds, previous to the game being roused' (*The Costumes of Yorkshire, in* 1814, by G. Walker, 1885, p. 77).

This description answers well, barring that the dogs are pointers and standing at point. But the article also relates that this was hawking only as revived by Colonel Thornton, and, therefore, was probably carried on under novel conditions. Anyhow, it is the first example I have found of the use of pointing-dogs with the hawk in England.

And now I have shown my readers all that I know concerning the pointing and setting-dogs previous to their arrival in Great Britain, and previous to their wonderful improvement and development with us. Other nations have always recognised our skill as breeders of dogs. In the classical days, Gratius and

# THE POINTER

Nemesian, whom Gesner the German naturalist quotes (*Historiæ Animalium*, p. 249), praised British dogs in their verse. Gaston Phébus said that the British had made greyhounds their own (*Deduiz de la Chasse*, chap. xx.). Argote de Molina extols our hounds for their qualities in following deer by scent (*Libro de la Monteria*, cap. xviii.). The Bishop of Senès pays us a frank tribute :—' Let us admit that we do not take enough trouble in the choice of the sires and dams to supply ourselves with good strains of dogs, as the English do ' (*La Nouvelle Agriculture*, p. 233). La Blanchère recounts that ' it is not to-day that the presumption of the English dog having a better nose than our dog, has arisen in the land. Under Louis XIV., when La Fontaine published his *Fables*, 1668, it was believed ; since the poet could say, while giving flatteries to Elizabeth Montague, widow of Mr. Harvey, " Your folk excel the rest in penetration ; even the dogs derive from their abode a better nose than dogs of our poor nation " ' (*Les Chiens de Chasse*, p. 147).

Britannia's work in the construction of the pointer has been done by adaptation, and by blending materials ready to hand, rather than by any heroic creation of the Genesis order. She has created no doubt, but, like Shelley's poet, she has created ' by combination.' Still, although in the case of the dog himself Englishmen may have but moulded the clay, they can look with pride upon having actually *invented* ' backing,' which is the key to the harmonious co-operation in work of two or more dogs ; and by that achievement have transmuted the *chasse cuisinière* of King Louis into a noble and delightful science.

# CHAPTER II.
## LATER HISTORY.

I HAVE shown how the English pointer originated about the commencement of the eighteenth century, and have given an occasional glimpse of him for the eighty years or so succeeding. I have now to concern myself with the second phase of his existence, which also covers a period clearly defined and of about the same length,—from the time of Colonel Thornton to the establishment of dog shows.

This era, notwithstanding its high importance, is unfortunately difficult to write about. For though, before its commencement, pointers had become an old-established breed of fixed type and exceeding repute, and early in it reached their zenith, the hopes of getting much intimate knowledge of either its dogs or its sportsmen are alike disappointed. Possibly, from the inherent exclusiveness of the sport, there has never been a shooting Pepys! Of course, there is much to be thankful for in the books of such practical pointer-owners as Taplin, Lascelles, Johnson, Oakleigh, Craven, Lacy, and St. John, but most of them are strictly impersonal in their writings, and have abstained from those gossiping anecdotes which would have taught us so much of their canine environment.

As, during this period, nearly every family of position had its own breed of pointers, it is obviously impossible to enumerate them all; but I will make mention of some of the most eminent breeders, breakers, and kennels of pointers that then existed, and will try

# THE POINTER

to give, at all events, a list of those races that have appreciably bequeathed their blood to later times. I have found it impracticable to arrange these references chronologically, but I have preserved a sort of rough sequence subservient to district.

Colonel Thornton (born 1757, died 1823), though he wrote several books of travels, &c., tells but little of pointers, and, I believe, nothing of his own kennel. It is clear, however, from contemporary writers, from the Gilpin picture (Plate IX.), and from the high prices that they commanded, that his dogs must have been first rate.

In his *Sporting Tour through the North of England and Scotland*, published in 1804, the following passage is worth attention :—

'The Duke of Hamilton, when we arrived, was not returned from shooting, in which he excels, being one of the best shots in Scotland. He is also a keen sportsman at every other amusement, but this country not being well adapted to fox-hunting, he has given up his hounds, and has paid great attention to his pointers and greyhounds, both of which are excellent. I found his grace agreed with me in opinion that, after moor-shooting, partridge has not the same charms' (p. 260).

Occurring on the same page, the remark that 'no man can have any species of dog clever without some sort of pains, and in general they neglect them in Scotland,' unfortunately might be written in a book of to-day. The Colonel adds that 'his grace' had every reason to be a sportsman, as he possessed the Island of Arran, 'probably the best shooting place in the world.' This Arran has for over a hundred years been the favourite shooting ground of the Dukes of Hamilton; and their pointers, isolated there, were of the best,— their purity of blood being most jealously guarded. The late Duke (the twelfth), grandson of Colonel

## LATER HISTORY

Thornton's host, was also fond of his pointers, but insisted upon introducing some violent out-crosses, notably one with a lemon-and-white dog, which he brought from France. For the appearance of his dogs this proved a disastrous alliance, as I can testify personally. While Mr. John Mackenzie (keeper on the island since 1857) writes, 'the Duke was very keen for the breed of the French pointer, of which I never thought much, and I am quite sure he in a measure spoilt our kennel of pointers.' He also states that Brodick Castle Sandy, an eminent stud-dog that I bought at the death of the Duke, had 'none of the blood of the French pointer,' though he thought very little of Sandy compared with his father, Dan, which he thus describes: 'Dan was, without exception, one of the best dogs I ever saw on the hill, full of quality, could work every day in the week; and he ran at such a rate that the ground almost shook under him.'

The breed of pointers at Cannon Hall, Yorkshire, was one of the oldest and most renowned; it still figures in some old pedigrees. Here is an extract from a letter (dated November 23rd, 1894) of Colonel Spencer Stanhope :—

'I believe the (Cannon Hall) breed was here at the time my grandfather succeeded his uncle, Mr. Spencer, in 1783. They were celebrated in the time of my grandfather, Walter Spencer Stanhope, for their steadiness and general good qualities. His keeper, George Fisher, who was still alive when I was a boy, was well known as a trainer of pointers. They were liver-and-white, not large in size, but very shapely. My grandfather kept them up well under his keeper, George Whitfield; but, in the year 1842, hydrophobia occurred in the kennel, and, I think, only one bitch survived. Since that time we have gradually given up keeping pointers, and now they are not used on the South

# THE POINTER

Yorkshire moors. Some of the old breed, more or less pure, were kept up in the neighbourhood, but I have not seen any for some ten years past, and suppose they are now practically extinct.'

T. B. Johnson, in the *Sportsman's Cyclopædia* (1831), remarks that 'there are many good pointers in various parts of England, and particularly in Yorkshire' (p. 652); and no doubt it has been the influence of such strains as the Cannon Hall, Colonel Thornton's, and Sir Tatton Sykes's (study Plate XVI.), that has engraved quality in the pointers of this county.

Here is some account, by a friend of his, of Mr. Johnson's treatment of his pointers, which 'were allowed to follow their master into the field as soon as their strength would enable them, before they could manage to surmount the ditches, over which they had frequently to be lifted. They taught or broke themselves into the business they were intended to pursue, and were never terrified by the whip of the professed dog-breaker. The author of the *Sportsman's Cyclopædia*, &c., generally contrived to have his whelps brought forth in the latter end of February or the early part of March; and, as soon as the hay was cleared off the ground, he allowed them to follow him into the fields, where they immediately began to hunt, and very soon to set young partridges, which might be found running in the after-grass towards evening, very steadily. This was adopting the admirable maxim, Train up a child, &c., and thus, without trouble, his young pointers might be said to educate themselves; and it may be justly observed that self-acquirement, or self-acquired education, uniformly makes the most lasting and the most perfect impression on the mind. Towards the latter end of the month of September they were shot over, and taken out regularly during the remainder of

## LATER HISTORY

the season' (*The Sportsman*, 1836, vol. iii., No. 4, p. 185).

'Mr. Daniel Lambert was born on the 13th March, 1770. He was extremely active in all the sports of the field till he was prevented by his corpulence from partaking in them, when he bred cocks, setters, and pointers, which he brought to as great, or perhaps greater, perfection than any other sporting character of the present day' (*Anecdotes*, by Egan, 1827, p. 137).

Shortly after Daniel Lambert, was born the famous Sir John Shelley (1783). Says Egan (p. 218), his 'celebrity as a first-rate shot and breeder of sporting dogs (in which he is wholly unrivalled) is already well established;' while Lacy vouches for the breaking of his pointers :—

'Many years ago Sir John Shelley hunted two brace at once, which were in the highest state of discipline. At the report of his gun the whole four dropped instantaneously as though they had been shot; and when two brace of birds, in a turnip-field, were brought to the ground, each of these accomplished and symmetrically formed animals was called by name, and was told to "bring that bird," the one nearest to him; when each in his turn retrieved his proper bird, brought it to the hand of his master, and laid himself down until all received the signal to rise' (*The Modern Shooter*, p. 144).

This incident shows wonderful breaking, but not more so than Richard Lawrence tells us of. 'A gentleman in the county of Stirling, lately kept a greyhound and a pointer, and, being fond of coursing, the pointer was accustomed to find the hares, and the greyhound to catch them' (*Sportsman's Repository*, 1820, p. 120). But my friend, Dr. Court, caps this story by averring that he himself, about thirty-five years ago, went out shooting with the Duke of Portland's keeper, who had

## THE POINTER

with him a brace of roan pointers and two greyhounds. The pointers found the hare, pointed, backed, and remained down while the greyhounds coursed her. A feat of steadiness (as an Irishman might say) still more singular in the plural.

A story of a famous south-country dog is given by Lawrence on the same page as the one just cited :—

'There is a very good likeness, by Cooper, in our Sporting Reference Book, *Wheeble and Pitman's Magazine* for October, 1815, of Don, the then reputed best pointer in the county of Sussex, the property of Jasper Bates, Esq., of Parnshurst, in that county, and perhaps afterwards a stallion of high repute. He appears by his portrait to have been of the light breed, and his characteristics, most valuable indeed, were first-rate speed, a nose nearly Spanish, &c. He exhibited twice the following extraordinary proof of superior nose and ability as a pointer : whilst in the act of returning with a cock pheasant in his mouth, which his master had shot to him, he found and stood a hen pheasant.'

The following information from the same work showing that the price of a thoroughly reliable brace was, in 1820, much the same as it is to-day, is also interesting :—

'With regard to the average run of the times, for the price of a good, fair, marketable dog the following advertisement from Herts in the early part of this season is given as a specimen : "Superior pointers. To be sold, a brace of black pointers, now in the hands of the breeder, a gentleman who has declined shooting. They are of the first-rate description, range high, find their game in fine style, particularly staunch, never tire, and, in fact, possess all the qualifications of pointers, without a blemish. They have been shot over two seasons. Price fifty guineas"' (p. 117).

At the end of the eighteenth and the beginning of

## LATER HISTORY

the nineteenth centuries flourished Messrs. W. A. Osbaldiston, R. B. Thornhill, and R. Lascelles, all sporting authors, rich men, and reputed to have owned pointers of excellence; but, except from some casual references to his dogs in the writings of the last named (of which I have fully availed myself in subsequent chapters), there seems nothing to be gleaned,—no records kept.

Mr. Philip Gell, of Hopton Hall, Derbyshire, born 1773, owned a famous kennel. He used to take his pointers regularly every year to Scotland, and was a thorough enthusiast. At his death, in 1841, he left his kennel to Mr. Tom Taylor, who had entered his service in 1820, when eleven years old, and had become his favourite keeper and breaker. The following year (1842) a draft of about ten pointers and six setters was sold from this legacy. Messrs. Brearey & Co. of Derby were the auctioneers, and the total realised was upwards of 700 guineas, one brace alone making 130 guineas. After this Mr. Taylor went in for pointer breeding extensively and with great success. He frequently had in his possession over a hundred pointers at a time, and once sold as many as seventy at one of his periodical sales. He was a judge, in 1866, at the Cannock Chase field-trials, which were held the first day on partridges and the second on grouse; and he died at Hopton in 1891. For these particulars of a remarkable career I am indebted to Mr. Chandos Pole Gell and to Mr. Walter Taylor.

Mr. Taylor's first sale at auction is the earliest of which I can get any details, as, although we are told that at the death of the second Duke of Kingston (1773) his 'celebrated breed of black pointers, considered superior to all in the kingdom,' were 'sold for immense sums' (*The Complete Farrier*, by Lawrence, 1816, p. 400), unfortunately there seem not to be any

## THE POINTER

records either of these dogs or of their ultimate dispersal, although the Duke was so fond of them that he actually constructed an underground passage from his house to his kennels!

On October 1st, 1844, there was another epoch-making sale at the death of Mr. Thomas Webb Edge (b. 1788) of Strelley Hall near Nottingham, the pointers being of nearly identical blood with the Hopton breed. Mr. Edge was closely connected with Mr. Gell, was cousin to Mr. Hurt of Alderwasley, Derbyshire, and uncle to Mr. James Holden of Ruddington, Nottinghamshire, and to Mr. George Moore of Appleby, Leicestershire. All of these were pointer-lovers, whose dogs figure largely in many pedigrees. Mr. Moore bought several pointers at his uncle's sale, and at Appleby the prestige of the race was maintained well into the show-period. Among other purchasers was the fourth Duke of Portland, who at the advice of his sons, Lords Henry and George Bentinck, refreshed his kennel by the acquisition of the famous five-year-old stud-dog Rake, and two brace of puppies. With these Lord Henry achieved remarkable results, culminating perhaps in Mr. Price's Belle, a great trial-winner about 1872. Mr. T. Statter also established a valuable kennel with his selections from the nineteen pointers offered.

The Alderwasley strain was shortly after this nearly exterminated by rabies, and finally, in 1863, was dispersed by the sale of four brace and a half at Tattersall's for 141 guineas.

There resided for very many years (till his death, about 1860) in Derwent Street, Derby, Mr. W. Statham, a veterinary surgeon, commonly known as the Old Doctor. He was a wonderful judge of a pointer, owned and bred them in great numbers, and used to deal in them. He had dogs out at walk all over the

# LATER HISTORY

neighbourhood. His strain was chiefly derived from Hopton, Strelley, Alderwasley,—and Shipley, where the Mundys had always some good dogs.

Mr. W. Sheild, of Whittingham, in sending me a typical photograph of an old Staffordshire pointer, described him as follows:—

'I enclose a photo of the picture of the old pointer belonging to my uncle, Wm. Princep of Newton near Tamworth. I can remember the dog and horse being painted about the year 1848, when I was about twelve years old. Major was one of a strain which my grandfather had kept up. The colour was liver, with small white ticks all over the body. Major had, as you will see, a little more white on him. The dog was very fast, as were they all—could beat any field of reasonable size while one walked across it. The outline of the dog is correct I have no doubt, though the ears have been lifted; feet were large, as used to be the case with all pointers. I shot over the last of the breed in 1858, as good a bitch as one could wish for. She was stolen, and we could never trace her. They all had the clean-cut head and fine stern' (November 12th, 1895).

Then, at Renton Abbey near Stafford, Lord Lichfield had an excellent kennel of working dogs, and he was one of the prime movers in the establishment of Field Trials, most of the very early meetings being held on his property.

In Yorkshire, besides those I have already mentioned, Lord Mexborough, the Blands of Kippax, and Sir Harry Goodricke, all had famous breeds dating from early in the century.

Northumberland is represented by the wonderful black pointers belonging to Admiral Mitford (b. 1781, d. 1870), and Cumberland by the liver-and-white Edenhall strain, which survived till recently, but now

# THE POINTER

(1902), Sir R. G. Musgrave writes, is unfortunately extinct.

In Lancashire, the pointers at Knowsley were bred most studiously by the thirteenth Earl of Derby (b. 1775, d. 1851). I have in my possession a portrait of one of his dogs, Quiz, named and dated 1812, by Barenger, who was himself a sportsman. The dog is a much-marked black and white; he is lightly made, and has great quality, with a beautiful eye, perfect legs and feet for a pointer, and a very fine but half-docked tail.

Of the same county was the Croxteth race, which belonged to Lord Sefton (the third Earl, b. 1796, d. 1855), and no blood from any kennel has been of more service to posterity. Though the breed at its fountain-head became degenerate before it was finally dispersed in the seventies, yet most kennels where there was an admixture of its blood were found to have also valuable pointer-like characteristics.

In Shropshire there never was a more noted sort than that kept at Woodcote, about which Colonel Cotes has sent me the following interesting account:—

'My father was born at Woodcote near Newport, Shropshire, in 1799, and had a good kennel of pointers. I have often heard him say that, when he was a boy, they had a capital breed of pointers there, worked by the old keeper, Andrew Penson, and that they were supposed to be as good as any in the county. The kennel book begins in 1817, but only gives a list of the dogs as they were entered. In 1825 there is a note of a bitch named Venus that came from G. J. Serjeantson of Hanlith Hall, Yorkshire, and, in the same year, Sylvia, from Sir E. Dodsworth, who had a celebrated breed of pointers at Newland Park in the same county. I can remember my father saying that he offered Sir E. Dodsworth 100*l.* for three pointers that he had in 1826, but he would not sell them. My

## LATER HISTORY

father, however, got another pointer from him in 1832, and in 1838 a bitch, Quail, and she was put to Lord Mexborough's Flint. He also got bitches from Lord Stamford, Lord Henry Bentinck, and others, to breed with his Woodcote strain. He was a very good shot, and used to take up his team of dogs (five or six brace) every year, for about thirty years, to High Force, to shoot with the Duke of Cleveland. I can quite well remember his team of pointers forty-five years ago. They were all lemon-and-white, long, low, medium-sized dogs, with lots of quality and plenty of bone; I have never seen a more even lot. My brother, after my father's death in 1874, kept them on till 1885, when they were all sold at Aldridge's, and I regret to say that I did not buy any of them. They averaged a good price: about twenty guineas each.'

Colonel Cotes has a picture of two of these pointers, painted in 1833 by W. Smith; it represents them, as described above, of the finest quality, with typical head, ears, tails, and bone; but whether Providence or the artist be responsible for the pattern, they are distinctly ill-favoured in their hind-quarters.

Sir Vincent Corbet, Mr. H. Powys, and Mr. Noel Hill of Berrington, had also some excellent pointers in this county about the middle of last century.

It is improbable that the Woodcote records were known to 'Stonehenge' when he wrote the following passage:—

'The pedigrees of our pointers seldom extend beyond two or three generations, and even Mr. Edge in his day could hardly have gone farther, nor could the breeders of the present time trace their pointers sufficiently far back to settle the question of their origin. The pedigrees of those bred by Lord Sefton are probably as well made out as any in the kingdom, but even they are far from leading to what is desired.

# THE POINTER

If a dog is traced up to any one of Mr. Edge's kennel, all is done which is now necessary, and, indeed, all that can be useful to the sportsman, however interesting a further investigation might be to the naturalist' (*The Dog*, 1859, p. 89).

It is impossible, however, that he can have seen the pedigree-books of Mr. George John Legh (b. 1768) and his son, Mr. George Cornwall Legh of High Legh, Cheshire, as these books are kept from 1828 with perfect accuracy and method.

In the same county there were the pointers of the Marquis of Westminster, an early competitor at the trials; of Mr. J. C. Antrobus of Eaton Hall, who also ran dogs at the first meetings; and of Lord Combermere, who frequently judged thereat.

Mr. Antrobus, describing the establishment of the breed formerly at Eaton Hall, writes that they sprang 'first from a brace of pointers given by Sir Charles Shakerley (b. 1792) of Somerford Park, Cheshire, to my father. I have a hazy notion that they were said to be Edge's breed. Then came an infusion of the Cornwall Legh stock, and later on we passed into the lemon-and-white, mostly descendants of a bitch of that colour given me by Mr. Thornycroft, the sculptor, father of Hamo Thornycroft. I do not know whence she came, but she was certainly well-bred.'

The best known of the old Welsh breeds was the Wynnstay, Sir Watkin Wynn's; but for many years the breeding and management of the pointers was left in the hands of a trusted keeper, Mr. W. Leighton, who in 1895 wrote to me that, 'at the time I left Wynnstay and sold part of the kennels to the present Sir Watkin, I destroyed all my pedigree books, &c.'

Sir Watkin had till quite recently a beautiful dog of the old Wynnstay blood, called Banjo O'Gymru, and still possesses his descendants. Indeed, as far as I

## LATER HISTORY

know, he is the only man in England or Wales who can boast pointer blood that has been in the family for fifty years!

It is sad to think that not a single one of the kennels that were famous at the beginning of the nineteenth century should have survived till the opening of the twentieth, for Colonel Cotes and Colonel Legh, though they may still own pointers, have entirely lost their old strains.

Among notable gundog-lovers we now come to Sir Richard Garth, who during all his long life has been enthusiastic about shooting over dogs, was one of the most successful competitors at the beginning of pointer and setter Trials, and was the breeder of the renowned Drake (Plate XVIII.). When he left as Chief Justice for Calcutta in 1875, he sold his dogs at Tattersall's. A passage from a letter to me (February 26th, 1902) gives proof both of his own former prowess and the excellence of his pointers :—
'I wonder whether my best day has ever been beaten : one brace of dogs, one gun, one gillie, one pony, from 9 a.m. to 5 p.m., eighty-eight and a half brace grouse, sundry hares, snipe, &c.'

Mr. Whitehouse of Ipsley Court, Redditch, was in his day an equally eminent pointer-breeder. In his strain of lemon-and-whites he contrived to concentrate by far the purest blood that remains nowadays in this country. He bred Hamlet (Plate XVII.), a dog equally remarkable in the field and at stud, and about him he writes to me : ' My old bitch Juno I exhibited at the second exhibition held at the Repository, Birmingham (1860), and won fifth prize. She was bred by a Mr. Tomes, of Cleeve Prior, Worcestershire, and was by a dog called Frank ; I believe he was bred by Lord Coventry. Juno was a wonderfully good bitch in the field. I do not know anything more about her

## THE POINTER

pedigree. Mr. Bird's Bob took first prize at the same show, and I put Juno to him; she had eight puppies. I kept Hamlet, Carlo, and Mona. Mr. Bird's Bob was a dog very wide across the nose: I dare say you have noticed that most dogs with a broad nose carry their heads high. All my lemon-and-whites were very hardy; they would stand any amount of work. I have shot over them in September from as soon as you could see in the morning till dark, and worked them day after day. I used to let Hamlet retrieve, and he was a very fair retriever, a good deal better than many retrievers I have seen. Just before I won the sweepstakes at Bala with Hamlet he was badly shot, and I was doubtful if I should be able to take him. I mention this to show you what a game old dog he was, and if you ask any one who was there, they will tell you that the longer he worked the better he behaved.' Now, Bird's Bob, which was the sire of Hamlet, was bred by Mr. J. Lang, the well-known gun-maker of Cockspur Street, London,—and Mr. Lang was as renowned for his pointers as for his guns, and used to command top prices for both. In this double calling, formerly not at all uncommon, his most eminent prototype was Mr. Page of Norwich, who wrote *The Art of Shooting Flying* (1767). Another of Mr. Page's followers is Mr. W. R. Pape of Newcastle-on-Tyne, and I fear he will prove the last. His breed of black pointers is celebrated, but he is chary of distributing it. The story of this kennel from his own pen (February 12th, 1894) is of great value:—

'It is now about forty years since I started to breed my black pointers, and have had them ever since. I got a black pointer bitch from Admiral Mitford, who had then a kennel of those pointers, which had a great name in this county. She was a perfect wonder in the field, so that I at last wished to get some pups to

## LATER HISTORY

oblige my sporting friends. I was told that in Spain they had the black breed, and a friend of mine was going out to Spain to look for ironstone and coal. I got him to get a dog for me. He was most fortunate in going to a large estate, where the owner had a kennel of pure black pointers, and gave my friend one, a fine dog. He had one of the most efficient heads I ever saw on a dog. He was powerful and heavy, very strong and healthy, and one of the most wise dogs I ever saw. I had him fourteen or fifteen years. His son, a dog from this pair, was a grand dog. I shot over him for thirteen or fourteen years, and gave him to General York, America, who shot over him three years longer, and his letters all say that he never saw such a dog on any game, and the General was a great dogman. I sent three young dogs out to America a few years ago. They were broken there, and all three took first prize at field trials. Those are the last I bred. I was once going to get a cross from Mr. Usher, but I was informed they had all white between forelegs, so I did not care about them. I only used them for my own shooting. Although I had many most handsome-looking dogs, I did not bother to send to shows. There was a show in Scotland that gave a prize to black pointers two years ago. This I was told by a gentleman to whom I had given a pair of pups. I had a lot of pointers before I got the black breed, but have never had any other sort since I got them. Those that went to America gave great satisfaction. I got up the first dog show that was held in Newcastle, 1859. Mr. Angus, a friend of mine, had a young black dog at the show, one of my breed, and, although the judges gave the prize to a liver-and-white dog, Mr. Walsh, the Editor of the *Field*, said in the *Field*, on reporting the show, that this dog, to his fancy, was the finest pointer dog there.'

# THE POINTER

There is very little mention of English keepers and breakers before the establishment of Trials, possibly because, in those leisure days, the masters themselves found time to *finish* their puppies as well as to work them when actually out shooting, only intrusting to the servants the removal of the rough edge. Still, such gamekeepers as John Mayer, who wrote the *Sportsman's Directory* (1815), and William Floyd, in the employ of Sir J. Sebright and author of *Observations on Dog-breaking* (1821), must have been worthy of all respect and attention. Pierce Egan (in his *Anecdotes*, 1827) gives a slight sketch of John Harris, a dog-breaker of his day :—

'Not that he thought a stubborn dog irreclaimable ; these, when once broken, were often the best of dogs in his opinion, and of his own opinion in these respects he was rather tenacious. To any one who seemed to question the making of an untractable animal about to be committed to his care, his constant reply was, " show me the dog with anything whatsoever of the breed of the pointer about him that I cannot break, and I will show you a man who has a lock of hair growing on the palm of his hand "' (p. 229).

Captain Lacy also, in *The Modern Shooter*, 1842, refers to two renowned breakers. 'I have seen Mr. Odlin, gamekeeper to — Turner, Esq., of Panton, in Lincolnshire, and one of the best dog-breakers in Great Britain, hunt five pointers at once, evidently in a state of complete subjection to the breaker's will. Mr. Brailsford, too, keeper to the Earl of Chesterfield, in Nottinghamshire, is a very superior artist in the nice science of reducing dogs to a perfect state of discipline in the shooting-field' (p. 145).

Of these two, the former is only recalled to us nowadays by the occurrence of his name in some old pedigree ; but the son of the latter, Mr. W. Brailsford,

## LATER HISTORY

was himself a breaker of high repute, and before his recent death sent me (May 11th, 1900) the following biography of his father :—

'Captain Lacy's reference applies to my father, and I may mention a few facts in relation to my father's progress through life which may be of interest to you. My father changed, at advanced salary, to take charge of a large tract of shooting at Morley, Stanley, and West Hallam, held by good old Mr. Jeffrey Lockett of Derby, and where for many years he had a very superior kennel of setters. From Mr. Lockett he moved, about 1833, to take charge of Lord Chesterfield's large shootings at Gedling and Bingham, and here he took some of his black setters from Mr. Lockett's, and with some black-and-white pointers which he found at Gedling, he now formed the best mixed kennel of working dogs I have known in my large experience. Hares were so numerous at Gedling then that from 200 to 400 were killed in a day's partridge-shooting, and one day, which I can well remember, Count d'Orsay and Colonel Anson killed, in Stocksfield (?), fifty brace of partridges and 150 hares; and I have actually seen hares jump over the dogs' backs when in work.'

Another famous dog-breaker, Mr. John Armstrong, was born about 1800 at Bew Castle, in Cumberland. He was of Scottish descent, and his father was a well-known farmer, who employed him first as shepherd and afterwards as topsman. When he was in his twentieth year, his fame as a dog-breaker reached the ears of Sir James Graham of Netherby, who sent for him. The result of their first interview was decisive, as, according to his son, when Sir James had catechised him thoroughly, he wished to see him working his brace of setters, 'after which he said, "John Armstrong, I am quite delighted with both your dogs and

# THE POINTER

yourself. I will give you forty guineas for your dogs, and, with your father's consent, I depute you from to-day as my head keeper and lands bailiff." An appointment he held, with honour and distinction, for forty-five years, nor ever changed, nor wished to change, his place.' Mr. Edward Armstrong, the son, worthily sustains the traditional tastes of his sire, even to the present day.

Then there was Mr. Elias Bishop (b. 1809, d. 1882), another of the celebrities of the golden age of pointers, who commenced at the age of fifteen to shoot over his father's dogs. He was bailiff and steward to Mr. George Morgan, Biddlesdon Park, Bucks; but he was not a game-keeper, though he ran a setter at some Trials in 1869, and won with it. He possessed a first-rate strain of pointers, which he had inherited from his father, who was a tenant-farmer; and this breed he duly passed to his children, who, like so many others, improved it away and lost it. Four of his sons, Elias, James, Charles, and Edwin, are eminent in the Trial world, and there are still Bishops of the fourth generation coming on as breakers. The first named of the sons writes:—'I can well remember my father when he shot over as many as three brace of pointers at one time; those were the days of stubbles up to your knees, and mowing machines not thought of.'

Last, but not least, among the notable breakers, I must mention Mr. Ecob, my father's old keeper. His methods of training I used to watch and wonder at. He had a mysterious, innate power over his pupils, such as I have never seen in any one else. All dogs loved him instinctively—but they had to obey, though his magnetism prevented their ever being cowed by him. He was so busy with his other duties, for he was my Mother's factotum, that his breaking had to be

## LATER HISTORY

done at lightning speed, and he always schooled his puppies two together. In consequence, though there was not always time to teach beautiful quartering, all his dogs backed in a fashion unknown nowadays. To exemplify the man's extraordinary breaking, I remember that once he procured a brace of wild Irish setters, perfectly ignorant and unbroken. He commenced with them one Monday, and eight days afterwards some one came down to buy a brace of well-broken dogs, tried these setters all day, carried them off with him, and wrote, after the season, to say how delighted he still was with them.

I have now followed the fortunes of the pointer down to 1860, to the end of the second period, and have even traced the history of some families a few steps further, into the reign of Dog-show and Field trial. In my next chapter, as I pursue his after-career, an ungrateful task to any one who loves a real pointer, I shall not interfere with particular dogs or their owners, but shall confine myself to general criticisms of Shows and Trials, with their effects on the modern pointer, and shall show that degeneration in him was a necessary consequence of the methods of the Kennel Club. The interests of this body, ranging from lap-dogs to life-savers, were far too wide to permit of its ever being a satisfactory legislator for the gundogs; and the votaries of no other branch of sport have been so insane as to submit to its jurisdiction, or to get their dogs mixed up in such an olla-podrida. For, in a club like this, the shooting men must be in a minority, and laws will be passed that may be good for barzois or bulldogs, but will spell ruin for sporting-dogs. The Jockey Club is entirely distinct from the Shire-horse Society; though thoroughbreds and cart-horses, both being *working* varieties of the same animal, have more affinity than exists between sporting

## THE POINTER

and fancy dogs. It, therefore, follows that when a 'Hybrid Committee,' in 1874, met to design a stud-book for the Kennel Club, they should have hit upon a scheme that, while advantageous to the 'idle' breeds, was fatal to the well-being of the pointer. For—all show-winners, without any guarantee of their working qualities, were admitted free of charge into this precious publication, and thus were given, even from the first, a numerical majority of twenty-to-one over the trial-dogs: but not long afterwards, *work* was thrust still further in the background by the revocation of the early stud-book rule of free-entry for every dog that had competed at a Trial.

A stud-book for a working breed based on looks alone must always be a stumbling-block to the unwary and a laughing-stock to the knowing ones, who remark sneeringly that, for true working quality, you must avoid a pointer with a number to his name.

By placing the description of the black pointers of Scotland in this chapter, I do not wish to infer that there is any very old Scottish breed of that colour, nor that the race was originally in any way distinct from strains of the same colour in other parts of Great Britain. Their importance for us lies in the fact that they were established long before the commencement of the show period, and are to the present day unaffected by the demoralising influence of the Stud-book—in short, are still quite *behind the times*. They have ever been bred for a pointer's legitimate purpose ; and, therefore, I think that in this division is found the proper context wherewith to associate even their recent history.

In Scotland the keepers were always greater personages than in England, as Colonel Thornton found to his annoyance at the Duke of Hamilton's, and they really owned the dogs in nine-tenths of the cases. This

## LATER HISTORY

state of things, though to the historian disastrous from the consequent contempt of written pedigrees, no doubt tended to preserve the practical qualities of the race. And as these keepers were, like the poet, born not made, they received their pointers from their forebears, only to hand them on eventually to their sons.

Mr. John Bishop (head-keeper to Mr. Pollock of Auchineden near Glasgow), who has since 1895 been keenly interested in my work, and whose invaluable assistance I here gratefully acknowledge, writes in February of that year :—

'I have been to see three kennels of pointers. First, a kennel of liver and whites, that I heard was a grand lot ; they were just Devonshire houndy dogs not worth any comment. Second, a kennel at the Trossachs, Perthshire. This is the kennel of the old black strain I wrote you about. One keeper tells me this kennel of dogs has been bred from the best working black dogs for years. The present keeper has had charge of them for two years only. He has had a lot of experience in other large kennels, where he was kennel-boy and under-keeper. He says he never saw game-finders like them, or better at backing and going down-wind. He says he has seen them throw themselves on their side in stopping. They are all black in colour, most of them have a heavy dewlap. The best in the ten is very throaty or dewlapped—her breast or brisket projects about four inches from her forelegs, giving her the appearance of being loaded at the front, not loaded at the shoulder, feet and legs fair, tail not very well carried. This bitch has a beautiful expression of eye. Ears too large for what is wanted now—they nearly meet under her neck. Third, I went to Kirriemuir in Forfarshire, and saw a kennel of ten black pointers at Cortachy Castle. They are bred from the dogs the Black Prince shot so many birds over in a short time. They are

# THE POINTER

dogs of a light build, rather fine in bone and snipy in muzzle, tails badly carried and not well set on, light in eye and flat-sided—still they look like work. One bitch I liked : she had a fine coat and ear, good feet, but her eye was a shade light, and her tail was a bit ring-shaped. I expected to see something good at Cortachy, as I knew he got two black pointers from Mr. Gordon of Aikenhead about twenty-eight years ago, and I sent him a dog of Mr. Lindsay's about twelve years since. He told me he had the finest dogs ever he owned, by that dog of Mr. Lindsay's. He regrets now he parted with them. He got big prices for them, and they all went.'

Now this letter having been the starting-point of my investigations, I cannot do better than analyse and expand its information.

Its 'kennel at the Trossachs' belongs to Mr. James Graham of Auchray Lodge, and the purity of the breed is most carefully preserved ; in fact the 'projecting brisket'—a malformation which, though unsightly, in no way impedes them at their work—only occurs among purely-bred pointers. This breed, says Mr. J. H. M. Graham, was originally an offshoot from Mr. Gordon's of Aikenhead. Mr. Gordon's kennel enjoyed in the North much the same reputation as Mr. Edge's in England—his dogs were the *ne plus ultra* of pointers. And when Mr. Bishop, as a mere lad, entered his service in 1869, he found 'fourteen brace of black pointers, almost without a white hair on them.' Here is his further description :

'Mr. Thomas Gaunt, head-keeper to that eminent sportsman, John Gordon, Esq. of Aikenhead, Cathcart, near Glasgow, had the largest kennel of black pointers in Scotland, and it was considered *by far* the best. I was second keeper, and had all to do with the dogs, so I can remember all about them. Mr. Gaunt brought

## LATER HISTORY

the breed from South Wales : they were all black, and bred from blacks for many a year before. He was then, in 1839, with a gentleman named Summers Harford, Esq., who had a shooting near Merthyr Tydvil. He came, in 1842, with the same gentleman to one of Lord Eglinton's shootings (Cloughern, East Kilbride). When there, he bred with an old pointer-dog, which Mr. White, head-keeper at Douglas Castle, owned. This dog was black just by chance, his strain was black and white; and Mr. Gaunt always said when a black-and-white pup came that it was Mr. White's sort. He afterwards brought the breed to Aikenhead, in 1846, and bred black ones only, as Mr. Gordon liked them best. The Aikenhead black pointers soon became famous, and bitches came from all parts. Mr. Gaunt just took a pup, which he went and picked, from bitches he approved of, so he soon had the best of all. The kennel that he thought most of was the Earl of Wemyss's at Gosford. They had also a breed of black double-nosed pointers, but he only bred from them once, as they were clumsy and soft. Mr. Lloyd, head-keeper to the Duke of Hamilton, had a large kennel of black pointers about thirty-seven years ago, but the most of them came from Aikenhead. Mr. Kirke, head-keeper to John Graham, Esq. (father of Mr. James Graham) of Skelmorlie, had a large kennel of blacks about 1850, and I fancy long before that ; he also brought his bitches to Aikenhead. When taking the pointers from Aikenhead to Riemore (Mr. Gordon's Highland shooting), I walked them through Dunkeld, and it took me hours, from English sportsmen, who were staying there, examining them, and asking all about their work. They said they had many a time heard of the black pointers, but never before had the chance of seeing such beauties.

The Cortachy Castle breed belonged to Mr. Carnegie, the head-keeper to Lord Airlie, and ' the Black

# THE POINTER

Prince,' mentioned by Mr. Bishop, was the Maharajah Dhuleep Singh.

Lord Home possessed two separate stocks of pointers, the one at Douglas Castle, Lanark, the other at the Hirsel, Coldstream ; the former of which, Mr. Gaunt says, was not entirely black in 1842, but became so afterwards. For the late Mr. Amos, head-keeper at Douglas, in writing to me about Sweep, a first-rate dog that Lord Home lent to me in 1895, gave his pedigree as by Lord Lothian's Sancho out of a bitch of their own, whose ancestors were 'all jet black, very handsome, and good ones.' And Mr. James White, present head-keeper at the Hirsel, writes (December 1901) that 'James Craw, who succeeded his father as keeper *here*, and left nearly fifty years ago, kept black pointers, and was a great authority. His successor, William Reid, also kept them.'

Mr. W. McCall of Ferniehurst, Jedburgh, head-keeper of Lord Lothian, writes (January 1902) that he first got his noted strain ' from a keeper on the neighbouring estate of Hartrigg (Lord Stratheden and Campbell's), 1864.' He says that he has had the breed in his own possession for thirty-six years, and that his son William, keeper at Glen of Rothes, is also possessed of it ; that he has at different times used dogs of Lord Home's at the Hirsel, of Sir William Elliot's at Stobs Castle, Hawick, of the late Lord John Scott's, Spottiswood, Lauder, of Sheriff Rutherford's, Edgerston, Jedburgh ; that latterly for many years he has bred with the Douglas Castle dogs ; and that he first saw black pointers in 1852, when he went as under-keeper to Drumlanrig Castle, which belongs to the Duke of Buccleugh.

At three places belonging to the Duke were kennels of black pointers maintained : at Drumlanrig, Dumfriesshire, at Bowhill, Selkirk, and at Dalkeith near

## LATER HISTORY

Edinburgh, where Mr. Lindsay, the head-keeper, took a special pride in them.

The late Mr. Usher, who had the handsomest black pointers that I ever saw, attributed much of their excellence to the Bowhill dogs. In a letter to me about them, written in January 1894, he said :—

'I have had these dogs for fifteen years and have got a reputation for them. My first was a bitch, called Ruby, which I got at a sale, and which got a first prize at a show. She was very handsome and very good. I have been careful in breeding, by sending my bitches to be served by good dogs. There are several noblemen who use these pointers—the Duke of Buccleugh and the Earl of Wemyss, I know, do ; and Rap VI. was out of a bitch called Kate, by the Duke of Buccleuch's best dog. Rap was very handsome, and was the best dog I ever had on the hill ; on a beautiful day, it was a fine sight to see him at his work. It was the Duke's dogs at Bowhill, Selkirkshire, that served my bitches.'

The Stobo Castle breed was also remarkable for its beauty, but some years ago Sir Graham Montgomery informed me that it was extinct.

Mr. D. M. Forbes, of Riemore Lodge, Dunkeld, whose dogs are famous for splendid heads and fine quality (Plate XXII.), gives the following account of them, dated September 1899 :—

'I got the first of my black pointers from James Craw about sixteen years ago. Craw was for about forty years head-keeper at Netherby, and he told me that these pointers were descended from two that were got more than fifty years ago, one from the Earl of Home's and the other from the Marquis of Lothian's kennels. It is but right to tell you that, though I have kept black pointers as a rule, one of the two progenitors named was black and the other liver or

## THE POINTER

liver-and-white, and occasionally a liver or brown pup still appears in a litter of pups, though the parents may be quite black. They have always, however, been most excellent dogs, and I have never found an indifferent worker in a litter. Every pup I have reared has invariably turned out a good one.'

This James Craw may very likely have been the man of the same name mentioned by Mr. White as having left the keeper's situation at the Hirsel, ' nearly fifty years ago.'

Mr. John Millar, of Whitehill Kennels, Aberdour, whose father kept a public kennel there and was keeper when a young man to Lord Wemyss, writes (January 1902) very explicitly. His father kept, as far back as 1831, a rough pedigree-book in which he recorded the names and full particulars of the dogs that he bred with. 'I do not know where my uncle, who was so long keeper at Gosford, got these pointers to begin with, whether they were there when he went, or whether he took them with him. But as he was associated with the black pointer before going there, it is very likely that he took them with him; for the Millars took them with them to any new place they went, as a thing connected with themselves. I never saw anywhere such models as they, and oh! such wisdom they had. If I was an artist I could yet paint from memory a perfect likeness of some of the model bitches we had; and as for true incidents, I believe I could give you matter to fill a whole volume itself, and such that would make you cry and laugh in succession.'

Mr. John Simpson, head-keeper to Lord Overtoun, Overtoun Moor, Dumbartonshire, procured a black bitch in 1858 from W. Millar, the father of Mr. John Millar, and from her ' bred the best kennel of pointers in Argyllshire.' He thus describes its foundation :—

'At that time I was young and anxious to dis-

# LATER HISTORY

tinguish myself, and I took the bitch to Eglinton Castle and got her warded by a son of Lord Eglinton's famous Grouse, the finest dog of his time. I was not very sure about her holding to that dog, as the heat did not leave her quickly, and I gave her one of my own dogs. However, to make sure, I wrote to Mr. Kirkland, the keeper, telling him about it, and he wrote back to say that, if there was a black-and-white pup in the litter, they were got by his dog, and so it turned out.'

I myself can testify to the excellence of the work of these Scottish pointers—indeed I have never seen an out-and-out *wonder* that had not got some black blood in his veins; and though I do not like their colour on the moor, I tolerate it because of their extraordinary cleverness.

If science and good luck brought gifts to the wedding, a blending of these blacks with the pied breeds of England might be followed by a regeneration all round; as, for want of an outcross, the Northerners are dwindling in size and constitution, while the Southerners are lacking in distinctive character. And there need be no fear of the cross proving too drastic, as the Scottish race is already full of English blood, absorbed at the best period.

No doubt, at present, the future looks rather gloomy for the pointer, but as ''tis darkest before dawn,' the present century may accentuate some streaks of light faintly wavering on his horizon.

He is not yet half-way through the third stage of his existence, and if there were a sudden reaction—his would not be the only case on record of re-establishment after forty years' wanderings.

## CHAPTER III.
## SHOWS AND WORKING TRIALS.

SHOWS and working trials for pointers are both the products of the last half-century; the former, open at first to pointers and setters alone, were instituted in 1859 at Newcastle-on-Tyne, while the first of the latter was held near Bedford in 1865. The shows were received with much enthusiasm, and at the outset, no doubt, did good. No one at that time had dreamed of keeping a pointer unfit for work or even unbroken, and the periodical exhibition of the handsomest working dogs of the different strains, collected together for comparison, should have tended without doubt to the perfection of the race. But the late Mr. W. Brailsford, in a letter to me about the starting of the Stafford trials in 1866, writes as follows:—'Another object was to bring to the front the best working strains of pointers and setters, as several dogs that had carried off prizes at dog-shows, after their introduction by my father, were worthless as field-dogs, and it seemed to me that a working test was the only reliable one to breed dogs of high character.' 'Stonehenge' corroborates this in 1877 with:—'From their institution at Newcastle in 1858 there has been a growing feeling of dissatisfaction with the awards of the judges' (*Dogs of the British Islands*, book iv., chap. i.). So, apparently, the idyllic state of affairs did not last very long!

Clever people soon fancied there was 'money in' the showing of so-called sporting-dogs; and the show type strayed farther and farther from the lines of the

## SHOWS AND WORKING TRIALS

old working pointer, until it touched the bottom about 1880, when the show-men, ignorant of the first principles of the pointer, could actually believe and applaud a writer who dared to sum him up thus :—'How can I better describe him than by saying he should be formed to a great extent on the model of the foxhound' (*The Dog*, Idstone, p. 118). But by this time Shows had multiplied like fever-rash — dog-showing had become a commercial profession—and doubtless the admixture of alien blood, alloying the gold, was found necessary to a dog that had to bear the constant strain of the show-bench.

But what was the Kennel Club doing all that time, may be asked ! Nothing, absolutely nothing. A nineteenth-century Gallio, it 'cared for none of those things.' As long as the pointer classes at its numerous shows were well filled, it was content. It still held Trials once a year, under the most cumbrous, ill-adapted rules that could be conceived ; but, as the entries kept on dwindling, the question of abandoning even these was mooted. From that catastrophe, however, I myself who was at that time a member was instrumental in saving it.

To give an instance of the apathy of the Kennel Club as regards pointer matters : it is not more than a couple of years since it first allowed the title of champion to be gained at Trials, though some of us had been clamouring for it long enough. It offered the title of champion as a reward for winners at Dog-shows, but there was no championship allowed for work even at its own Trials! On the same principle, I suppose, we should give our servants wages not for their skill, but for their looks! If the Kennel Club had demanded any proof of the working capacity of the show-ring winner before he assumed the title of champion, their custom would not have been so de-

# THE POINTER

moralising ; but, even if the conditions of its championships had themselves been sound, its method of granting them would have been absurd.

At the present time (1901) secretaries of Shows are invited to apply to the Kennel Club by a certain date, asking for these championships to be allotted to them. Then, however poor the entry, the judge is expected to award them, unless he withhold all first and second prizes from the classes. My suggestion was that a two-year average of the individual entries at the big shows, in each particular breed, should be taken ; that on these averages should be based the minimum number of dogs for the future award of championships, as by this method the rule would work automatically ; and that no pointer should be dubbed a champion until he had gained a championship both at a Trial and a Show. To give a casual example of the working of the present plan :—at Preston (1895), where there were thirty-three pointers, no championship ; at Edinburgh (1895), twenty-eight pointers, one championship ; at Darlington (1896), eleven pointers, two championships !

No doubt the sins of the Kennel Club against the pointer have been less of commission than of omission ; but, as if to emphasize its contempt for *work*, it excludes from its stud-book any mention of the field-trial classes at its shows. It is odd that a club founded more or less in the interests of the English sporting breeds should so soon have forsaken them to run after foreign dogs that are useless in England ; but, as Dr. Caius remarked over three hundred years ago, 'We English men are marvellous greedy gaping gluttons after novelties, and covetous cormorants of things that be seldom, rare, straunge and hard to get.' He knew his fellow-countrymen then—and now !

I do not wish to suggest for a moment that as a

## SHOWS AND WORKING TRIALS

dog-show club pure and simple the Kennel Club has done amiss, for (again like Gallio) it appears to police its kingdom effectually enough, and its registration of dogs' names and pedigrees is emphatically a benefit to all. It is as a guardian of the English working-dogs, and as a bulwark against the seething whirlpools of 'fancy,' that it has proved such a failure.

To turn to the other Societies connected with the pointer, there is the National Pointer and Setter Society (often called the Shrewsbury Society), the oldest of all, which has, I believe, held Trials regularly since 1866. It has had little to do with the retrogression of the pointer, except in so far as its Trials, in common with those of the other Societies, have been tainted by the omnipresent spirit of fancy. Indeed, it has always held itself superior to the dog-show element, and it was the inventor of the sportsmanlike 'spotting system,' now adopted by all the other Societies at their Meetings.

The Pointer Club was another Trial society, but solely for pointers. It held its first Meeting in 1889 and after that date held them annually, until, Mrs. Dombey-like, it finally flickered out at the birth of the International Shooting-dog Club in 1895. The Pointer Club was never a very vertebrate affair, and one of its definitions, 'that the type of pointer as described by "Stonehenge" be adopted,' is as ambiguous as anything from Delphi! I have three editions of 'Stonehenge' now before me, 1858, 1867, and 1882: the pointer described is different in them all, and the illustrations make the confusion worse confounded.

The International Shooting-dog Club, springing as a phœnix from the ashes of the Pointer Club in 1895, has certainly shown itself more anxious for the well-being of the gundogs than its older relatives. It

# THE POINTER

has brought out an excellent set of Trial rules (grafted on those of the National Society), has regularly held autumn Trials on grouse, and from the first has encouraged brace-stakes.

It soon changed its rather truculent title into the International Pointer and Setter Society, and more recently has united with the Sporting Spaniel Society and the Retriever Society as a section of the International Gundog League. The League has started a yearly dinner where all gundog-lovers may meet, and has also instituted a badge for its members as a pledge of unity of object. But these things, though very well, are not enough. The League must hold an annual dog-show for gundogs, it must establish a stud-book open to trial-winners and certificated dogs alone, it must support *local* Trials, and it must see that the judges carry out its excellent rules. It might also with advantage establish certificated stud-dogs in different localities at a reduced fee. Captain Lacy, about 1840, foreshadowed in a remarkable manner the actual establishment of the Societies:—' The grand cause of the continued superabundance of ill-bred dogs, and the difficulty of procuring good-bred and first-rate ones, is the want—as far as I know, the entire want—of the establishment of societies professedly for the purpose of promoting improvement in the breed and training of pointers and setters!' (Lacy's *Modern Shooter*, p. 145). Let us hope he will prove an equally true prophet of the benefits that he does imply are to follow—in spite of that qualifying ' professedly.' Of one thing, however, I am certain,—that, if these good times ever do come, to the League will belong the credit. But it must press forward, as the other Societies will have to try to keep pace with it; and glorious will it be if the gundog, after receiving for long enough nothing but harm from Shows, and very

# SHOWS AND WORKING TRIALS

mixed blessings from Trials, at last begin to reap real benefits from them both! The title of International, which seemed a few years ago happily chosen on account of the League's membership of all nations, its Continental Trials, Officers, and Committees, is now alas! rendered practically meaningless through the six months' quarantine imposed by the Board of Agriculture, which, while granting exemptions to the performing dogs of the music-hall, has refused so far any privilege to gundogs entered for Trials, though from the very nature of their calling they have to be not only under close supervision, but also in perfect health!

Nevertheless, its full title is retained by the Society in the hope that some day the official eyes may be opened, and that the liberties of the pointer may not remain entangled in bureaucratic red-tape.

The 'fancier' at the shows has long been recognised, and sportsmen have always deplored his influence among the gundogs. By the name of fancier they define a harmful person whose mania it is to be unable to see any useful or beautiful point in an animal without longing to develop it abnormally to the ruin of all symmetry : such a being would be safe nowhere but in a dove-cot, where his efforts might at least be buried under piecrust. Sometimes he exaggerates useful qualities till they become useless : his hobby otherwhile is to engraft foreign characteristics on his victims.

The seed of the 'pointer-fancy' was sown at the first dog-show ; it was germinating when pointers were forced to do the double duty of the show-ring and the field ; and it was in full bloom in the days when men regardless of the proper use of gundogs, and lusting after Show-prizes, bred pointers as like foxhounds as they could get them. The designs of fanciers are also

# THE POINTER

furthered by those who after buying a dog or two at high prices have been pitchforked into the office of judge by some astute show-secretary, alive to the fact that a novice in the judging list and a large entry frequently form a sequence. But such a man seldom has a knowledge of dogs, perhaps he has never even seen them at work, and has no notion of the exquisite balance that makes perfection of form in the working breeds. So when actually in the ring he is panic-stricken by a sudden sense of his own ignorance, and clings in his alarm to any feature prominent enough to catch his eye.

The press also is not guiltless in this matter. Very often unfortunate reporters are sent down to write essays on gundogs without even knowing the sporting A, B, C, so they fall a prey to the smooth-tongued fancier, who is ever ready to hymn the particular fad of the moment. Even their inept criticisms fade, however, when compared with the doings of the anonymous reporter-cum-exhibitor-cum-judge, a monstrous trinity that is a perpetual scandal, be the conduct of this composite person ever so pure. All honour, then, to those editors who order the reports of Shows and Trials to be signed, and to those reporters who obey!

So much for 'fancy' at the Shows: but, though it may appear still more out of place at the Trials, it is there too! At their commencement Trials for pointers and setters were started unfortunately, because unnaturally, with the so-called single stakes, *i.e.* stakes in which two dogs, strangers to each other and handled by different men, work in direct competition. Thus there soon arose among the breakers such keen rivalry to secure points at any cost that quartering, backing, roading the game, style, and obedience to signal were sacrificed. The judges of the period joined in this

## SHOWS AND WORKING TRIALS

rabid point-worship, some no doubt because it simplified their duties, others from the flashiness of this kind of work; until the ideal 'trialer' came by breeding and breaking to be a sort of machine with a good nose, very fast, and immovable on the point till the birds were flushed for him. He dashed into the wind straight down the middle of his ground, showing what his admirers were pleased to call his 'bird-sense,' which meant finding those birds lying in his course and ignoring all the rest. Thus was bird-sense substituted for common-sense; and though the hare-foot was condemned, the hare-brain was in the ascendant. Such dogs were, of course, quite useless on the grouse-moor, as I found out by bitter experience; and I fear that the uselessness of costly trial-winners has turned many a promising 'dog-man' into a 'driver.' That dogs no good to shoot over can win at Trials is proof positive of rottenness in the system, and even 'Stonehenge' himself had to own:—' In any case, to count up the number of times each competitor finds a brace of birds, and decide by that alone in a trial limited to minutes, is, in my opinion, to give chance too great a " pull "' (*Dogs of the British Islands*, 1883 ed., p. 89). And as evidence that 'fancy' had not altogether ceased from troubling even in 1901:—a setter in one of the Stakes was awarded a first prize at a moment when she had galloped far out of sight both of judges and handlers.

I fear that nothing now will put a check on the popularity of the single-stake. Its element of luck, its excitement, and its standard of partial breaking are very attractive to most; although nearly all the in-and-out runnings at Trials, and the dissatisfaction arising therefrom, are attributable to this form of trying dogs. The brace-stake, in which the two dogs that work together belong to the same owner and are

## THE POINTER

worked by one man, was started later. It demands work identical with the work done out shooting, but it has never yet created enthusiasm among the many. If brace-stakes were judged carefully, there would be the same continuity in the awards as is found at spaniel trials : a greater gain, perhaps, to the breeds of pointers than to the coffers of the trial-giving Societies. Anyhow, the brace-stake is treated as a rule with scant courtesy, sandwiched in anywhere, and the braces are given but one trial each. For it is subordinated completely to the racing single-stakes ; and actually the National Society goes out of its way to bar expressly a win in a brace-stake from qualifying a dog to compete in its champion stake !

I have often heard it said that if there were less chance and uncertainty in the running of the dogs it would affect trials injuriously. My own opinion is entirely against this ; though no doubt the scale of prizes would have to be remodelled, the offered money cut down somewhat, and the immense first prizes abolished by utilising the surplus among the other prizes to make them more proportionate. For, as long as competitors look on a stake as a kind of lottery, they may be attracted by a lump sum ; but if the best dogs were generally in the money, they would require that money to be more widely distributed. To make it clearer, if the breed is to be encouraged, and the production of good shooting-dogs adequately rewarded, when A, B, and C, all good dogs and about equal in merit, are left in at the end of a stake, A ought not to win more than double what B does, because of the judges' (often vacillating) decision. I dare say I shall be blamed for telling unpleasant truths, but I see no other way of getting justice for pointer and setter, and nothing is to be gained by paltering any longer with matters so vital to them. The time-

## SHOWS AND WORKING TRIALS

honoured way to rouse sleepers is by 'shouts and shakings.'

At length I can turn to a task more congenial, that of criticising and discussing the methods of judging at Trials, taking as my model the admirable rules of the Pointer and Setter Society (I.G.L.). A judge at a Meeting, if he conscientiously do his duty, has no sinecure; and especially on a grouse-moor he must be both mentally and bodily an exceptionally endowed person. If wind or limb give out and he lag behind, or if he relax his attention for one moment during the day when dogs are running, in that moment a flush may pass for a point or a cast may become a chase, and vitiate the equity of a whole stake. And in addition to his physical qualifications, he must be right-minded enough to recognise that by accepting this office he becomes the servant of the competitors as a whole, bound to give his own ripe judgment; and that if he fail to do so through idleness, fear, or favouritism, he fails also in common honesty.

Of course there are still extant undesirable types of the judge, but they are certainly becoming rarer. I will only mention three of these, which may be distinguished as 'feudalist,' 'foretelling,' and 'faddish.' Of the first of these is he who apparently considers that the prizes are to be *presented*, not awarded, by him, and that his beneficence, not his judgment, is to be called into action. He will complacently put forward that he 'does not care for that colour in a pointer,' and that he 'never fancied Irish setters,' as reasons for excluding them from the prize-list. Of the second is he who will say openly at lunch-time, when the dogs have run once, that such-and-such a dog must win, that he knew as much the moment he clapped eyes on it, &c. And after this pronouncement let that dog commit the gravest faults, let another

## THE POINTER

perform never so well, the judicial prophecy will be fulfilled. Of the third is he who analyses the motives of the dogs in their work, and arrogates for the poor beasts brains as complex as his own. Such analysis may be interesting in one's own kennel, with unlimited time at one's disposal and cumulative experience of each dog's individual record; but at a trial it is quite out of place, and in a public money-stake manifestly unfair. The best judging is of the plain, straightforward, 'under your nose' sort, taking care that all the decisions can be proved by *rule of gun*!

It was, I suppose, in the expectation of getting judging of this kind at the Trials that the 'spotting system' was first invented. It derives its name from the judges being allowed a practically free hand, being allowed to 'spot' the winners how they like. If the judges are strong and thoroughly capable, I think it the best of the three systems, but if they are not first-rate—infinitely the worst. It throws all responsibility on them—they can retain, they can dismiss the dogs as they choose; and until the announcement of the prizes at the finish the spectators can but guess at the progress of the stake. I consider the secrecy of this system, and its consequent dullness to the lookers-on, its chief defects.

The 'heat system' was undisguisedly a gamble. It did not pretend to discover any but the best dog; and it magnified the element of luck even as regarded him. Still it was much more interesting, and much more likely to captivate and educate the casual visitor to the Trials. The method of conducting this system is, or rather was, to draw by lot into pairs, and so run, all the competing dogs, in order to pick out the better one from each pair. These selected dogs were then drawn together, and again chosen from. And similar procedure was continued, until only one dog

# SHOWS AND WORKING TRIALS

remained in the stake. This one of course took first prize, while the one last put out by him had the second, and so on.

But no community with any lingering respect for the traditional uses of gundogs would have tolerated this system for long; so the Kennel Club eventually replaced it by the 'modified heat system,' which allowed the dogs that had been beaten in any of the heats by the absolute winner to compete afterwards for the other prizes, and authorized the judges to pronounce at pleasure any particular trial to be 'undecided,' admitting both competitors into the next round. But before that time most trial-men had become so impatient of the farcical results of the crude 'heat system' that they would not give these modifications a chance.

Myself I believe that, granting the necessity for holding single stakes at all, the modified heat system could be made, with a few improvements, the most satisfactory of all; it is so much more lively, and much more helpful to any ordinary judge. If, for instance, to its existing regulations power were added to dismiss both dogs after a trial, and if when ties were over dogs that had not met before in any heats might be run together, this system would I fancy come again into vogue.

Having now explained the earlier systems, I will proceed to review the Trial laws of the I. P. S. S.; of which code Rules 1 and 2, embodying adequate formulas for the organization of single and brace stakes, do not call for any comment.

Rule 3 dictates a minimum time for the duration of each trial in the first round, ensures that the prize-winners shall have run together, and insists that no brace-stake shall be decided before all meritorious braces have been tested twice. This last is a most necessary addition of the present year (1901), to guard

## THE POINTER

the braces a little against the chances of unequal conditions. But it is a significant fact that as yet no other Society has accorded them even this elementary courtesy!

Rule 4 forbids any prize to a dog that will not back of his own accord. As a rider to this, the judges might well be requested to call up the backing dog after a point, and let the two start level for the fresh cast: otherwise a willing backer is so heavily handicapped. I remember a notable instance of this; when a pottering little bitch, running with an admirable setter, got a point at once and was backed, then a second and a third in rapid succession, going straight up the field, while the dog got further and further behind. The bitch won on this, though she was not worth the dog's shadow!

Rule 5, I really must quote in full :—'The Judges will, in making their awards, give full consideration to the manner in which the ground is quartered and beaten, and are requested not to award a prize to the dog of any owner or handler, who does not beat his ground and work exactly as he would do were he actually out shooting.' O admirable rule, — more honoured, alas, in the breach than in the observance!

Rule 6 is to protect a dog from the evil consequences of detention on point by the judges as a provocative of non-backing in his rival.

Rule 7 also deserves to be printed in full :—'The judges shall not decide the merit of a dog's running from the number of times he points game, backs, &c., but from the style and quality of his performance as a whole. Dogs are required to maintain a fast and killing range, wide or narrow as the necessity of the case demands; to quarter the ground with judgment and regularity, to leave no game behind them, and to be obedient, cheerful, and easily handled.' Here is a

## SHOWS AND WORKING TRIALS

spirited demand for a perfect judge and a perfect trial dog! In 'the style and quality of his performance' is included the style of galloping, style on point, and the very beauty of the dog ; and that these traits are most desirable is easily proved. We go shooting with dogs to enjoy ourselves, and their 'gallant' ranging with high head and wanton tail will charm away fatigue from many a barren stretch of moorland, while their grace and beauty on point will add that zest to the occasion which begets straightness in the powder. I know that some sportsmen nowadays affect total indifference about their dogs' appearance, but if they appreciate the good looks of their wives and their horses, why, in the name of consistency, not of their pointers! It is probable that if dogs are 'quartering' well, 'they will leave no game behind them.' Still this reiteration is good if it check that fatally common want of breaking, of which leaving game behind is one of the most tell-tale symptoms.

Rule 8 :—in this the Judges are given plenary powers over the breakers, with a clause permitting the latter in certain cases to invoke judicial protection from their opponents. Now the 'not keeping together' of the actual competitors is one of the offences specified by the rule, and yet judges are for ever complaining that these two *will* wander apart. But that they might be easily checked is certain, if they were subjected to firm discipline and the rule for their guidance acted upon. The breakers themselves would respect the judge who enforced it, provided that all were treated alike ; for to succeed as a breaker, a man must be sensible and well aware of the value of discipline. And, after all, these men are not always the ones to blame, for I have seen them worried without reason by a bullying judge, and even told to drag their dogs off points that were perfectly in bounds.

# THE POINTER

Rule 9, ordaining that a gun shall be fired over the aged dogs as well as over the puppies before awarding them recognition in any stake, is timely and excellent. Formerly, only the puppies had to be 'tried by fire;' though the reason of this I could never discover!

Rule 10, granting certificates of merit to dogs outside the prize-list, furthers the scheme for doing good to pointers and setters, as the trial classes at the shows are recruited largely from certificated animals, and the number of 'hall-marked' dogs in the country is thus materially increased.

Rule 11 is simply to protect the Society, as also are Nos. 13, 14, 15, 16, 17 and 18; for this reason, therefore, though sound and necessary, they do not enter into the scope of this chapter.

Rule 12 that enjoins, when the first round is finished, the hoisting of a red or a white flag 'at the end of each individual contest, to indicate which of the two competitors has shown the greater merit in that particular trial,' has now unfortunately become almost a deadletter. It is a pity, as it would so much illumine the dark places of the spotting system; and if systematically employed, it would help to sustain that interest in the actual trials which has drooped since the abolition of the heat system. But judges, like setters, are apt to *keep their flags down* when nervous: though, protected by the sentence 'the hoisting of the colour of a dog whose performance on that one occasion has been the more meritorious will not necessarily imply that his opponent is debarred from winning in the stake,'—there seems small cause for alarm. Besides, they seem to forget that by not hoisting a flag at all they are really declaring, according to the Rule, that 'there is a total lack of good work.'

Before closing this chapter I will add my own method of avoiding the dangers that beset the judge

## SHOWS AND WORKING TRIALS

at a dog-show ; as I know several eminently qualified pointer-men who have declined to officiate, in their bewilderment at those Limit, Novice, Maiden, Junior, &c., classes, thick as leaves of autumn, and scared by presentiments of weary exhibits recurring less like dogs than decimals. Happily, however, there are certain 'tricks of the trade,' which easily enable a man to give his decisions according to his mind and keep him out of the various pitfalls.

When the steward first of all announces to you, the judge, that the competitors are in the ring, ask for the numbers of any absentees and note them, both on your own part of the page and on the detachable slip, which will have to be sent to the secretary's office as soon as your awards are made. Then order the dogs to walk in single file round the ring, the man being on the further side of each dog, while you take a bird's eye view from the centre. Halt them, and make a dog-to-dog inspection, straightway collecting into a given corner all dogs that are good enough to be certain of a 'Very Highly Commended' at least, and sending back to their bench the hopelessly bad ones ; but be sure to take the numbers of these latter and to mark a cross against them in your own portion of the book. Try to 'corner' at least two more than are wanted for the prize-list ; and then proceed to judge the moderate dogs remaining in the ring, doling out to each a 'Highly Commended' or a 'Commended' according to his deserts, before you consign him to his bench. When the last one is disposed of, marshal your selected dogs ; and, after making them again circle round you, thoroughly examine them and try their paces one by one. Next mark and send out the 'V.H.C.' division, and finally the prize-winners in reverse order, so that 'the last shall be first.' In any case, whatever order you may adopt, always stick to the same one in dismissing exhibits, as to try to mystify

# THE POINTER

exhibitors and spectators is both childish and discourteous. Employ the interval between the classes in making up your book, *i.e.* in finding out which dogs that you have judged are to come again in future classes, and making notes of their previous positions opposite their numbers in the fresh class. Thus you will never reverse your decisions unwittingly, and will not fatigue yourself needlessly by judging dogs more than once at the same Show; for one *thorough* examination will give more satisfactory results in every way. To save time and space it is a good plan to make notes, while you judge, in the body of your judging book. There is as a rule but one line available for each entry, but this is sufficient if you make use of the signs plus and minus to express your likes and dislikes. For examples, ' + ' head, coat, tail, would mean that those parts were good, while ' − ' before them would reverse that opinion. The following axiomatic remarks may also be useful when judging pointers in the ring :—

Do not look too long at the bad dogs—they will spoil your eye.

Do not needlessly keep a full ring—it will muddle your brain.

If you do not like a dog, pick two definite faults in him—and 'out' him.

If a dog puzzle you, take him (and his man) unawares; and if he still puzzle you, take his chain in your own hand.

Till you have tried his paces, pronounce no dog a 'flyer.'

Remember that the *tail*, though it affect not his quarterings, is the pointer's family tree; but the *head* is the pointer himself.

## CHAPTER IV.
## CHARACTERISTICS OF THE POINTER.

FROM the first chapter there will have been gained a sufficient knowledge of the materials that were blended together to compose the English pointer, the present chapter is concerned solely with his attributes.

The *Sportsman*, in 1836, remarks of this dog that 'like the Arabian horse, he may be regarded as an exotic, which, in the hands of the English sportsman, has attained a degree of perfection which will be vainly sought in those countries of which he was originally a native' (No. 4, vol. iii., p. 131). It is just this 'perfection' that I have now to describe and consider—a perfection that required a hundred years of practical work, attention, and combination to mature. For though the pointing-dog first touched the shores of England in the beginning of the eighteenth century, the *pointer* did not, to judge from the average excellence of type in contemporaneous pictures, reach his zenith till the opening years of the nineteenth. In describing this precious heritage from our forefathers, I glory that his worth is to-day acclaimed by the whole sporting world ; even Italy, France and Spain, the very countries that have contributed to his manufacture, vying with each other in the cult of the British pointer.

I am about to establish his characteristics as far as possible by quotations from old English writers, so as to leave for the future no shadow of doubt about the type always admired by the most prominent sportsmen. This type is now rare : because fine old races of animals,

## THE POINTER

unlike old wines and furniture, do not placidly await the re-awakening of good taste, but during periods of neglect tend to disappear and die out. Fortunately, however, the true pointer is not yet extinct, though he is nowadays to be found more often in the highways and byways than with number and pedigree attached to his name.

For the sake of brevity I will quote in full only those descriptions which seem specially interesting either from the personality of the author or the individuality of his style, while the others I will cite as occasion may require to give evidence on controverted points (*i.e.* head, tail, feet, coat, &c.), about which a consensus of opinion is necessary; but in my abridgments I shall never withhold any passages that may appear to run counter to my own theories. As a rule the ancient cynography is wonderfully in accord with the old English writings that came afterwards. For instance, the Spaniard who wrote the *Dialogos* (sixteenth century), though hardly mentioning the looks of pointing-dogs, insists on the necessity of the greyhound foot; while the Italian, Biondi, also of the sixteenth century, emphasises the fact that their muzzles must be concave rather than convex. Perhaps this unanimity arises from the fact that the English have cherished the lore of the Continental nations from the time that Edmund de Langley, Duke of York, translated the work of Gaston de Foix in the fourteenth century, till the times when *La Chasse au fusil* was embodied in an *Essay on Shooting* (1789), and Colonel Thornton made the generous admission that the 'sportsmen of France in point of science far surpass us' (*A Sporting Tour in France*, 1806, p. 32).

The characteristics of the pointer may be divided for convenience into two parts, those always patent to the eye, and those revealed at intervals by his actions; though except to simplify description such a distinction cannot be sustained, so constant is the action and reaction of body and mind where true symmetry is found.

# CHARACTERISTICS OF THE POINTER

By symmetry in a pointer, I mean a condition of perfect development: the harmonious growth and correlation of brain with body and scenting power, of part with part, of limb with limb, there being no deficiency —no excess. Perfection is found in the very centre of his potentialities; and beauties in the abstract, if disproportionate to him, must be reckoned blemishes. Virgil's *medio tutissimus ibis* applies even to pointers ! The form and proportion that are most elegant in the pointer are also the most useful; for where each bone, each muscle, each fibre—in short, the entire machinery —is most nicely adjusted, perfect motivity and highest beauty will also reign. Every part of his anatomy has some meaning, some use, which should be learned by man before he ventures to meddle: the HEAD contains the intellect and scenting power; the BODY and LIMBS form the galloping apparatus; and the TAIL denotes purity of race. It has become a sort of catchword to say a pointer must be made like a foxhound or a hunter. But he cannot be compared properly with either foxhound or hunter, as his duties are the very opposite of theirs. Some points of resemblance there doubtless are; but for all that a symmetrical pointer must be made like a pointer, and like nothing else in the world.

The *Sportsman* (1836), in an article on sport generally, treats of him thus: 'A dog for the purpose in question (the pursuit of the grouse, &c.) should have an elegant lofty range, should possess considerable speed, as well as strength and spirit to endure long and fatiguing exertion. For such a combination the well-bred pointer is well, we may say pre-eminently, calculated; for, although there are sportsman to be met with who prefer the setter to the pointer on account of his superior strength and hardihood, yet we cannot give in to such an opinion, since, as these qualities, the capacity of enduring exertion or fatigue, are the result of animal organization, so, when the pointer is bred as he ought

# THE POINTER

to be, he will be found equal to the setter in strength and endurance, superior in the acuteness of his olfactory organs, and steadier also' (No. 4, vol. iii., p. 184).

But to abandon generalities, here is the figured outline of a dog's profile; by no means put forward as a model of form, but intended to enable my readers to recognise readily the part under examination.

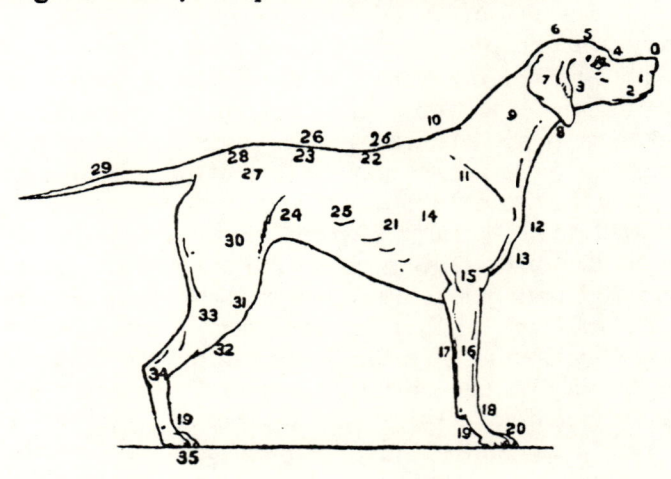

INDEX TO FIGURE.

| | | |
|---|---|---|
| 0. Nose or Nostrils. | 14. Girth. | 26. Chine or Backbone. |
| 1. Muzzle. | 15. Elbow. | |
| 2. Lip or Flew. | 16. Foreleg. | 27. Hip or Haunchbone. |
| 3. Cheek. | 17. Back-sinews. | |
| 4. Stop. | 18. Knee-joint. | 28. Croup. |
| 5. Forehead. | 19. Pastern. | 29. Tail or Stern. |
| 6. Occiput or Poll. | 20. Forefoot. | 30. Thigh. |
| 7. Ear. | 21. Ribs. | 31. Stifle-joint. |
| 8. Throat. | 22. Back. | 32. Stifle. |
| 9. Neck. | 23. Loin or Fillet. | 33. Gaskin or Second-thigh. |
| 10. Withers. | 24. Flank. | |
| 11. Shoulder. | 25. Floating or Back-ribs. | 34. Hock. |
| 12. Breast-bone. | | 35. Hindfoot. |
| 13. Chest. | | |

# CHARACTERISTICS OF THE POINTER

I will next reproduce, in chronological order, some typical descriptions of the make and shape of the pointer for the last two centuries, until the establishment of dog-shows.

'The pointers I best approve are not small nor very large; but such as are well made, light, and strong, and will naturally stand. A small pointer, though ever so good in his kind, can be of but little service, particularly through a strong piece of turnips, broom, or heath; and the feet of a large, heavy dog will soon be tired by his own weight' (*Art of Shooting Flying*, by T. Page, 1767, p. 80). Mr. Page was a gun-maker; and the insistence with which this extremely simple little sentence was copied, even by Squire Osbaldiston and Mr. Thornhill, shows in what repute his authority was held.

'The most proper dog, and what is generally used for partridge shooting, is the pointer, a dog extremely well calculated for the sport. If the pointer be staunch, and have a good nose, he will seldom pass in common fields within forty yards of a covey without intimating by a point pretty near the exact line they be in. The small light dogs are, for many reasons, to be preferred to the large, heavy Spanish breed, as they hunt the ground over quicker, quarter it better, and will go over two or three times as much as the heavy sort without being tired or losing the skin off their feet' (*A Treatise on English Shooting*, by George Edie, 1772, p. 11).

[Written of a setter.] 'He should be rather tall than otherwise, flat ribbed, and longish in the back; for a dog, where speed is a principal requisite, must, as well as a horse, in the language of the turf, "stand upon ground." The short back, home coupled, is much admired by many. "Do but observe how close he is put together, all of a piece throughout. That is the mould for a long day," &c. But this is a vulgar

# THE POINTER

error, exposed from daily experience; the quickness of his stroke, with a wanton stern, gives the appearance of speed indeed, but if we note the space described in a given time, we shall correct our first opinion immediately. The same will hold good of the pointer' (*A Treatise on Field Diversions*, R. Symonds, 1776, p. 12).

'The properties I expect him to possess are, a round but not large head; wide open nostrils; full staring eyes; thin long ears; stern very fine and thin and as smooth as silk' (*Angling, Shooting, and Coursing*, by R. Lascelles, 1811, p. 137).

'Let his muzzle be open, flew jawed, rather short, full hazel eyes, called hare's eyes; his poll rising to a point, his ears long and falling down between the neck and the jaw-bone, which is called being well hung; neck and head set on straight, so that when he points his nose turns up rather above the horizontal line; deep in the shoulder and well let down; elbows well in; straight and large legs; small feet, a little pointed, standing true, and the balls small and open; narrow withers; back a little hooped, broad loins, deep in the fillets and gaskins; short from the hock to the pastern joint, flat sides, fine floating veins, straight croup, stern set on high and straight, being very fine. Ill-bred dogs you may know by their being fox-muzzled, small eyes, fan-eared, bat-eared, short necked, head set on like a pickaxe, broad withers, round shoulders, elbows out; small legs, feet out, called cat-footed, thick balls; round barrel, round croup; clumsy stern, set on low, sickle-hammed,' &c. (*The Sportsman's Directory*, by John Mayer, game-keeper, 1815, p. 23).

'They [pointers] should be remarkable for the exquisite sensibility of their olfactory organs (or what a sportsman would call the goodness of their nose), as well as for the gallant style of their range; not the

# CHARACTERISTICS OF THE POINTER

speed with which they run, but their mode of running, that is with their heads well up and their sterns constantly moving, since nothing looks worse than to see a dog run with his nose to the ground and his tail carried between his hind legs. They should have well-formed straight legs and a small close foot, deep chest, full blood eyes, fine stern, round back, thin long ears, hanging loosely from the head, altogether the middle size' (*Dictionary of Sports*, by H. Harewood, 1835, p. 256).

'The pointer should present a round, well-marked head, neither small nor large. His face should be open, his nostrils large, and his eyes full; his ears should be thin, and of a due length, but they should in every case hang close to the head; for if they fall back we should suspect the get. His coat we would have very fine. The thighs should be full without being coarse, and they should be surmounted by a fine taper stern' (*Encyclopædia of Rural Sports*, by D. P. Blaine, 1852, p. 300).

'First, the form of the head, which should be wide, yet flat and square, with a broad nose, a pendulous lip, and a square tip. . . Fourthly, a fine stern, small in the bone and sharp at the point, like the sting of a wasp, and not curved upwards. The form of the stern, with a vigorous lashing of it from side to side, marks the true-bred pointer as much as any sign can do so; and its absence distinguishes the foxhound cross, which gives a very heavy stern, with a strong curve upwards, and carried over the back; or the too great amount of greyhound blood, marked by a small stern also, but by one whose diminution commences from the root, whilst the genuine pointer's is nearly of the same size till within a few inches of the point, when it suddenly tapers off' (*Manual of British Rural Sports*, by 'Stonehenge,' 1856, p. 567).

# THE POINTER

I will now proceed to give a detailed description of the form of a perfect pointer, illustrated with excerpts, where necessary, from the old writers.

## THE HEAD.

'A narrow-headed dog cannot possess a good nose, because, owing to the compression of his cranium, the requisite quantity and due expansion of the olfactory nerves, to constitute acuteness of smell, are rendered impossible. The sense of smell arises from small white cords, which are called the olfactory nerves, and without resorting to anatomical technicality, it may be stated that these little white cords form a sort of bunch at the upper part of the nose, and spread thence over the brain, and descend to the nose and the lips in proportion as the head is capacious or otherwise' (*The Shooter's Preceptor*, by T. B. Johnson, 1842, p. 5).

'Above all, look to the head, "the knowledge-box," as it is vulgarly but most aptly called. It ought to be broad between the ears, which should hang down close, with a fall or dent under the eyes; the nose long and not broad; the nostrils very soft and moist' (*Recreations in Shooting*, by Craven, 1846, p. 27).

*The Head* is the nucleus of the pointer; and *the Skull* is his nucleolus, the very centre of his being. It is spheroidal in form and, whether looked at from the front or from the side, presents a rough semblance to a Norman or round arch; in full face the spring of this arch commences behind and just below the temples, in profile—at the base of the stop and the back of the occiput, which must be high and developed. Of great importance is the chiselling of all the purposeful elevations and depressions on the surface of the skull, for these may be valued as nature's hall-marks. As regards its proportions, I need add little to the descriptions of the pre-show writers, except that in a symmetrical

# CHARACTERISTICS OF THE POINTER

head the eye is placed halfway between the nostrils and the occiput ; and that the term 'broad head' refers to breadth of forehead, and does not include the broad cheeks that rather betoken pugnacity than intellect. Skulls that I find typical are one on the bitch in Plate XIV., and two more at the top and the left-hand of Plate XXII.

A 'dished' face, *i.e. the Muzzle* concave in form, is a sign of facility in scenting. The reason may be easily seen. A pointer carries head and neck outstretched in his gallop, and the higher the nose is presented to the wind the farther off it will perceive the body-scent that is gradually rising from any neighbouring birds. If he have a houndy or even a straight face, in order to raise his nose sufficiently he will have to constrict his windpipe, and he will thus be in discomfort : the most frequent cause of a pointer flushing, when he is going fast, is a badly formed muzzle. It should spring from the skull at a slight angle, and though fine at base it must not taper, the jaws ending level and square with *the nostrils*, which are spongy and spreading.

*The Lip* or *Flew* though amply developed appears as thin as paper. It is beautifully shaped in the best dogs, with a graceful curl at the corner of the mouth. Muzzles enveloped in much coarse flew, giving the effect of a bread poultice, are to be avoided. For an example of a perfect lip I will refer to a white bitch (Plate IX.); and, indeed, her muzzle is a perfect model, which redeems the ugly effect of ears that have been 'rounded' like those of a foxhound.

*The Eyes* are to be bright, full, and gentle in expression; they vary in tint from the lightest hazel to the darkest brown, according to the colour of the coat. The test of their being correct lies in their looking rich, soft, and harmonious. Black, yellow, green, and white are not desirable colours for the iris.

# THE POINTER

*The Ears* must be attached high up on the head, and lie closely to it without folding; but, when on point or otherwise excited, the dog will lift and advance them somewhat. They must be rather pointed at the tip, of fair length, very soft and thin in leather, and have their veins visible. It is somewhat difficult to find a satisfactory illustration of the correct ear, not so much from the scarcity of dogs as of draughtsmen, pointers' ears being proverbially hard to portray. My selections are Titian's standing dog (Plate III.); Oudry's bitch (Plate VI.), perfect in the quality and carriage of ears which are, however, too long; and Miss Maud Earl's pointer's head on the left (Plate XXII.).

## THE TRUNK.

'If lumber be, as it is, odious, weediness is even worse' (*Modern Shooter*, by Captain Lacy, 1842, p. 171).

In a pointer, *the Neck* is long, rounded, and muscular, springing gracefully from his shoulders, and attached to the head in such fashion that it is easier for him to carry himself in one continuous curve from shoulder to nose, than in the right-angled position natural to most other breeds. It must also be free from those superfluous folds of skin underneath, the presence of which constitutes 'throatiness.' *The Shoulders* are long and sloping, running smoothly into the back, with the two blades convergent at the withers; they must work quite freely and flexibly as in galloping down hill, or in scrambling about rough places, supple shoulders are indispensable.

*The Breastbone* is bold without being unduly prominent, and the width of *the Chest* is sufficient for stability without hindering speed. *The Girth* must be ample, the ribs descending as low as the elbow-point and being rather convex in form. The outline of *the*

# CHARACTERISTICS OF THE POINTER

*Back* inclines to undulate from the withers till it joins the loins. *The Ribs* themselves are strong and elastic, and gradually taper away towards the loin and flank, where they become the *Back or Floating Ribs*, ceasing about half-way between the withers and the root of the tail. *The Loin or Fillet* must be lengthy, powerful, and decidedly arched, for this is one of the most potent factors in the speed and endurance of the dog. *The Chine or Backbone* must be strongly jointed, as it is the axis of the whole body. *The Hips or Haunch-bones*, at the junction of the thigh with the body, must be well formed and nearly on a level with the chine, placed wide apart and standing out distinctly, with a tendency to be ' ragged; ' as on their position and prominence much of the power and leverage of the hind-quarters depends. *The Croup* must be long and level, modifying the curve of the loin.

## THE LIMBS.

*The Elbows* of the pointer must be strong, muscular, and truly parallel, so as to work just clear of the body. If the shoulders be long enough, the elbows will be ' well let down,' and the back of them will be in place directly under the withers. *The Forelegs*, extending from the elbow to the knee-joint, must be straight, and consist of an ample—not excessive—amount of flat bone of close quality, far removed from the round bone of the foxhound : indeed, if a transverse section be made, it will be found to be rather oval in shape. *The Back-sinews* must be strong, wiry, and clearly defined, and *the Knee-joint* must not project in front and only a little on the inside of the leg, as undue prominence reveals weakness and ill-rearing. *The Pasterns* are lengthy and perceptibly finer in bone than the leg, and must slant somewhat. This is to give such a buffer-like spring and elasticity to leg and foot as not to tire

## THE POINTER

and shake the dog over hard and uneven ground, when he pulls up suddenly on scent, or when he doubles at full gallop. Short, thick pasterns on a pointer are an absurdity, meaning, as they must do, defective agility.

*The Feet* are oval, with long, narrow, arched toes, and the cushion underneath but slightly developed.

'Such a formation of the feet [the "round cat-foot"] is perfectly in unison with the mechanical or animal organization of the cat kind, but when the structure of the dog is considered, and the strongly marked difference of the progressive motion of the two species taken into account, the admirable adaptation in the one case, and the glaring incongruity in the other, cannot fail to be impressed on the mind with the most unqualified conviction. The cat (and so of all animals of the cat kind) is, like the rest of creation, formed for its mode of life. The round foot and well-developed toes of the cat enable it to creep stealthily upon its prey, while by this peculiarity of formation it retracts or draws in the instruments (the talons or claws) by which it is to seize and secure it. When within reach, the cat springs upon its victim, the propulsive force of which results from the form and extraordinary power of the hind legs or quarters. In this operation, or rather combination of operations, the cat is assisted by that flexibility of body, particularly of the backbone, that contraction and tension, which will be vainly sought in the canine tribe. In fact, the two animals are so distinctly marked in form, manner, and motion that the peculiarity of the one, the round foot for instance, becomes preposterous, if not monstrous, in the other. For a correct idea of the perfection of the foot of the pointer, we should steadily keep in the view the long, wiry, narrow toe, and, indeed, the altogether exquisite formation of the foot of the hare. . . . . The hare has no ball to her foot; the dog cannot be divested of this

## CHARACTERISTICS OF THE POINTER

cushion-like appendage; but, in breeding, nothing should be neglected that will be likely to reduce its size and softness (so conspicuous in the Spanish pointer) as well as to lengthen and harden the toes. When the foot of the pointer is formed so as to approach as nearly as possible that of the hare, his limbs strong and straight, his chest "low dropping," loins broad, &c., he will go through a lengthened degree of exertion which would be regarded as impossible by those who have paid but slight attention to the subject' (*The Sportsman*, No. 4, vol. iii., p. 184).

' In breeding pointers, the foot of the hare should be imitated as far as the limits of nature will admit; the ball of the pointer's foot should be as small as possible; his toes long, narrow, and wiry. Very short bulky toes (which constitute "the round cat-foot") in the dog may be compared to very short upright pasterns in the horse, and are equally contrary to the true principles of speed' (*The Shooter's Preceptor*, by T. B. Johnson, 1842, p. 149).

' The toes should be close to each other, long, wiry-looking, and, if I may so speak, well gathered up or arched; the balls or soles of the foot should be small, hard, tough, and not too fleshy. The foot altogether, in form, should not be (and, indeed, cannot be) round, like that of a cat, but will be longer in front,' &c. (*The Modern Shooter*, by Captain Lacy, 1846, p. 170).

' My purpose is to protest strongly against the hound-foot in a pointer, which seems, from a jumble of judges at many recent dog-shows, to have found favour with pointer exhibitors. If we take fairly into consideration the momentarily quick turns a fast pointer has to make in working at great speed a moderately sized stubble or other field, and his pulling up suddenly on point, the common-sense view of the case would decide upon an expanding foot as a necessity, and for both pointer and

## THE POINTER

greyhound, nature has given the strength of claw and grasp of foot suited to their work. Hound-work, as we all know, is so different, and the round, close foot, with strong muscular formation, is admirably suited for hound endurance; but where is the expansion for quick and sudden turns at great speed ? And I wonder how Mr. Garth's Drake, the fastest pointer in his field-trial work we have ever seen, would have fared in his sudden points when going at sixty miles an hour? Why, he would have been head over heels time after time, and could not have made the grand displays in instantaneous pointing which delighted all who witnessed his work' (W. Brailsford's letter to the *Stock-keeper*, March 1st, 1895).

And even 'Idstone,' of all writers on pointers the most extreme in his worship and advocacy of the hound type, had to admit that he was 'almost a convert to the hare-foot' (*The Dog*, 1882, p. 118).

The hare's foot is obviously, therefore, the model for the pointer's foot, and is allied and correlated with a long sickled stifle and great propelling power—all three contributing to twisting and turning, speed and stamina. A cat-foot is more adapted for straightforward running, and is generally allied to a straight stifle.

*The Stifles*, extending from the stifle-joint to the hock, must be well bent, since on the length of the outline of his hind-quarters, between the hip-bones and the hocks, will depend the endurance of the dog, as this formation, in conjunction with an arched loin, gives the maximum of speed with the minimum of labour : to suit such a scheme, *the Hock*—bony, flat, and cleancut—must be 'well let down.' *The Thighs* are well developed, rich in muscle, and of large surface; and *the Gaskins*, the under-thighs, which extend from the stifle-joint downwards, must also be muscular and deep.

# ILLUSTRATIONS

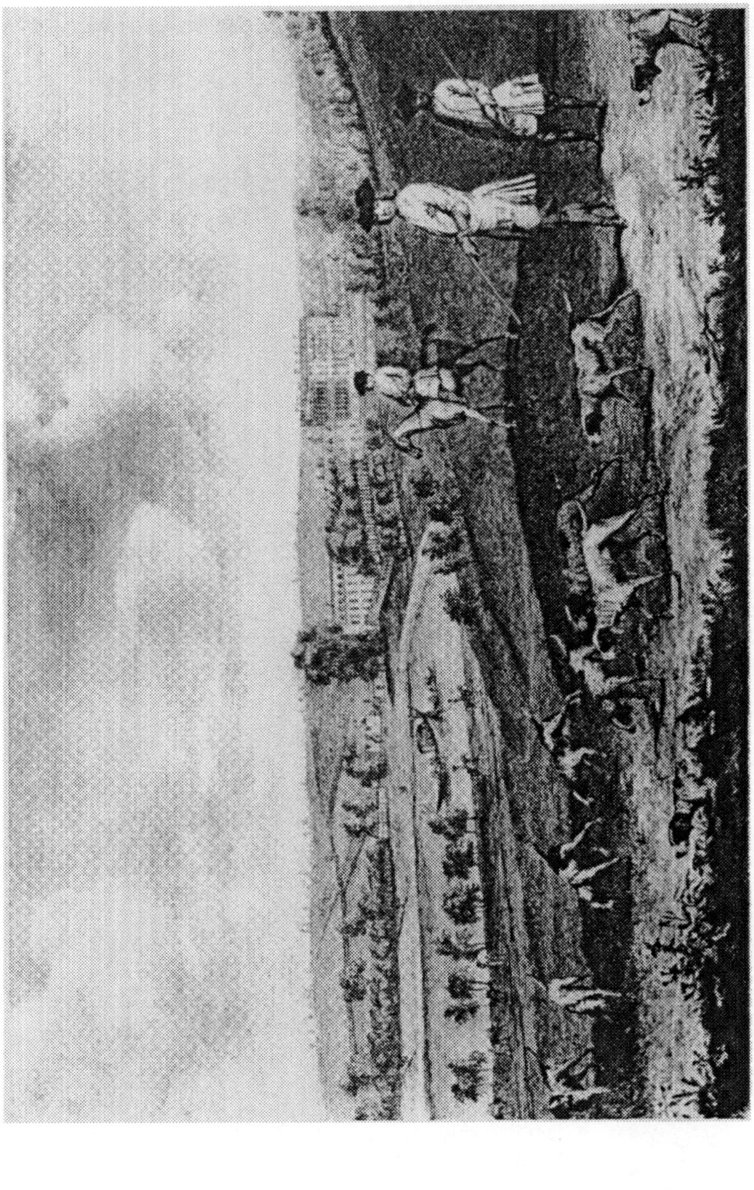

PLATE I.

From an etching of an oil painting, both by Tillemans (born 1684, died 1734). The original, a large picture, is a portrait of the Duke of Kingston among his pointers, with a view of his home, Thoresby, in the background. It is dated 1725 (Redgrave's *Dictionary of Painters*).

The colouring of the picture is very beautiful; and all the pointers are liver-and-whites of a uniform type—the type of the royal pointing-dogs of France, from which I have shown elsewhere that the Duke, being so much at the French Court, had every opportunity of deriving them. This is, as far as I know, the earliest picture of pointers in England, and in date is probably intermediate between the two examples from the Louvre (Plates V., VI.).

*In the Possession of Earl Manvers, Thoresby Park.*

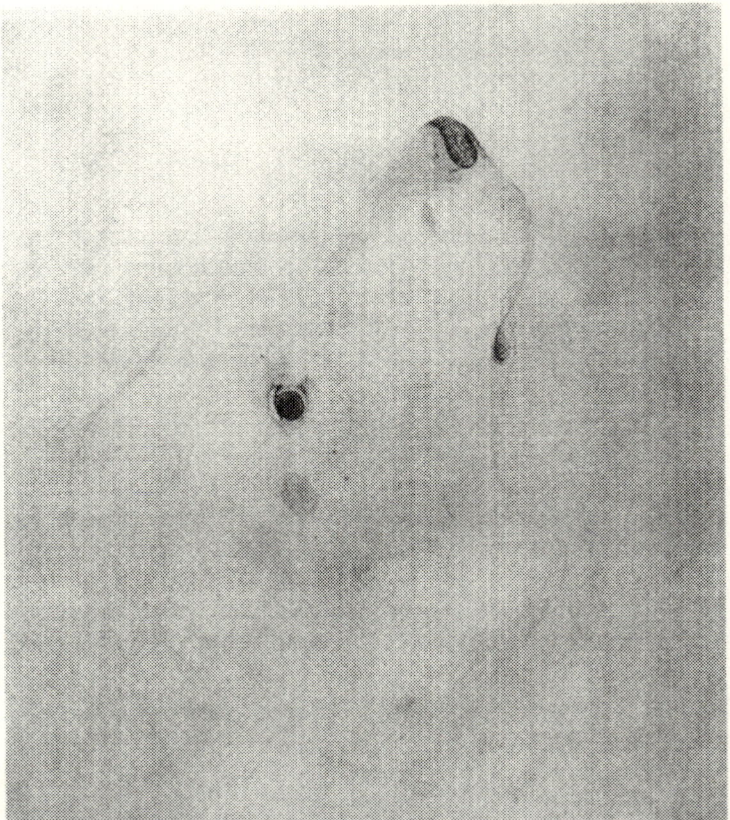

## PLATE II.

From a pencil sketch, of the Veronese School, by Vittore Pisano, called Pisanello (born 1380, died 1446). It is of the head of a pointing-dog, whose eye, nostril, and curl of lip have been touched in with pigment. The model was evidently of high quality, though an unfortunate blur on the muzzle rather detracts from its shapeliness : observe, however, the beautiful profile of the skull. The dog was evidently light-coloured, as the nostril is flesh-coloured and the eye orange.

The original sketch is so faint and rubbed that, although indications of lines appeared on the negative that are to the naked eye invisible on the drawing, I was obliged to have some of them slightly emphasized for the sake of a satisfactory reproduction.

*In the Receuil Vallardi, Museum of the Louvre, Paris.*

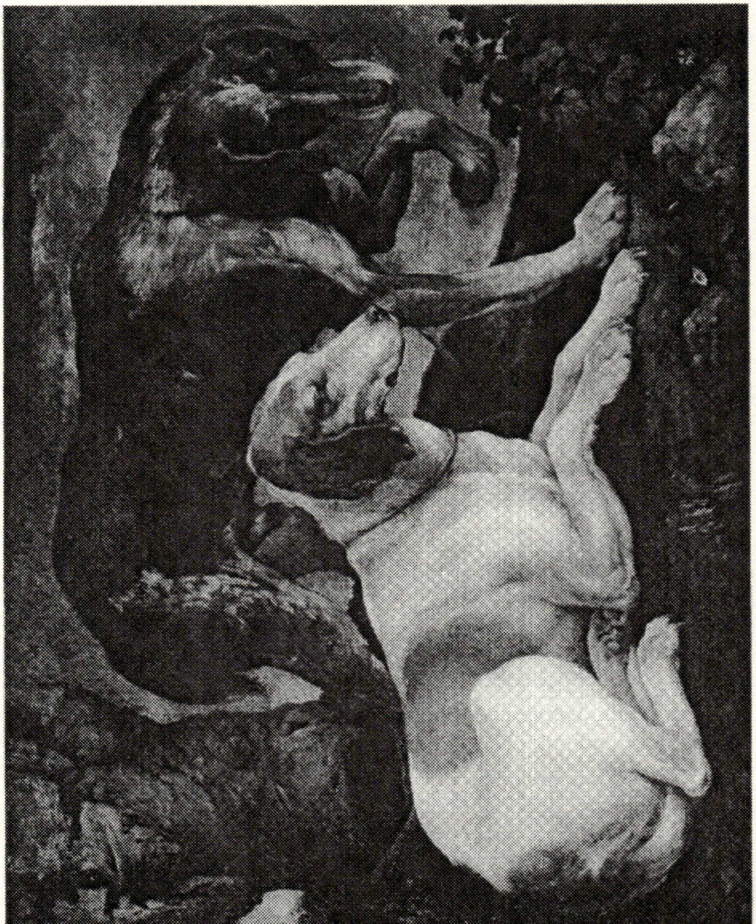

## PLATE III.

From a painting, of the Venetian School, by Titian (born 1477, died 1576). Here are represented two dogs of pointer character. The standing dog is liver-roan in colour, with touches of tan about his face and feet; the one lying down is orange and white, with a black nose. The colouring of the whole picture is brilliant, but the lifted leg of one dog seems somewhat out of drawing.

This picture was engraved in 1792 by George Townly Stubbs, with the following dedication : 'The original picture, now in the possession of the Duke of Bedford, was brought to England by Wm. Beckford, Esq., to whom this print is dedicated by his most humble servant, G. T. S.' This is of interest; as it not only shows that Mr. Beckford parted with the picture in his lifetime, but it also establishes its identity with the 'drawing' described by Sydenham Edwards in his article on The Pointer :—

' In the possession of the late Mr. Beckford was a beautiful drawing, after Titian, of two pointers, which according to Mr. Beckford, were the same as those used in France : narrow head, fine muzzle, and light limbs, are very staunch and fleet; but from Scotland, where the French dog is not at all uncommon, I am assured he is a perfect model of the Spanish, only smaller and firmer in his make ' (*Cynographia Britannica*, 1800).

Mr. Fairfax Murray has lately called into question the authorship of this picture, and calls it ' certainly an early example of Jacopo Bassano, the Elder.' It may not be by Titian, but I feel convinced it is not by Bassano, of whose paintings I have made a special study; I, therefore, shall follow Mr. Beckford and shall leave it as a Titian.

*In the Possession of the Duke of Bedford, Woburn Abbey.*

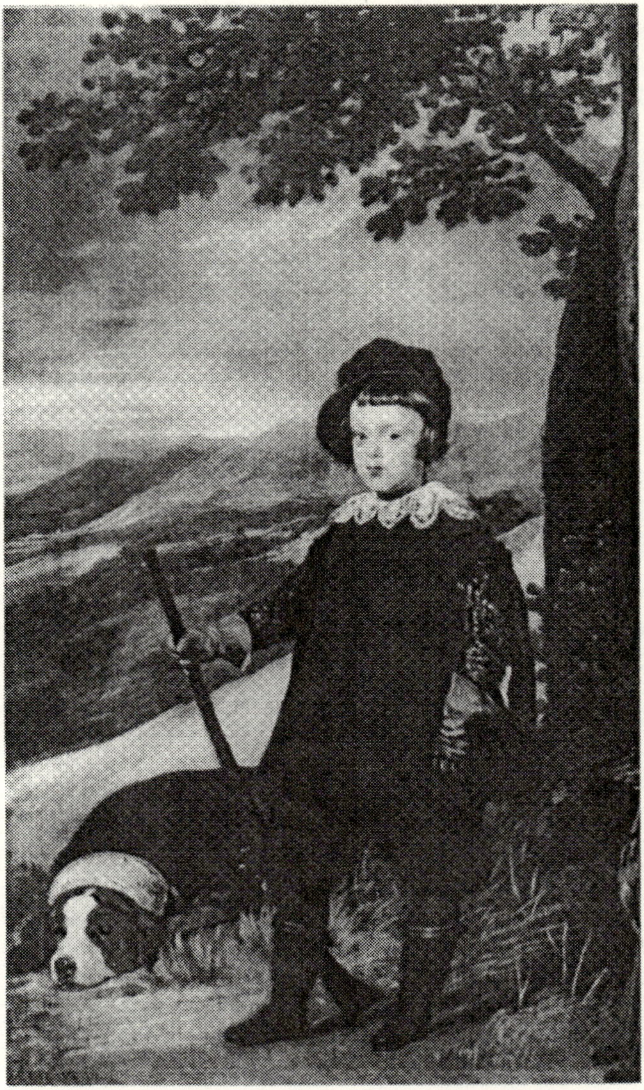

## PLATE IV.

From a painting by Velazquez (born 1599, died 1660). This picture, charming though it is, does not do justice to the partridge-dog, which is too much subordinated—besides being choked, like a masher nowadays, by his great white collar. One must be thankful, however, that he has not been treated with the same scant courtesy as the little greyhound in the picture, for early Spanish portraits of pointing-dogs are as rare as butterflies in winter.

A picture by Espinosa (1600-1670) was shown in London last winter (1901). It is the property of Mr. Ralph Bankes, and is a portrait of Don Alonzo de Canamas, a Valencian nobleman, with his right hand resting on the head of a sitting Navarrese partridge-dog, which is large, typical, and very dark liver-and-white ; but in his pendant ears and sombre expression he shows more of the hound than does the dog of Velazquez.

Of this Plate 'Evero' gives a capital description, which I append :—

'The painting is a portrait of the Prince Baltasar, a child of six, in the pose and garb of a sportsman ; on his right, lying down in an attitude common for sporting dogs when old, rests a fat Navarrese partridge-dog, which, had he been standing up, would have dwarfed the principal figure. His ear is thick, falling, and not very large ; his skull broad and well-developed, showing his great intelligence : of his docility one can judge by his submissive attitude. His colour is like the reddish-yellow of the natural wax, "*encerado*" as Espinar calls it, with pure white ' (*Paginas de Caza*, 1888, p. 14).

His nostrils are black, and in England we should call the colour of his body, orange.

*In the Prado Museum at Madrid.*

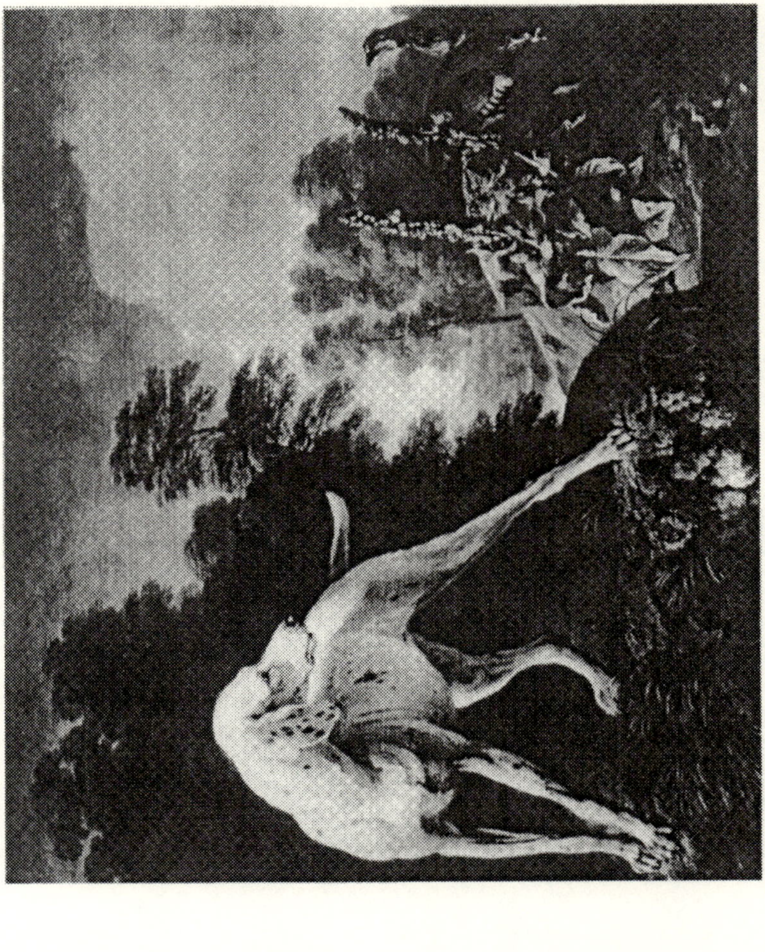

## PLATE V.

From an oil painting by Desportes (born 1661, died 1743). This picture is dated 1720, and is of a superb white bitch, slightly ticked with black, looking at a brace of French partridges. She is one of the royal breed of France, from which our English pointer seems to have derived his quality. Her shortened tail cannot rob her of her air of distinction.

'François Desportes was the first to paint, in France, sporting subjects and animals, and those of his pictures that we have preserved, besides their very great artistic quality, are witnesses to his perfect knowledge of his subject. Louis XIV. made him painter of his sporting establishment, and gave him a salary, with apartments in the Louvre. We have still at the Museum his fine portraits of the dogs (*chiens couchants*) so much loved by the great king, with their names written on the canvas in letters of gold.'—From M. Ch. Blanc's *Vie des Peintres* (*Histoire de la Chasse*, by Dunoyer de Noirmont, 1867, tom. 1, p. 254).

*In the Museum of the Louvre, Paris.*

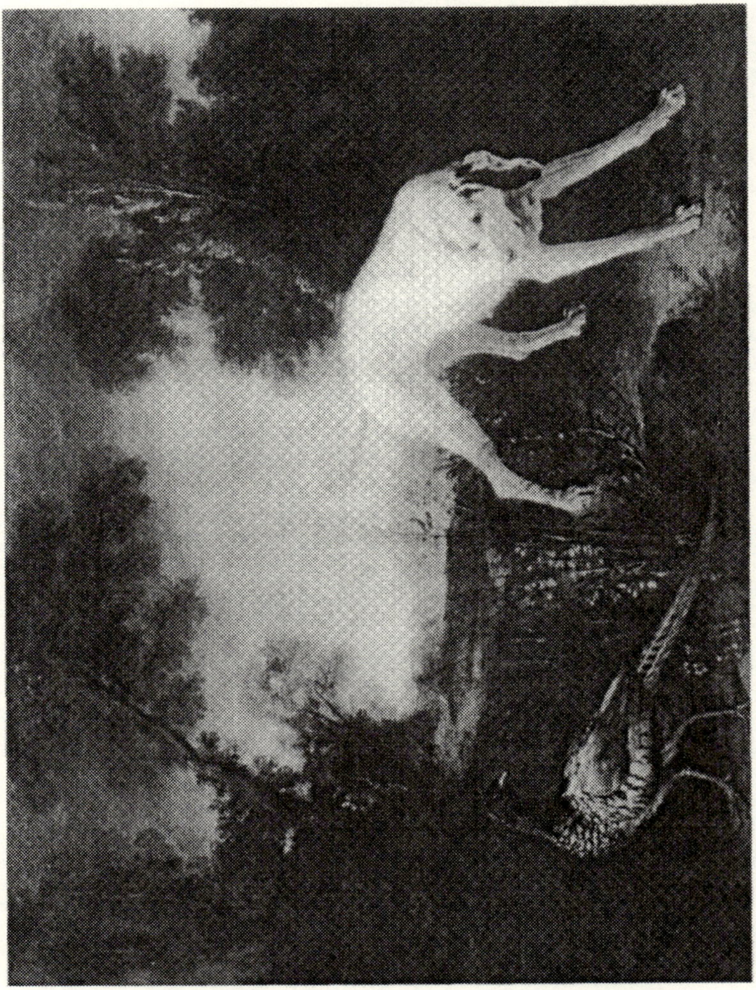

## PLATE VI.

From an oil painting by Oudry (born 1686, died 1755). This represents Blanche, a French bitch from the royal kennels, a lemon-and-white of the highest class, differing but little from the best of our English dogs, except in the length of her ears. This bitch presents one of the earliest examples of the liver-coloured nose.

'Oudry, younger by twenty-five years, was the rival and successor of Desportes. He was also salaried by the king, with apartments in the Tuileries. Louis XV., fascinated by his talent and the fidelity with which he represented his sport, was passionately fond of the work of this great artist. He passed long hours in his studio to watch him painting his hunting pictures, and had them reproduced in Gobelin tapestry, to be hung in his bed-chamber at the Castle of Compiègne, and in the Council Chamber. Oudry was invited to the royal hunts; the chief episodes of which he reproduced in a series of pictures as interesting to sportsmen as to lovers of painting. The dogs and horses of the king are there drawn with a truthfulness so striking, that Louis XV. used to amuse himself by recognising one after another, and calling them by name. Oudry also painted separate portraits of the favourite dogs of the royal establishment.'—From M. Ch. Blanc's *Vie des Peintres* (*Histoire de la Chasse*, by Dunoyer de Noirmont, 1867, tom. 1, p. 254).

*In the Museum of the Louvre, Paris.*

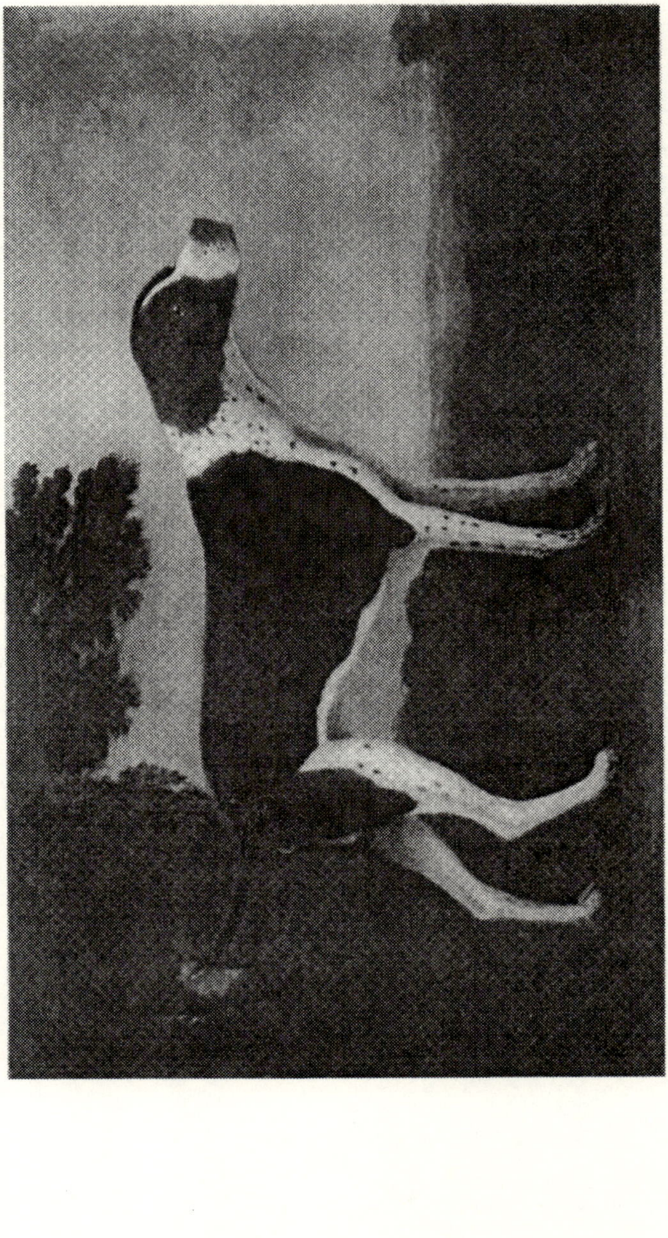

## PLATE VII.

From an oil painting by J. Wootton (born about 1690, died 1765). This is a life-size portrait of a liver-and-white dog. He has a splendid neck, a good eye, a fine tail (probably shortened), hare feet, and much quality all over. His hind-quarters appear too short and straight, and his flank too tucked up, but his colouring emphasizes these defects.

*In my own Possession.*

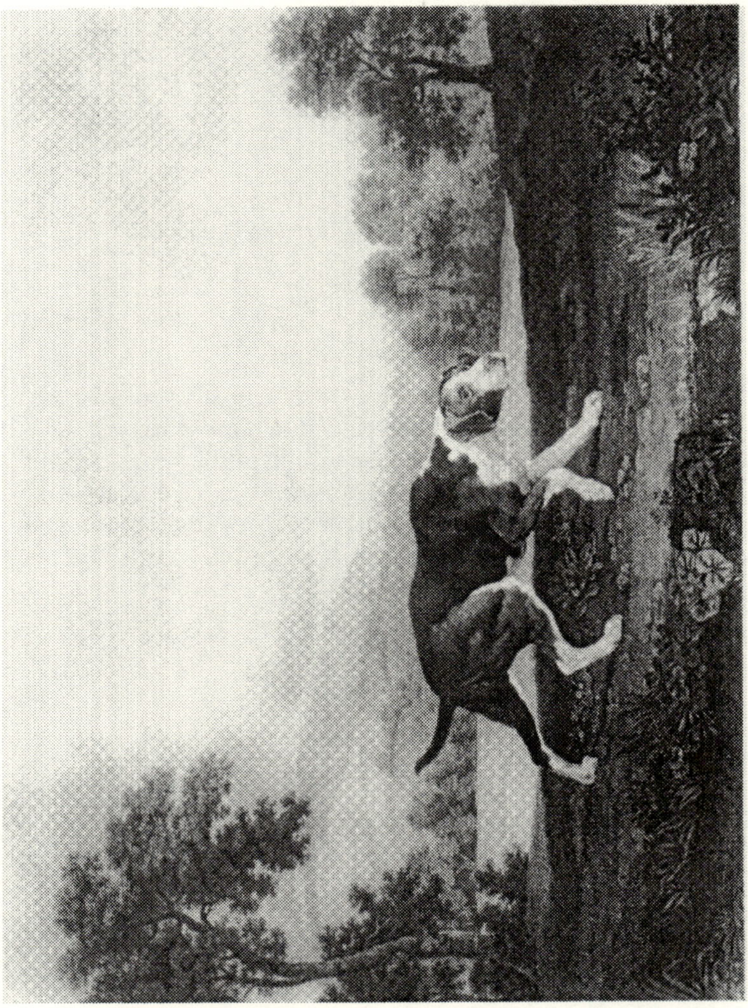

## PLATE VIII.

From an engraving, 1768, by N. Woollett, after G. Stubbs, R.A. (born 1724, died 1806). This is entitled 'The Spanish Pointer;' and the original painting is stated to be 'in the possession of Mr. Bradford,' but I have heard that this noble picture has since passed into the collection of the King of Bavaria. The muscular development of this Spaniard is very fine, but it is a pity his ears have been either rounded or else badly torn, as it destroys the character of his head.

*In my own Possession.*

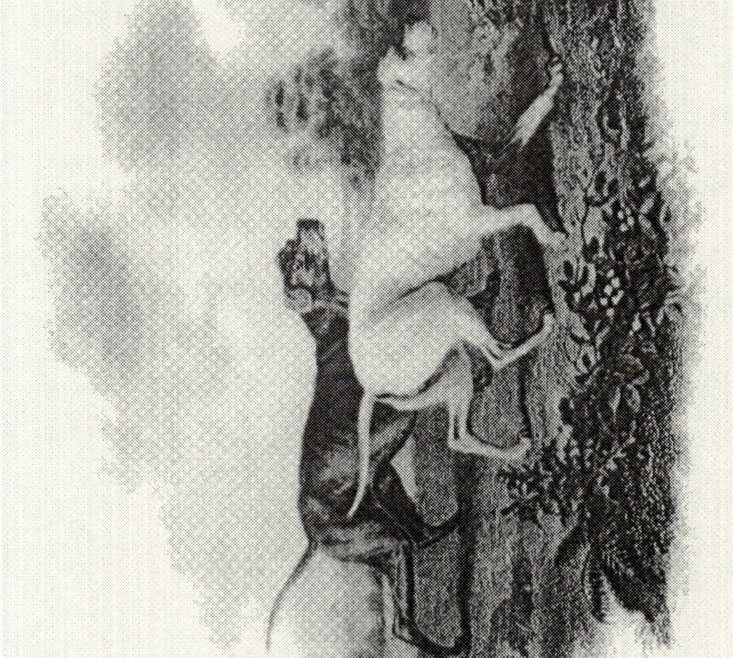

## PLATE IX.

From an engraving, 1802, by J. Scott, after S. Gilpin, R.A. (born 1733, died 1807). The sketch was made in 1772; and later it was used as an illustration for *Rural Sports*, where it is entitled 'Pluto and Juno.' Juno, the white bitch, is an almost perfect pointer, though she may perhaps fail a little in neck and shoulder, and her ears, like her companion's, have been rounded foxhound fashion, which detracts from her appearance. Her tail is quite correct in shape and size, and her muzzle and lip are models. Pluto, the black dog, has quality and substance wonderfully combined. The following is the description given by the Rev. W. B. Daniel :—

'The dog and bitch represented in the engraving were the property of Colonel Thornton. Pluto, although a very capital pointer, was celebrated for his pursuit of deer when encouraged to follow them. Many outlying deer were taken from this dog's hunting them, after very long chases. As a proof of both his and the bitch's steadiness as pointers, they kept their point when Mr. Gilpin took the sketch from which the picture was painted, upwards of one hour and a quarter' (*Rural Sports*, 1881, vol. iii., p. 338).

Pierce Egan relates how Juno was 'a remarkable bitch, which was matched with a pointer of Lord Grantley's for ten thousand guineas, who paid forfeit' (*Book of Sports*, 1832, p. 133).

*In my own Possession.*

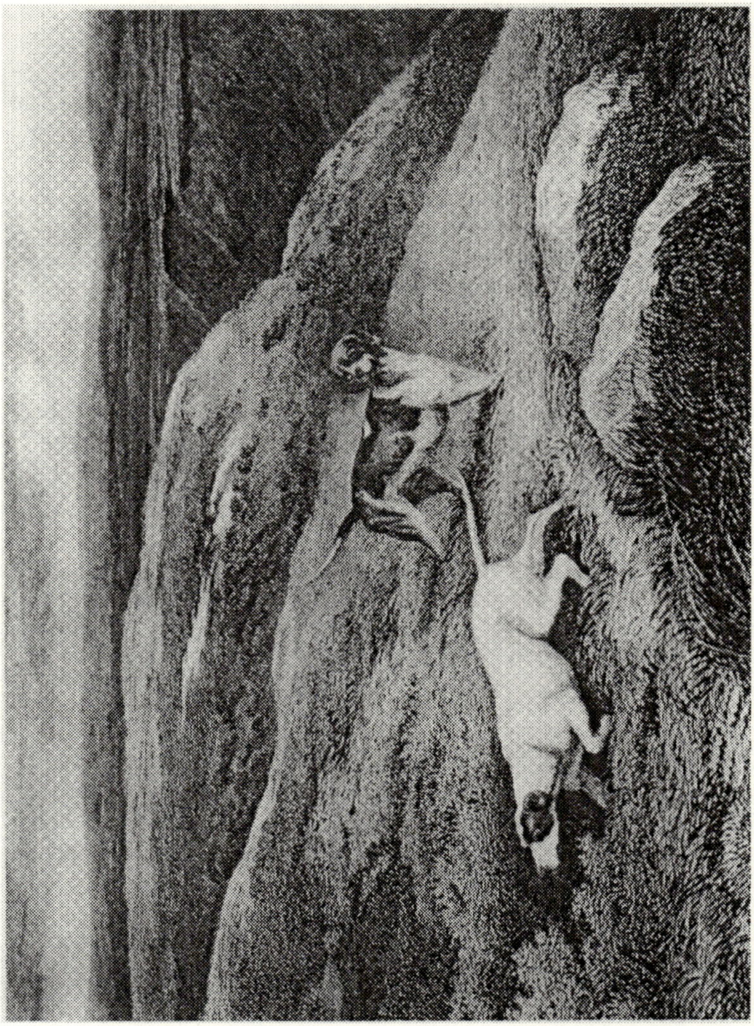

## PLATE X.

From an engraving, 1823, by Thomas Landseer, after P. Reinagle, R.A., who exhibited from 1773 to 1832. The original picture belongs to Lord Wenlock, and it gives portraits of pointers belonging to a former Lord Middleton.

A scene on the Yorkshire moors, in which the bitch, pointing in the foreground, appears to be ideal in neck, shoulders, girth, hind-quarters, and tail. Her head and eye are very good, but her ear does not seem natural. The backing dog is not a happy conception.

*In my own Possession.*

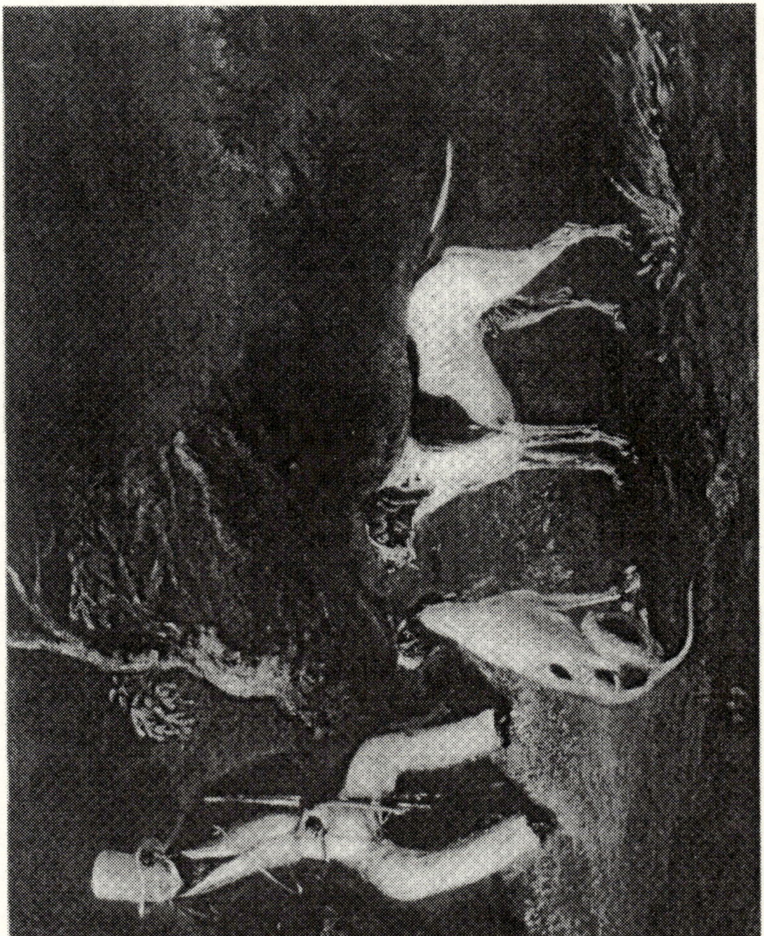

## PLATE XI.

From an oil painting by J. Jackson, R.A. (born 1778, died 1831). This is the corner of a large landscape : it is not the work of an animal painter, and yet how charming are the brace of pointers he has painted. The muzzle of the standing dog is too short, but otherwise he is quite a model, his feet and pasterns being especially typical : of the dog sitting down only sufficient is visible to bespeak quality and high-breeding.

*In my own Possession.*

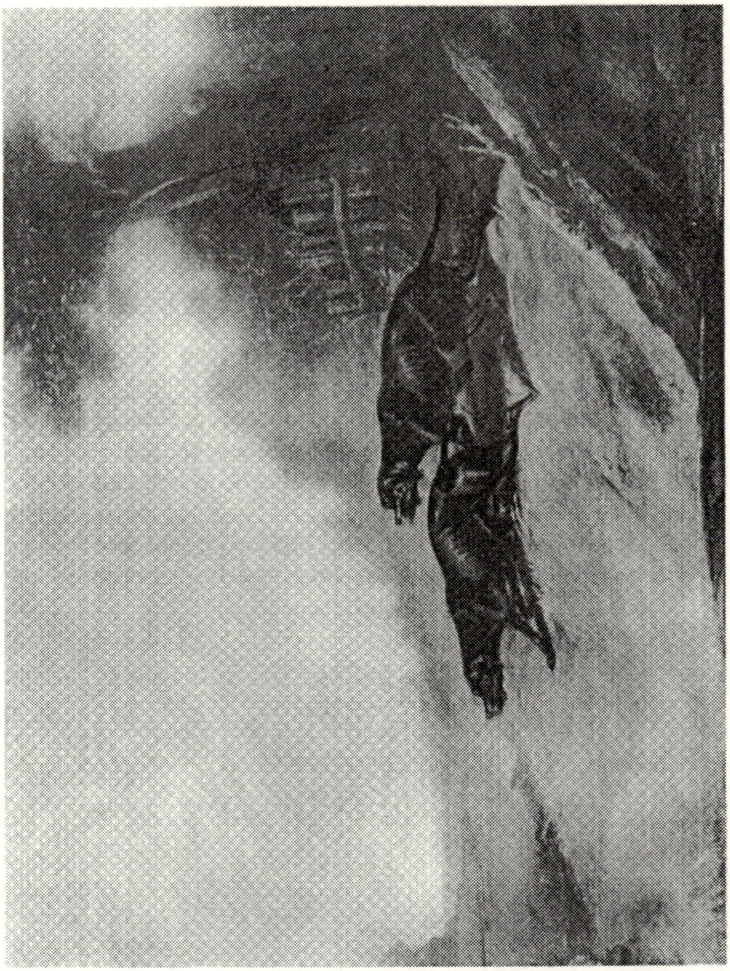

## PLATE XII.

From an oil painting, dated 1827, by C. F. Newton. The black pointers, the subjects of this picture, are beauties. Especially admirable is the pointing bitch, although the artist has somewhat failed in his foreshortening of the other's head. The two, however, are models of quality, and they possess the dished muzzles, the curl of the lip, the full eyes, the high-set ears, and the fine tails, that denote purely bred pointers.

*In my own Possession.*

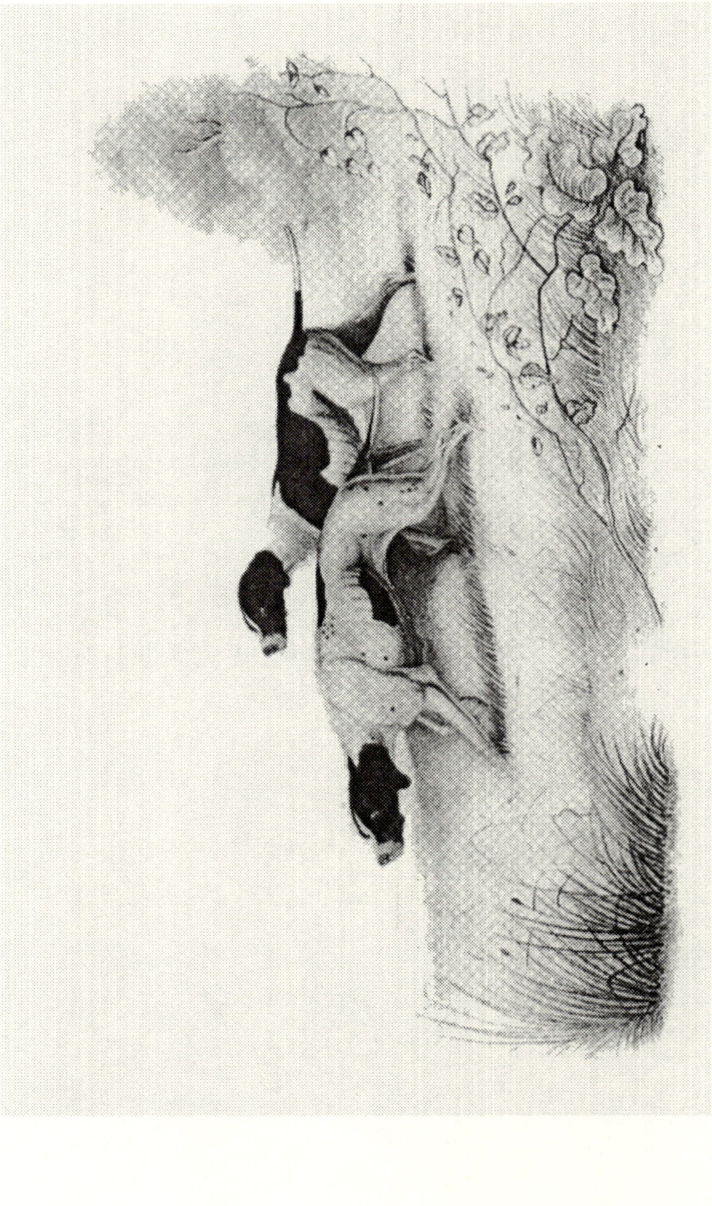

## PLATE XIII.

From a *Sporting Magazine's* engraving, 1831, by J. Scott, jun., after J. F. Lewis, R.A., who exhibited from 1820 to 1877. A brace of handsome bitches are represented in this scene; but the better of the two is without doubt the nearer one, as she has the more pleasing head : both appear to have had the tips of their tails removed.

*In my own Possession.*

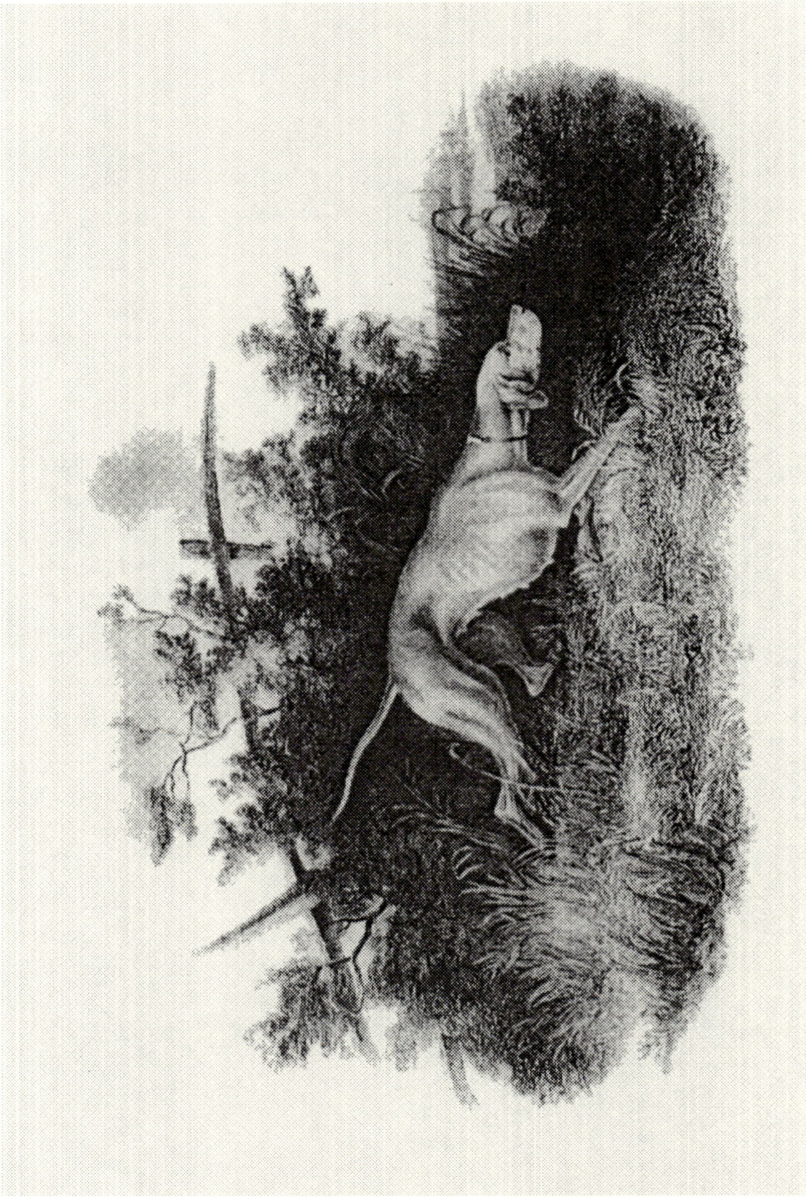

## PLATE XIV.

From a *Sporting Magazine's* engraving, 1834, by Richd. Parr, after G. H. Laporte, who exhibited from 1821 to 1873.

The bitch here portrayed was called 'Juno,' and her colour was a pale fawn. She was bred by H.M. George IV., and was owned by Thos. Scotland, Esq. She was 'a very remarkable worker' (vol. lxxxiv.).

She was also, as this picture testifies, a very remarkable bitch to look at! If there are faults in her, they lie in her rather low-set ear, and her tail being too thin at the root. *In my own Possession.*

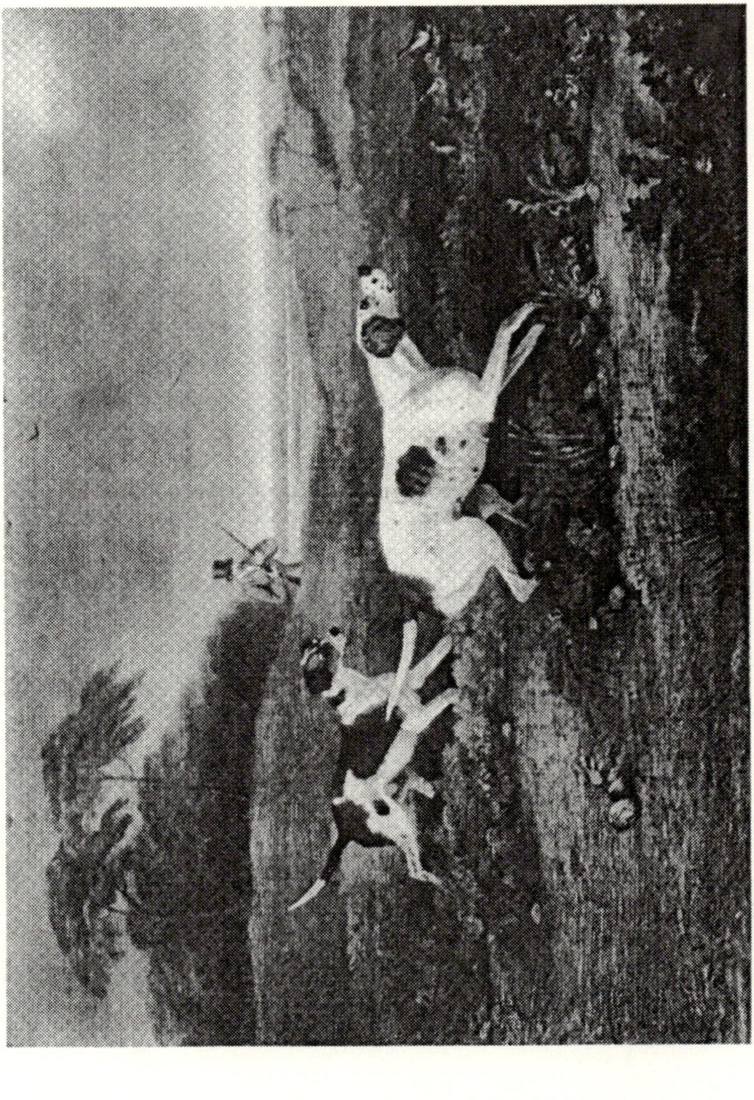

## PLATE XV.

From an oil painting by Henry Alken, jun. (born 1809, died 1892). A black-nosed orange-and-white bitch, having made a point, sees the partridges begin to run, and, if tempted, she is steady. To be ideal, this symmetrical bitch only needs a skull more arched ; but the backing liver-and-white is merely a rough indication of a pointer.

*In my own Possession.*

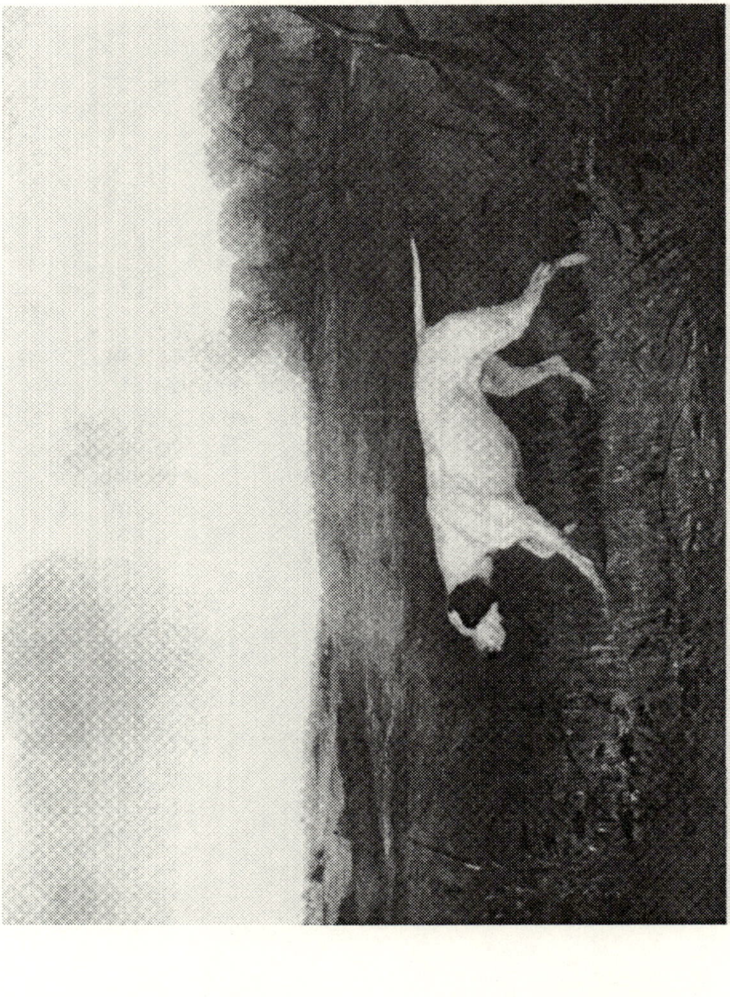

PLATE XVI.

From an oil painting by W. Shayer, who exhibited from 1829 to 1885.

This notable portrait, signed but unfortunately not dated, is of 'Tasso,' a liver-and-white dog belonging to Sir Tatton Sykes. He must have been a superb pointer in all but his muzzle, which is not enough dished ; but though his plainness of face may arise from a mistake of the artist, he is certainly rather wanting in lip.

*In my own Possession.*

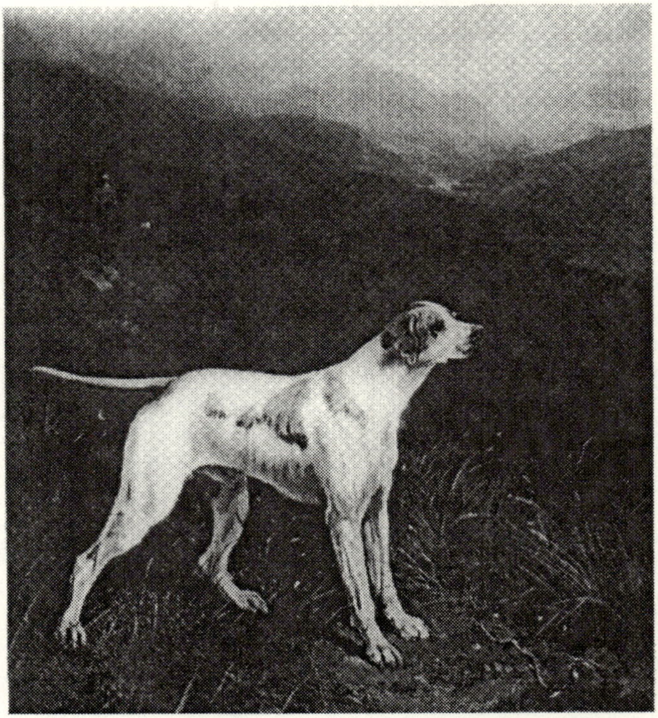

## PLATE XVII.

From an oil painting, dated 1868, by George Earl. This is a portrait of Champion Hamlet, a renowned pointer, that was bred and owned by Mr. J. H. Whitehouse, with whom the artist had the advantage of shooting over him several times. He is proved to have been a highly-bred pointer by his work, by his appearance, and by his success at the stud.

*In my own Possession.*

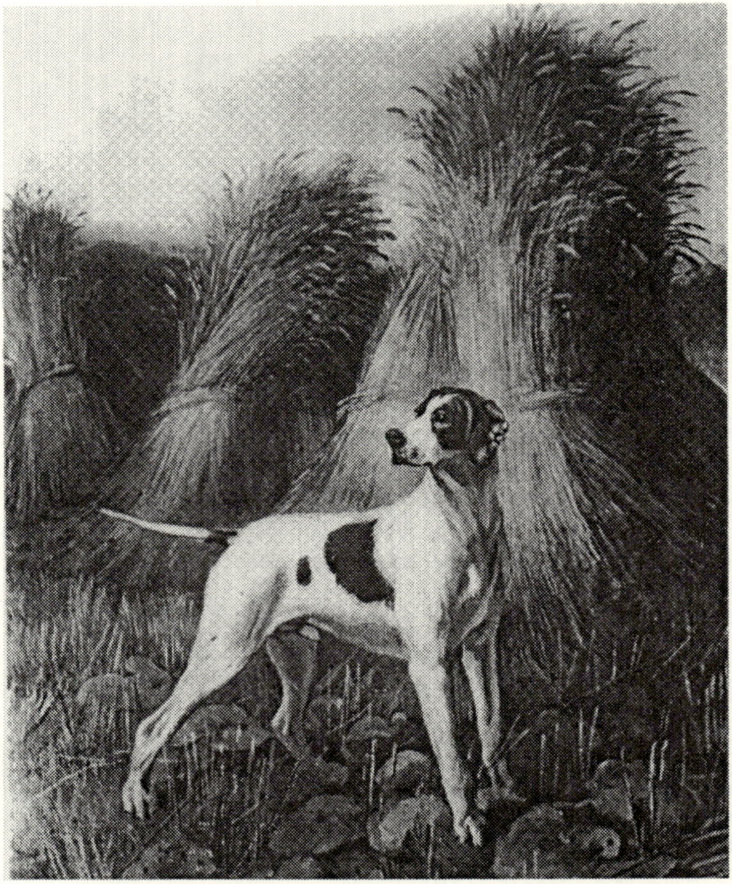

## PLATE XVIII.

From an oil painting, dated 1875, by George Earl. This is a portrait of Champion Drake. He was bred and owned by Sir R. Garth, Q.C., and was one of the most sensational winners of Trials that has ever lived. Drake's legs and feet are here made too wooden; but his head, despite an injury to the picture spoiling one ear, is nice, though both skull and stop are rather lacking. I fancy that the artist must have tried to idealise the dog; as I am told that he possessed an ample head, but that it was not famous for beauty.

*In my own Possession.*

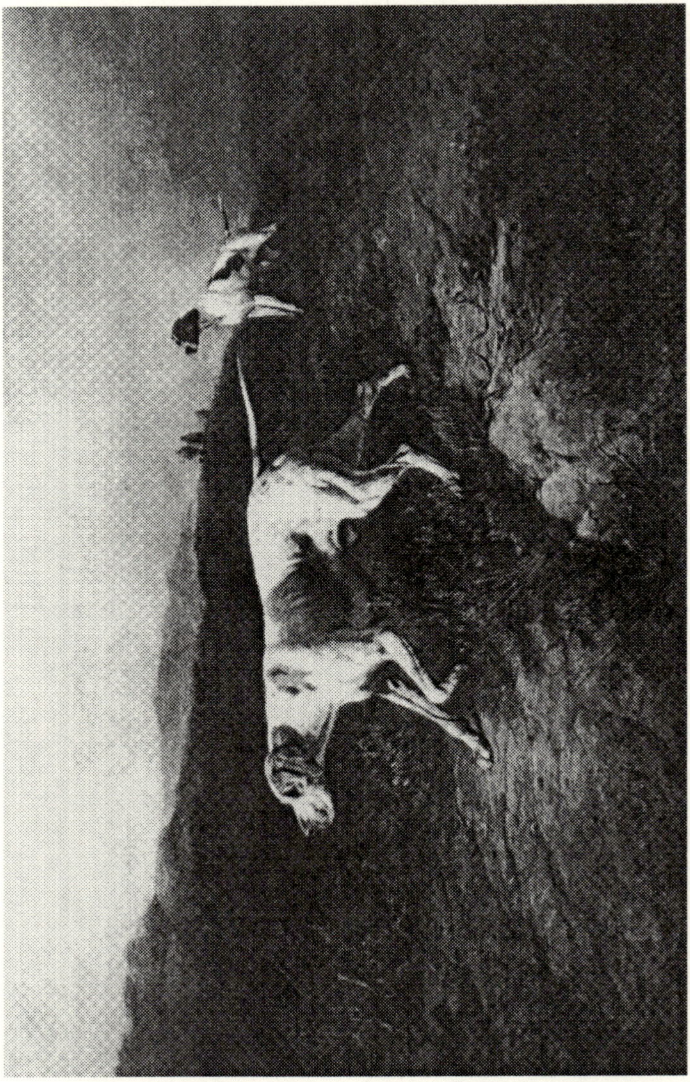

# PLATE XIX.

From an oil painting, dated 1897, by George Earl. It was reproduced on October 22nd, 1899, in *Land and Water*, with the following description appended :—

'The lemon-and-white dog, on game in the foreground, is champion Aldin Fluke, the winner of two prizes at trials, although he ran only on three occasions: he has also obtained the highest honours on the showbench. He is in appearance a great slashing dog, without a suspicion of lumber, although he measures twenty-seven inches at the shoulders and weighs sixty-seven pounds. His long sickled stifles, his fine wiry pasterns, his tapering prehensile toes, guarantee his faculty of traversing the roughest ground with speed and safety, while his shoulders, heart-room, loin, and muscle, ensure his extraordinary powers of endurance. His head is very pointer-like, without any appearance of the hound in it: the eyes are large and round ; the skull well developed, with pronounced " stop ; " the muzzle squarely finished, slightly inclined upwards, and furnished with wide nostrils ; and the ears, full of quality, placed high on the head. Nor does he belie his appearance, for in sagacity and keenness of nose he has few equals, while his long, easy stride is practically untiring ; and he is still, though in his tenth year, a prime favourite of his master. He is a litter-brother of champion Belle Chance, a bitch similar in colour, and relatively of equal beauty. The liver-and-white bitch, which is backing in the picture, is Bride II. of Pitcroy, bred by Mr. Pelham Burn, and bought by Mr. Arkwright from him. She has in her veins a combination of several old Scottish strains and of the Rev. W. Shield's old sort. She was a good and reliable worker, a prize-winner wherever shown, and a successful brood bitch. With its mellow colouring and soft, hazy atmosphere, this picture is a most poetic example of contemporary British art ; but, as a representation of a shooting scene, it becomes a real master-piece. It is the production of a painter who is himself a sportsman and a dog-lover, who is permeated by the fascination of shooting over dogs, who has studied the pointer at work with keen appreciation, and who has here reproduced with fidelity a familiar incident of a day's sport. What a contrast to the well-intentioned, and often well-painted, sporting pictures by fireside artists, who huddle together the pointing dog, the backing dog, and the game in a proximity that, if true, would only show such want of nose and breaking in their favourites, as owners should be ashamed to commemorate ! '

*In my own Possession.*

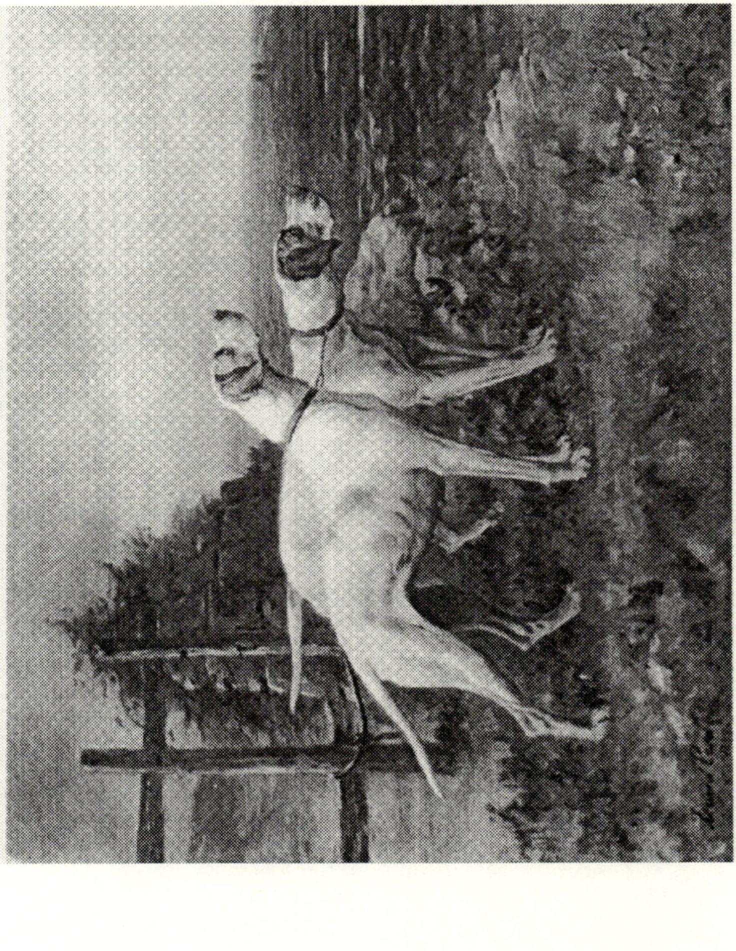

## PLATE XX.

From an oil painting, dated 1899, by Miss Maud Earl.

The picture contains portraits of two of my pointers, champions Sandbank and Seabreeze. I will not describe them, beyond saying that Seabreeze, in the foreground, is pale lemon-and-white, while bright orange-and-white is Sandbank's colour. The picture is entitled 'The Promised Land,' and it represents the brace waiting for their turn, and watching with envious eyes the shooting in the distance.

*In my own Possession.*

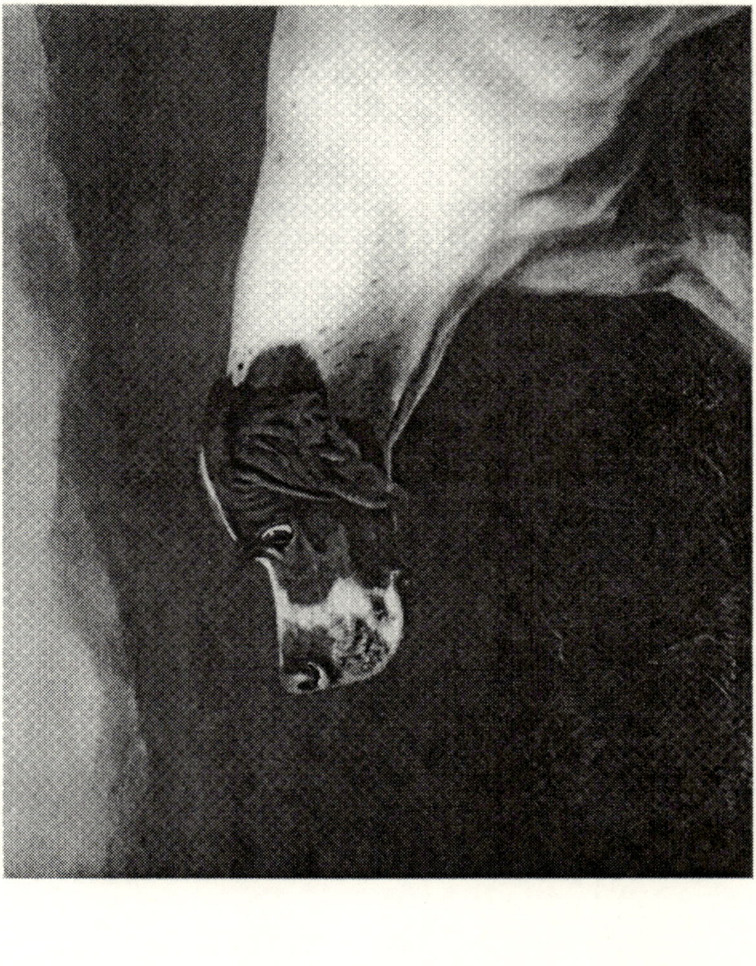

## PLATE XXI.

From an oil painting, dated 1898, by George Earl. This is the portrait of the liver-and-white pointer, Seashore, a litter-brother of Seabreeze (Plate XX.). It is a most forceful presentment of a wonderful head and neck. *In my own Possession.*

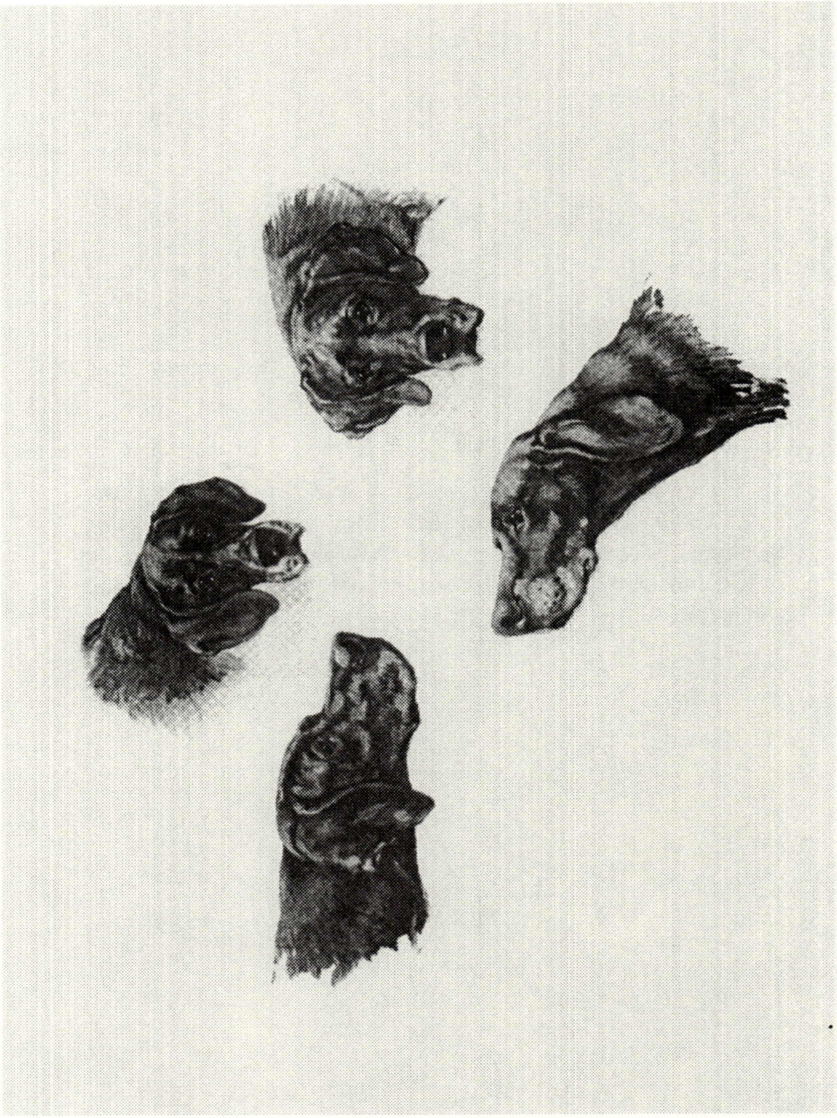

## PLATE XXII.

From studies in oils, painted 1901, by Miss Maud Earl.

These are the portrait-heads of a brace of first-rate black pointers belonging to Mr. D. M. Forbes ; and, alas ! pointers of this beautiful type are now very rare. What I may term the eastern and western heads are likenesses of a dog called Lorne, and, I think, his profile at all events approximates to my idea of perfection. The northern and southern heads represent his daughter, Kate—maybe rather too long in the ear and too fine in the skull, but very lovely. These dogs, like Sandbank and Seabreeze (Plate XX.), have had the advantage of the portraiture of Miss Earl—a lady who, in addition to her other qualifications, combines enthusiasm for the pointer with an intimate knowledge of his anatomy.

*In my own Possession.*

# CHARACTERISTICS OF THE POINTER

### The Tail, the Coat, and the Colour.

*The Tail* of the pointer must be moderately short, with thick bone at the root, very gradually tapering to a fine point. It must be covered thickly with smooth, glossy hair, and must be carried straight, on a level with the back, the 'pot-hook' curve being very objectionable. When questing it is wantoned and lashed without ceasing, but when pointing it is held rigid, either quite straight or with a slight 'pump-handle' curve.

There is nothing for a pointer more necessary than a tail of the right shape, of the right length, of the right carriage, and of the right covering. It is more convincing warranty of pure blood and high breeding than reams of written pedigree. There is a saying about the pedigree being carried on the back, but in this case it is told by the tail. The head is invaluable for showing the character of a dog, but for a certificate of blue-blood apply at the other end!

*The Coat* is dense, and hard, and as smooth as glass, with a sheen on it. It is of the same length on the white as on the coloured places; and if you run your fingers the wrong way through it, it must instantly resume its former appearance, and must by no means hide the wonderful development of sinews and muscle that distinguishes the well-bred pointer. One sometimes hears persons complaining that he is too fine-bred, or that he has not a coat to suit all weathers, &c.: they might just as sensibly find fault with the thoroughbred horse. A ploughboy cannot do the work of a philosopher, though he may have a harder constitution. What is not worth taking care of, is not worth having; besides, the pointer is by nature a rich man's possession, a luxury like the grouse-moor itself.

## THE POINTER

There is a very wide latitude allowed in *the Colour of pointers*; white, black, liver, fawn, lemon, orange, red, and virtually almost any colour with or without white. In fact, John Mayer (1815) includes even brindle in his list as follows:—'Whole colours are black, white, lemon, yellow, whey-coloured, dark brindle, brown, &c.' (*Sportsman's Directory*, p. 112). For my own part I venture to doubt the orthodoxy of the brindle; but still more do I 'suspect the get' of liver or black-and-white dogs with tan markings about them, because there is no mention of them in the old books, because I have never seen a typical pointer of this motley, and because, though I have repeatedly crossed yellows with liver and black-and-whites, and lemon-and-whites with blacks, I have never bred one single tricoloured puppy. I well remember to have seen, when a child, some beautiful mouse-grey-and-whites of Lord Sefton's breed, but at present they, like the pure whites, seem in abeyance.

The nose of the lemon-and-whites may be either black or liver-coloured: these colours are equally correct. Just now there seems a prejudice against the former. But why? The earliest pictures show these dogs to be black-nosed—for instance, the painting by Titian, fifteenth century (Plate III.), and the Velazquez, seventeenth century (Plate IV.). Again, in an example of Stubbs, eighteenth century, and in a painting by Seymour, eighteenth century, which belong to me though not included in the present book, the noses of lemon-and-white dogs are also dusky. Besides, on the other hand, the earliest liver-coloured nose that I have found on a lemon-and-white is in the eighteenth century picture by Oudry (Plate VI.), while I have seen no specimen of it in British art earlier than 1840, the date of a painting by Thomson of Nottingham. I must, therefore, from the evidence before me, find for

## CHARACTERISTICS OF THE POINTER

the superior antiquity of the black nose, though personally I prefer liver-coloured nostrils, as they seem more harmonious. But when it comes to a matter of penalising a pointer at a dog-show because his nose is black, the height of absurdity is reached!

Lastly, I must touch on the effects of *Instinct* and *Nose* on the character of a pointer, as these, with the *Body* and *Limbs*, complete the handmaidens of the BRAIN.

His instinctive ideas are concentrated on the one idea of sport, and to keep him in proper bodily and mental condition sport he must have, or failing that, its best substitute—hard exercise. It is almost piteous to watch him diligently working bare ground, even gravelled or paved spaces in default of other, to make assurance doubly sure, and deeming it better worth to quest hopelessly than not to quest at all. It is this obsession by the one idea that makes him so poor a 'pal to knock about with,' and so impatient of lolling in his master's rooms; for he does not thrive as a house-dog, nor anywhere else without constant movement. The pointer differs essentially in his temperament from the spaniel, or even from the setter, which can be contented anywhere as long as he is basking in the master's smile; and to a disposition like his it must be torture to be chained, Ixion-like, to the eternal round of the shows—to a life of enforced inactivity in a tainted atmosphere!

He is by nature one of the most nervous and sensitive of all dogs. For instance, any sudden noise, such as the banging of a door, will make him jump for yards; but I think this is due to his day-dreaming propensities when at leisure, as it is only the unexpected that frightens him, and he will face composedly enough whatever he may be prepared for. The sound of a gun, if he have been thoughtfully initiated, never

# THE POINTER

cows him at all, nor does a severe flogging properly administered; but a stone thrown at him will terrify, and the flicking of a whip-lash will drive him to frenzy.

Many a pointer, in his passion for sport, is quite oblivious of feminine charms, like the '*Venator, teneræ conjugis immemor*' of Horace. Indeed to such lengths is this coldness sometimes carried that I have known excellent dogs that have absolutely refused to procreate; and, similarly, many bitches are very unwilling to yield to the periodical demands of sex. I worked my own spaniel, though she was in season, among my pointers during August, 1900, without one of them finding out her condition, or taking the slightest notice of her.

Having thus shown that the pointer exists simply for sport, those natural qualities have to be considered that caused him to become the chosen assistant of man in one of its branches. To commence with, a fine passage from Captain Lacy illumines the subject.

'The two symptoms of most felicitous augury in a young dog are decision, depending upon superior nose, in going straight up to his game, with his head erect, the moment he catches the scent; and his backing another dog instinctively from the first. Again, if when he come to a decided point, he, what is called, "chap his point," and never stir till the birds rise, so much the better; but if he dash in immediately afterwards, no matter, as he may soon be cured of that. I by no means deny that dogs which do not display these early and marked indications of future excellence may ultimately turn out well, or even first-rate; but this is the best sort of stuff to go to work upon, and these are the dogs to be selected from a litter where the shooter breeds his own, and keeps the whole to choose

# CHARACTERISTICS OF THE POINTER

from. The best temper for a dog to have, is the mean between the extremes of the timid and the resolute; in fact, he should be high-couraged without being sulky, vicious, or shrinkingly timid. A sulky dog is not worth a halter, and a very shy one I should always be shy of accepting' (*The Modern Shooter*, 1842, p. 168).

Now, some wonder if a 'superior nose' be really separable from a superior intelligence; but if Youatt, a professional man, confirming the opinions of many eminent laymen, can be credited in his anatomy and deductions, the matter is settled by the following as being primarily one of nerve:—'The olfactory nerve in the dog is the largest of all the cerebral nerves. The relative size of the nerve bears an invariable proportion to the necessity of an acute sense of smell' (*The Dog*, 1845, p. 107).

'There are many dogs that will point the first day that they are taken out, and there are others which will both point and back the first time by natural instinct' (*Essay on Shooting*, 1789, p. 256).

'It has been supposed by some that dogs which slip so naturally into the method of pointing acquire afterwards too much set; this, however, is quite a mistaken notion: ill-bred dogs will frequently be guilty of the incurable fault just mentioned; in fact, an ill-bred dog is very seldom worth keeping' (*The Sportsman*, No. 4, vol. iii., 1836, p. 185).

With the above remarks about natural pointing and backing, I entirely agree; the best pointers that I have known started, without exception, by doing these duties of their own accord.

'Chapping the point,' or 'chewing the scent,' is another infallible proof of the inheritance of old pointer blood. It is so called because the dog when on the point has the appearance of munching something, and

## THE POINTER

this movement is accompanied by slaver from the mouth, a sign of his actually enjoying the taste of the scent on his palate. For this diagnosis I am indebted to a medical friend of mine; and I must say that the possession of this power is most desirable, as it enables virtue to be its own reward.

'A pointer or setter, to deserve the name, should hunt high but steadily; quarter his ground with truth and judgment; turn to hand or whistle; drop to hand, bird, and shot; back at all distances; be steady from hare, yet follow a wounded one if necessary; and recover a dead or wounded bird well' (*Sporting Magazine*, September 2nd, vol. v., by 'A Quartogenarian,' 1832, p. 9).

One is inclined to comment on the above that evidently 'there were giants in the earth in those days,' and that, though of value as a 'counsel of perfection,' one may with profit omit the sending of one's pointer after a wounded hare! Nevertheless, I myself had a pointer—only one though—that might have been so sent with safety. Because, in addition to ordinary duties, he regularly acted as retriever both from land and water, and as spaniel too, for he was an expert at springing 'flappers' from the rushes; and despite these irregularities at home he continued year after year to win at the field-trials. He was by an old black pointer, also father to another whose case is even more remarkable. He, by some curious trick of heredity, was a self-taught and perfect 'circler' as described in the *Dialogos* and *Arte de Ballesteria*. He would point staunchly enough when the birds lay well, but when they were at all 'jumpy' he would never stop still for a moment, and actually would give you with his head the sign of their whereabouts as he passed. These traits must have descended to the brothers from their black blood, as the mothers' families showed no traces

# CHARACTERISTICS OF THE POINTER

of such genius. But a dog known by the author of *Kunopædia* seems to have possessed a tithe of the same gifts. He writes of 'an old dog who, as the associate of a keen and practised poacher on the moors whom I once knew, had acquired a deal of self-taught sagacity; and I have seen him, when baffled upon a haunt, and unable to make out an absolute find, nay, I have seen him almost on the first touch of haunt, take a sweep off, in something between a crouch and a run, as hard as he could go, deaf to every call, as though he were mad, two hundred yards or more directly *down the wind*, in which quarter it is evident that experience had taught him to look with more of certainty to find, or towards which he had, in any dubious case, been immediately led off by his knowing director, and then come crouching up, with no part of him but his head visible, in a right line to meet you' (*Kunopædia*, by W. Dobson, 1814, p. 105).

'A pointer cannot be too fast, if his nose is good; but many of the very swift dogs are sometimes apt to run over the game' (*The Shooting Directory*, by R. B. Thornhill, 1806, p. 63). This is very true, as far as it goes. But the pointer that hunts faster than his nose lacks instinct and intelligence, and, in short, is a second-rater. A good dog regulates his pace day by day according to the quality of the scent, and it is curious to see mere puppies doing the same thing. They instinctively carry their heads to the wind also, and nothing disquiets a good puppy more than to find himself in such relation to the wind that his nose will not serve him. Of course, an old dog that adds craft to instinct will quite enjoy a cast down-wind; and wonderful is the manner in which he feels for the scent as he goes along like Agag—delicately, stopping at the slightest whiff for the assistance of his master. In fact, so subtle does he become in the use of his nose,

## THE POINTER

and so little chance has grouse or partridge against him, that one feels that there was not extravagance, but inspiration, in that sixteenth-century Spaniard who, when he saw how the very winds seemed to serve the clever pointing-dog, proclaimed him 'Lord of the Air!'

# CHAPTER V.
## BREEDING AND SELECTION.

WORKING dogs are of all the domestic animals the most interesting to breed, as they alone, in addition to the physical, have mental qualities that require solicitude. The voices of the ancients are on this subject as suggestive as usual, and pre-eminent among them are some sayings of Sir John Sebright, the dean of scientific breeders :—

'Were I to define what is called the art of breeding, I should say that it consisted in the selection of males and females, intended to breed together, in reference to each other's merits and defects' (*Art of Improving the Breeds*, &c., by Sebright, 1809, p. 5).

'We must observe the smallest tendency to imperfection in our stock, the moment it appears, so as to be able to counteract it, before it becomes a defect' (*id.* p. 6).

'Animals must degenerate by being long bred from the same family without the intermixture of any other blood, or from being what is technically called *bred in-and-in*' (*id.* p. 8).

'I do not by any means approve of mixing two distinct breeds, with the view of uniting the valuable properties of both. This experiment has been frequently tried by others, as well as by myself, but has, I believe, never succeeded. The first cross frequently produces a tolerable animal, but it is a breed that cannot be continued' (*id.* p. 17).

The above are fundamental axioms for the breeding

## THE POINTER

of live stock in general, and, as far as they go, are thoroughly pertinent to the production of the pointer.

Next in point of antiquity comes Colonel Thornton's method; but in practice I hardly think that even he could have been so reckless and haphazard:—

'I scarcely ever found one pointer in fifty answer my expectations, either for shape, bone, or action; and the different modes of breaking, if they are not whelps, make them irreclaimable; but it only costs a little time and a little money, at least to see such as are well recommended, and the greater opportunity the greater chance of success; if well-shaped dogs or bitches, they can be bred soon, and they may make gamekeepers' dogs' (*Sporting Tour*, &c., by Colonel Thornton, 1804, p. 279).

When we seek the keynote to Mr. Lascelles's breeding operations, we learn that this was *nose*:—

'As a fine nose is the first thing I look to in a pointer, I am always particularly careful that both sire and dam are thus gifted. I think it one of the greatest proofs of bad blood for a dog to take much breaking; mine all stand naturally, and they are not only the highest-couraged, but the fastest rangers. This I attribute to nothing so much as to their having the finest noses, which gives them a confidence beyond the possibility of abuse' (*Angling, Shooting, and Coursing*, by Lascelles, 1811, p. 136).

Of Mr. T. B. Johnson's precepts and practice we possess two accounts: one written by a friend, one from his own pen. Both are important, and interesting enough for insertion:—

'At the period of which we are speaking, it was the custom or fashion, or both, to regard a large, expansive head as not merely the reverse of beauty, but a sort of blemish; and, inconsiderately adopting this monstrously ridiculous idea, he [T. B. Johnson, about

## BREEDING AND SELECTION

1815] found himself, after several years' experimental crossing, in possession of a set of dogs with compressed heads, considered *handsome* forsooth! giddy and uncertain to a most vexatious extent; because being thus deprived of a sufficient breadth and expansion of the requisite organs (of smell) the operative functions were inadequate to the due and satisfactory performance of that duty which they thus vainly essayed to perform; in the language of the school, *their noses were bad*. However, reflection induced him to *bark back*; he was convinced there could be no effect without a cause: what, therefore, was the source whence the Spanish pointer derived his unequivocally acknowledged superior powers of smell? To use the words of the would-be-thought genius, whose *spurious inventions*, however, will not give to his memory an enviable immortality, it "struck us like lightning," that the large expansive head of the surly Spaniard would afford him the desired information. Therefore Chance, five years old, a genuine Spanish pointer, was immediately condemned. Dissection exhibited the small white cords which constitute the olfactory nerves or organs, or rather perhaps which receive and convey the impression of scent to the brain, in vast numbers; hence the superiority already noticed. However, for satisfactory elucidation more sacrifices were rendered indispensable; in short, after the examination of a variety of heads, it was found the olfactory nerves or organs were numerous precisely in proportion to the expansion of the head, and therefore, as the heads narrowed, the cords in question diminished, and consequently the powers of smell became inferior in the same degree; the Spanish pointer and the narrow-headed high-bred greyhound may be regarded as the two extremes: the experiments were delightfully satisfactory!

'The difficulty which presented itself was to unite

## THE POINTER

a head sufficiently expansive with a form calculated for celerity and endurance. In the course of his experiment, the writer to whom we have alluded, procured pointers from various parts of Europe, particularly from France, Spain, and Portugal; he had recourse to his sporting friends in this country, and introduced the Yorkshire and Leicestershire blood into his kennel: and after sixteen years of crossing and recrossing he produced pointers from whose performances he experienced the utmost satisfaction. He happened accidentally to meet with a pointer on board a Spanish vessel in the harbour of Liverpool, whom the captain represented as the best blood in Spain. It was the most shapely Spanish pointer which he had seen, and he therefore procured it' (*The Sportsman*, 1836, vol. iii., No. 4, p. 182).

'Having seen pointers much superior to my own, particularly in Yorkshire, I set about the business of improvement — of possessing pointers equal, if not superior, to any in the world. The head of the Spaniard was alone desirable from him, which it was requisite to attach to a strong, wiry, well-formed body, supported by straight, clean, bony legs; and feet, the toes of which should be hard, close, and narrow, the ball as small as possible. No very great time elapsed before I procured a Spanish pointer of great repute in regard to breed, and which I was credibly informed came from the favourite strain of the late King Ferdinand. The appearance of the dog was nothing in his favour; I entertained not the least doubt that, from family repute, he had not been bred out, had been produced on the in-and-in system, which I am well aware from experience is a very inadvisable plan. A dip of relationship, when judiciously managed, will conduce to the beauty and mild temper of the animal, without deteriorating the sagacity, the sense of smell, or any of

## BREEDING AND SELECTION

the essential qualities ; while a continuance of the same strain produces semi-idiocy and disease ; ultimately barrenness' (*Shooter's Preceptor*, by Johnson, 1842, p. 6).

'I proceeded in my experiments, keeping in view the qualities already pointed out ; after a number of crosses with selected individuals and an occasional conjunction of first cousins, I became possessed of pointers which gave me unqualified satisfaction, either as regarded nose, fleetness, powers of endurance, steadiness, obedience, good temper, beauty, and indeed in whatever can be desired in such an animal' (*id.* p. 8).

'My pointers were of middle size (in respect to height), presenting the capacious, low-dropping chest, widely-spread thighs, strong loins ; legs straight, bony, and clean ; toes narrow and hard, rather long than short ; ball of the foot small ; head as large as possible, broad and well formed, with plenty of lip. The best bitch I ever possessed was inclined to the roach back ; her powers of endurance, particularly on the grouse mountains, were superior to what I ever witnessed in any other dog—pointer or setter.

'During the process of my experiments, amongst other foreign dogs which I procured was one from Portugal, which, like his Spanish relation, was ill-tempered, unwieldy, &c., and, like him also, possessed a most acute sense of smell. Further, several "double-nosed pointers" came into my possession during this period. This grotesque ramification of the pointer was originally (I believe) from France' (*id.* p. 9).

The vulgar idea of the 'double-nose' is that it is distinctive of the Spanish pointer, instead of being an unsightly malformation peculiar to no country—no breed, but most commonly found in the south of France. I know a family of Irish red setters similarly distinguished, to the evident satisfaction of their owner.

# THE POINTER

Of course the nostrils are not really double, not even more expanded owing to this freak of nature; they are merely split in half by a deep furrow. Equally of course, dogs with this formation have got no keener scent than their normal relatives. In the standard Spanish Dictionary (*Madrid, Real Academia,* 1727), under the word '*Braco,*' is found the following passage:—'Properly this is the name of dogs and bitches that have the nostrils split and somewhat elevated, the muzzle blunt, and the ears large and falling over the face. Some say they come originally from the French *braque*; others think they may be from the *bracco* of Tuscany.' This does not prove much, but it seems effectually to disprove their Spanish origin, though a Frenchman, M. Baudrillart (*Traité des eaux et forêts*, 1820, pt. iii., p. 294), has it that 'there is still another variety of brach from Spain, which is most improperly styled *double-nosed*, because this dog has his nostrils separated by a groove. It seems that this variety, though it has been much cried up, has nevertheless a nose less sensitive than the French, or the English dog.'

'A young dog that carries his head well up when beating should be chosen in preference to one that hunts with his nose on the ground. It is not only the best dog that carries his head up, but game will suffer him to approach nearer than one that tracks them. The handsomest dog is that which shows the most breed, the most valuable that which affords the sportsman the greatest number of shots' (*The Shooter's Handbook*, by Oakleigh, 1842, p. 97).

'One great cause of the scarcity of well-bred, docile, and naturally steady pointers has been the fashionable rage for speed, to secure which, regardless of more valuable properties, the fastest pointers, setters, and foxhounds have been sought as stallions; while the old, naturally staunch, large-headed, fine-nosed breed, to

# BREEDING AND SELECTION

which the true-bred pointer belongs, has been proportionately neglected. The latter are fast enough in any sort of country, are incomparably the best for finding game, and for behaving over it with that steady caution which ensures the sportsman by far the greatest number of fine shots. I do not, however, allude to that heavy, clumsy, dead-slow species of dog which once prevailed, but to the improved sort, of a medium size and of good shape, bred from these, such as the black-and-white breed of the late Sir Harry Goodrick' (*The Modern Shooter*, by Captain Lacy, 1842, p. 169).

The following advice on choosing a pointer seems excellent when you can find such dogs to select from : ' Mark if he be a gallant beater, ranging high, going within himself, his head well up and to the wind, as endeavouring to catch a flying scent ; making his casts, turns, and offers, dashingly ; neither hanging on the haunt nor puzzling for a ground scent. See that he quarters his ground regularly, and independently of any other dog hunting in company, without leaving the corners of his fields untried. He must neither skulk, shirk, break field, follow, watch, blink, nor point at sight. He shall not be hard-nosed nor near-scented, but wind his birds at long distances ; keep his point staunchly ; back without jealousy ; crouch to bird, dog, or gun at a signal from the hand, or the word *Toho*, without caprice, or standing when you call ' (*Recreations in Shooting*, by Craven, 1846, p. 141).

I cordially agree with nearly all of the foregoing maxims, but I must add to them a few supplementary remarks. As regards mating your dogs, it is quite straightforward work to breed for the physical points, though you have, of course, as a preliminary to form in your mind the ideal up to which you intend to raise your stock. Let all your bitches be first-rate according to your own standard, or, if this seem a hard saying,

143

## THE POINTER

only breed from the first-raters. It is indeed a waste of time and place to trust to lucky nicks in breeding, they are so rare ; and even if you do fluke a wonder from a poorish dam, he will not be the sort of dog to benefit your kennel permanently. Not that I would pay too much attention to the shape of the grandparents, for the appearance of the couple concerned is the main consideration. I will give an illustration of this, which concerned my own dogs—not, indeed, the pointers, but some dachshunds. I bred two brothers of one litter, and two sisters of another litter, the two lots being first cousins to each other. The brothers were of opposite types, one inclined to be heavy-boned and houndy, the other somewhat elegant, arch-loined, and light ; the same variation occurred in the two bitches : all four were prize-winners. In due course I sold them. And it happened that the coarse, houndy couple were mated together, as also were the elegant, light-boned ones. The result was that the entire litter from the former had an intensification of the heavy characteristics, while the pups from the latter pair were quite as exaggerated in the opposite direction—so much so that a casual beholder would have guessed them to be not only of a different family, but almost of a different variety.

You must judge your brood-bitch dispassionately, to make quite sure of those points in which she is not perfect, and mate her with a dog of the same type, but excelling where she is moderate ; and, if you wish to establish eventually a true-breeding race, you must abstain from using sires, faulty in themselves, but famous because they have begotten a good pup or two.

In pointers, beware also of paper pedigrees, unless the dogs concerned carry confirmatory credentials in their work and appearance.

It is necessary to in-breed your dogs to a moderate

## BREEDING AND SELECTION

extent to gain uniformity of type, but avoid excess, and be careful to employ for such a purpose only animals that are sound in mind and body. Concerning this, let your motto be : In-breeding for out-shining, but in-and-in breeding for out-and-out folly!

Breeding from unbroken parents is, of course, trusting to chance, as no man can tell the undeveloped potentialities of a dog, and the further into the pedigree you have to dive to reach the working element, the more uncertain the result. Some dogs require breaking to develop their brain-power, while others are born essentially ready-made; and, though breaking is not necessary for the breeding animals themselves—because, if once the sporting instinct be there, it will remain latent for generations—yet a knowledge of individual character, only to be gleaned from their actual work, is indispensable to the man who is attempting to mate them advantageously.

Minute analyses of the work of each of his pointers should be from time to time entered in a book by the scientific breeder. For him the most fascinating problem to solve is how nearly he can breed his dogs ready-broken by nature, and only needing the finishing touches superadded. But this is a somewhat complicated matter, and demands critical attention at all times. The triumphs in this breeding for mind are not showy—you cannot parade them before a gaping crowd ; and, with the limited choice of blood now open to a pointer man, they are difficult to win, for there are so many qualities in a perfect pointer, that you must be careful not to let one drop while picking up another. Among those attributes that I have found innate in certain cases are the pointing, backing, and quartering instincts ; nose, obedience, initiative, indifference to fur, pace, dash, endurance, carriage of head, with style on point and in questing.

# THE POINTER

To select youngsters from a litter, take them when about six months old into a big field with their feeder, and walk along, allowing the pups to gallop how and where they please. Those of them that do not care to play with their brethren, preferring to hunt about by themselves, never following another, will make the best dogs. This test I have found infallible.

Sportsmen who are worthy of the name will never withhold from each other their particular strains of blood, they will try to keep their supremacy by superior skill in their blends, and by their nurture and education of the pups.

When you are forced to send your bitch on a visit to a dog outside your own kennel, let her be accompanied by a trustworthy attendant. It may cost a pound or two more, but the money is well spent in obtaining *certainty*, for strangers are sometimes careless, and the bitch may be shy and restless among them. The chief objection to breeding from outside dogs is that your knowledge of them can be but superficial; when, therefore, you can arrange either for a loan of them or for their purchase outright, it will be found more satisfactory.

# CHAPTER VI.
## ALIEN CROSSES.

SOME persons cannot leave well alone; and the world of the pointer, ever since the dawn of the nineteenth century, seems to have been troubled with more than its share of novelty hunters.

The hybridising of the pointer was started, no doubt, from some misty hope of bettering his work, though, up to the end of the eighteenth century, it seems to have been very little practised. In fact, the only reference of this date to it that I can discover is from the pen of Mr. Page :—

'The breed of pointers which has been mixed with English spaniels, such as are for setting dogs (in order to have such as will run fast and hunt briskly), are, according to the degree of spaniel in them, difficult to be made staunch, and many of them never will stand well in company' (*Art of Shooting Flying*, 1767, p. 85).

Now, as this sentence is distinctly unfavourable to the cross, and as Pye (1790) and Osbaldiston (1792) both become plagiarists for its precious sake, we can infer that the mischief done by crossing up to that time was infinitesimal. In fact, setter blood can never have been introduced into the pointer to a large extent, and I find so few mentions of it in sporting literature that I will deal summarily with the subject of this cross by quoting the two following passages :—

'A species of dog generally nominated the pointer, and Spain may be said to have originally sent forth a breed of these which, at the time, were superior to

# THE POINTER

every other. By a careful and judicious management, the union of this with the English setter has produced a kind, in my opinion, infinitely surpassing either' (*Angling, Shooting, and Coursing*, by Lascelles, 1811, p. 128).

'We have heard inconsiderate sportsmen recommend a cross with the setter. We have witnessed the experiment of this incongruous conjunction repeatedly : one good dog in five hundred may be thus obtained ; but in general the offspring of the pointer and setter are very unruly, very obstinate, and very rarely indeed worth the trouble of rearing' (*The Sportsman*, 1836, vol. iii. p. 185).

At first sight this difference of opinion seems remarkable. I gather from it that Mr. Lascelles, an exceptionally clever sportsman-breeder-breaker, as is proved by his book, had sufficient patience and ability to force a success, denied to most others. For my own part, if I were obliged to cross my pointers (which Heaven forfend!) with any outside blood, I should certainly select the setter, as the only breed that would not diminish the pointing instinct in the puppies *by one half*. A prospect, one would have imagined, sufficiently daunting to the thoughtful in any age!

How far more rational than the advocacy of any alien cross is the following passage :—

'With respect to the Spanish pointer, he is of foreign origin, as his name seems to imply, but is now naturalised in this country, which has long been famous for dogs of this description ; the greatest attention being paid to preserve the breed by many sportsmen, and those who have paid due attention to it have been recompensed by preserving the breed in the utmost purity. This dog is remarkable for the aptness and facility with which it receives instruction ; indeed, it may be said to be self-taught. The English pointer,

## ALIEN CROSSES

on the contrary, is very difficult to be broke in, the greatest attention being necessary to complete his education. A cross between these produces capital dogs, which are much esteemed for their goodness. The Spanish pointer cannot undergo the fatigues of an extensive range, nor is he so durable and hardy as the English' (*Shooting Directory*, by Thornhill, 1804, p. 51).

Evidently the homogeneous cross has always possessed the virtues here claimed for it, as it was the blending of two strains—the one from Navarre, the other originally from Italy—that produced the English pointer.

But it was in the last years of the eighteenth century that the crying sin against the pointer was committed, by mating him with the foxhound. Had he been crossed once again with the tender-nosed, sagacious, southern hound, the effect would not have been disastrous; but the dashing, harum-scarum foxhound was an exemplarily mischievous selection. I suppose that the idea of this cross originated from a superstition, indulged in by the many, that the foxhound was a sort of 'chosen' dog; and that it culminated in our own day with the efforts of fanciers to engraft an untypical appearance on the pointer for show-ring purposes. In the beginning there was no concealment about the matter, the cross was discussed with perfect frankness, though, of course, the hound-like appearances were obliterated as soon as possible. Latterly, however, the process was reversed, for great reticence was displayed in acknowledging hound-blood, though hound-type was openly advocated. Colonel Thornton, who kept both foxhounds and pointers, was the first to intermix the two breeds. I select quotations from Sydenham Edwards, his contemporary, on the subject:—

'The sportsman has improved the breed by selecting the lightest and gayest individuals, and, by judicious

# THE POINTER

crosses with the foxhound, to procure courage and fleetness' (*Cynographia Britannica*, 1800, p. 2).

'His high spirit and eagerness for the sport render him intractable and extremely difficult of education ; his impatience in company subjects him to a desire to be foremost in the points, and not give the sportsman time to come up, to run in upon the game, particularly down-wind' (*ib.*).

'The most judicious cross appears to have been with the foxhound, as by this has been acquired speed and courage, power and perseverance ; and its disadvantage, difficulty of training them to be staunch. I believe the celebrated Colonel Thornton first made this cross, and, from his producing excellent dogs, has been very generally followed' (*id.* p. 10).

But, as we have Lascelles's exhaustive book on pointers, written ten years later, with no mention of a cross between the pointer and the foxhound, though he mentions the setter cross and was himself in addition a hunting-man, the cross at that time cannot have been so 'very generally followed.'

It was very unfortunate that Colonel Thornton should have succeeded so soon in producing such an eminent dog as his Dash. This was an extraordinary worker, and was sold for a sensational price—enough to set half the breeders in England crazy to try the same experiment in breeding.

'Dash in his day was held to be the Eclipse of pointers, a character sanctioned by his high ranging over the moors, the vast expedition with which he cleared his ground, and the intuitive, heaven-born method, said to be almost incredible, in which he hunted enclosures for birds, which was by at once scenting and advancing upon them without the previous labour imposed upon other pointers of quartering his ground : add to this, he was a most staunch and steady backer,

## ALIEN CROSSES

or seconder, of other dogs' (*Sportsman's Repository*, Lawrence, 1828, p. 121).

'What are well understood amongst sportsmen by the term, "cross-bred dogs," we regard with contempt, though an extraordinary animal (one in ten thousand perhaps) has been occasionally produced. The late Colonel Thornton's Dash is the most celebrated of these semi-mongrels. Dash was produced by a cross of the foxhound with a highly bred pointer bitch. He was remarkable for his style of ranging upon the moors, as well as for his superior method of finding game; he was equally excellent in partridge-shooting, and backed other dogs as steadily as possible. This dog was sold to the late Sir Richard Symons for one hundred and sixty pounds' worth of champagne and burgundy (which had been purchased at the French Ambassador's sale), a hogshead of claret, an elegant gun, and a pointer, with the stipulation that if any accident befell him, as might render him unfit to hunt, he was to be returned to the Colonel for fifty guineas. Dash had the misfortune to break his leg; he was therefore sent to Colonel Thornton, who paid the fifty guineas and kept the dog as a stallion, from whom, however, a single whelp worth keeping was never procured. Nor was such a circumstance very likely: the stock of these cross-bred dogs is uniformly good for nothing' (*The Sportsman*, 1836, vol. iii., No. 4, p. 185).

'Colonel Thornton's celebrated pointer, Dash, was bred from a rather small pointer bitch and a shallow-flewed (fleet) foxhound, and his appearance indicated his relationship to the latter in a very preponderating manner—the lofty foxhound, not the low-stooping pointer. Yet he was acknowledged as a pointer of surpassing excellence both on the moors and in the enclosures, but as a stallion proved worthless, as might reasonably be expected (at least by those who have duly

## THE POINTER

studied the subject) from that almost indescribable *inharmoniousness which seemed to breathe around him.* I have used this mode of expression as the best calculated to convey my meaning, which may be more clearly understood, perhaps, by further stating that there are homogeneous crosses and heterogeneous crosses, the former desirable, the latter rarely answering the intended purpose. When, for instance, the English pointer (after breeding in the same family too long) becomes too light and his head too narrow, a dip of Spanish blood is advisable, or the heavier dog of this country may be employed for the requisite purpose, which I call a homogeneous cross; while a cross with the setter and pointer I deem heterogeneous, and when a capital dog happens to be thus obtained he is not calculated for pro-generation ' (*Shooter's Preceptor*, by Johnson, 1842, p. 147).

For my own part I often used to wish that the Colonel (good sportsman as he undoubtedly was) could look down—or up—to see what a mess this parlous invention of a foxhound cross had ultimately made of the pointer, since the fancy had taken to wallowing in that blood which he had used homeopathically. I wished him no further punishment than one good look round the pointer classes at a principal show! But the type is better now than it was ten years ago, when the pointer ring reminded one of a schoolboy's misapplied slate—overspread with *naughts* and *crosses*! Last Birmingham Show (1901) I spied a bitch of really distinguished appearance, and, as she hailed from an unexpected quarter, the pleasure was doubled. I have lately seen one or two others of the right sort also cropping up. So let us hope that they, like the snowdrops, herald a happy reawakening, when the pointer shall be, to use a Shakespearean expression, ' fancy free.'

Of course, as in the case of Dash, a violent out-

## ALIEN CROSSES

cross may produce a good, even an eminent animal; but it destroys all continuity in breeding, and is responsible for a large proportion of mongrels. One swallow does not make summer, nor one dog a team!

About crosses for the pointer I must add the following opinions, taken from the books of two of the most famous nineteenth century writers on Sport :—

'The further any dog is removed from the original Spanish pointer, the worse the dog is, and consequently all attempts to cross the pointer with any other breed must necessarily deteriorate the breed. Why, then, should the pointer be crossed with dogs which, in so far as the sports of the field are concerned, scarcely inherit one quality in common with him? Attempts, however, are constantly made to improve the pointer by a cross with the bloodhound, foxhound, Newfoundland dog, or mastiff, sometimes with a view of improving his appearance and bringing him to some fancied standard of perfection, but in reality inducing a deformity. One of these imaginary standards of perfection is, that to one part thorough Spanish blood the pointer should have in him an eighth of the foxhound and a sixteenth of the bloodhound. A cross will sometimes produce dogs which are, in some eyes, the *beau idéal* of beauty; but, however handsome such dogs may be, they will necessarily possess some quality not belonging to the pointer. For instance, a cross with the hound gives the propensity to trace hares, if not to give tongue. A thoroughbred pointer carries his head well up when ranging; he will not give tongue, nor has he much desire to chase footed game. The hound-pointer may sometimes be detected by his coarse ears, by his tail being curled upwards and being carried high, or by his rough coat. An occasional cross with the mastiff or Newfoundland dog is said to increase the fineness of nose, but it is converting the pointer into a

## THE POINTER

mere retriever. Another, and the main source of the often unsightliness of sporting dogs, is the allowing an indiscriminate intercourse between pointers and setters. Good dogs may be thus obtained sometimes, but they are invariably mis-shapen; they have generally the head and brush tail of the setter with the body of the pointer, and their coats are not sleek, and instead of standing at their point they will crouch. We are not willing to allow that the pointer is improved in any quality that renders him valuable to the sportsman by a cross with the hound or any other sort of dog; though we cannot deny that the setter is materially improved in appearance by a cross with " The Newfoundland," but what it gains in appearance it loses in other respects. Breeding mongrels, especially crossing with hounds, has given the game-keepers and dog-breakers an infinity of trouble which might have been avoided by keeping the race pure. The best pointer is the offspring of a pointer bitch by a pointer dog. Such a one is nearly broken by nature. The Spanish pointer seldom requires the whip, the hound-pointer has never enough of it. One of the main sources of the sportsman's pleasure is to see the dogs point well, &c.' (*The Shooter's Handbook*, by Oakleigh, 1842, p. 91).

'Pointing is hereditary in pointers and setters; and puppies of a good breed and of a well-educated ancestry take to pointing at game as naturally as to eating their food, and not only do they, of their own accord, point steadily, but also back each other, quarter their ground regularly, and, in fact, instinctively follow the example of their high-bred and well-brought-up ancestors. For my part, I think it quite a superfluous trouble crossing a good breed of pointers with foxhound, or any other kind of dog, by way of adding speed and strength; you lose more than you gain, by giving at the same time

## ALIEN CROSSES

hard-headedness and obstinacy. It is much better, if you fancy your breed of pointers or setters to be growing small or degenerate, to cross them with some different family of pointers or setters of stronger or faster make, of which you will be sure to find plenty with very little trouble' (*Wild Sports of the Highlands*, by St. John, 1846, p. 116).

'Dogs which bear too close an alliance to the hound or other varieties are very difficult to break, and when broken, though you certainly may shoot game to them, are, comparatively speaking, not worth having, for unless you at all times keep up the most rigidly strict and painfully exact discipline, their dormant mongrel propensities, "bred in the bone," will soon begin to show themselves' (*Modern Shooter*, by Lacy, 1842, p. 168).

No doubt there has been, throughout the last century, a certain amount of commerce with the hound, though chiefly confined to the kennels of those who owned both varieties. Of this the following are cases in point.

The Duke of Portland states that he has always heard that Lord Henry Bentinck crossed some of his pointers with a foxhound.

Again, that well-known sportsman, Colonel Welfitt, who owned both foxhounds and pointers, told me that he had put his pointer bitches to a foxhound, and while showing me the offspring remarked that they were 'handsome but very headstrong.' He bred these with two of my mother's pointers, Don (811) and General (4970), of Mr. Whitehouse's strain, and finally he presented us with a puppy, Don José (9019). This was a handsome sort of dog, and won several prizes, but he was impossible to break properly, and his puppies out of six of our bitches were not much better.

Mr. C. M. P. Burn, in a letter to me, says :—' Skirk-

## THE POINTER

ing, of Glen Rinnes, told me that a cousin of his, the late Mr. G. Ashton (Stormer Hill, Bury), who hunted a pack of his own in Lancashire, and had a moor in Glen Lyon, regularly crossed his pointers with his own foxhounds. He never found them really good workers until the fourth cross. His object was to get durability.'

As long, however, as pointers were kept for work alone, the hound-cross was comparatively harmless to the breed; for when a dog was a failure at his business, he was, of course, not bred from. But when the Shows set up an artificial standard of looks, when the Kennel Club did not require any certificate of work from a prize-winner, when wide was the gate and broad was the way into its stud-book, pointers received a blow from which they may never more recover—they lost their prestige. For when many sportsmen found that they could only get unruly hound-pointers, they discarded dogs altogether, took to other methods of shooting, and now their desire for even good ones is practically extinct.

Observe this suggestive sequence of events! First, the stud-book is established for purposes of 'blood and pedigree.' Secondly, eight years afterwards, Idstone, having announced that the hound should be the model for a pointer, proceeds with cautious innocence :—' I have a suspicion that we shall have to go to a distinct cross, probably that of the foxhound " diluted," if I may use such an expression, to the fifth or sixth generation, to obtain that courage and verve which are essential in an animal bred for field sports, nor can I see my way to any other remedy' (*The Dog*, p. 119). Thirdly, Mr. Lort, the celebrated Judge, openly recommends the cross to old Mr. Bulled, whose signed statement I hold :—

'At the Birmingham Show, in the year 1886, after

# ALIEN CROSSES

the judging of the pointers, the late Mr. W. Lort went round their benches with me. He then advised me to cross a foxhound with one of my pointer bitches, and said that he [Mr. Lort] had done so some years before, and by crossing the produce back to the pointer he had obtained hardiness, more bone, better legs and feet, &c. I, for my part, did not follow this advice, but I have always believed that Mr. Lort's Old Naso had a cross of foxhound in him. Mr. Lort, on the same occasion, instanced the name of one dog he had that was bred from the offspring of the foxhound and pointer cross, but I cannot remember the dog's name. Directly after that Show I told my son, John Lee Bulled, of Mr. Lort's talk with me, and my son distinctly remembers the fact.'

At a time when pointers were growing houndier and houndier, in the beginning of 1895, I wrote this sentence in a letter to the *Stock-keeper* :—' From many of his descendants I should imagine that Old Bang had some alien blood to counterbalance Hamlet's excellent strain in him, and his son, Bang II., had still more of the hound cross.' For this supposition I was ruthlessly attacked, ordered to produce my proofs, accused of libel, and what not! I had to wait three years, till January 29th, 1898, for my vindication, but it came at last in a letter to the paper, *Our Dogs*, from Major Lodwick (Queen's Park, Chester), of which, on my application, he afterwards gave private confirmation. I now give extracts from the original letter, which, it will be seen, was written by a stranger to me, and by one who somewhat dissents from my views on the crossing of pointers :—

' In your "Spaniel Sparks" for January 22nd, *apropos* pointers, where Mr. Arkwright is stated to have expressed his opinions concerning the crossing of pointers in Devonshire with foxhounds, perhaps it

## THE POINTER

may be interesting to some of your readers to know that I can corroborate what Mr. Arkwright states. I knew Mr. Sam Price, of Bow, Devon, intimately from 1880 up to the time of his death. I have shot times out of number with him over his prize dogs, and he told me more than once, I remember well, that a few years back he had obtained the services of the late Lord Portsmouth's staunchest foxhounds, and had introduced the strain into his kennel of pointers. Up to 1880, I think, Mr. Sam Price was recognised as the pointer man throughout England. He owned Ch. Bang, and got some huge figures for his dogs. I think I am right in saying that all the best pointers, in the South of England at any rate, are sprung from Ch. Bang. So Mr. Arkwright is quite correct, you see: but why should he be so severe now upon pointers that show this strain of foxhounds? Mr. Price gave me one of his pups, and two more my father bought, and since 1880 we have had this particular breed of pointer, and have bred very carefully from them, and for staunchness I have never met their equal.'

Mr. Price, therefore, with commendable candour, did not make any very great secret of the foxhound element in his pointers—an element that no one who knows anything of hounds could fail to observe in the demeanour as well as in the appearance of his dogs.

I once had a bitch of Mr. Price's breeding, called Sella Price, which was much inbred to Old Bang. She was a handsome bitch, and a prize-winner, but she had the fuzzy tail, the coat of two lengths, and the cat feet of her race. Sella was a good single bitch to shoot over, though rather soft, but she would never attempt to back. Usually she was perfectly steady, yet one day in her fifth season I sent her out with two of my friends and her usual handler, when she, for no apparent reason, ran up the first brood of grouse, and chased it

# ALIEN CROSSES

out of sight, loudly giving tongue. I never knew her guilty of this either before or afterwards. I kept four of her puppies, of which Tap and his brother were excellent, but the two bitches, though they would gallop about, were not possessed of the slightest sporting instinct. Tap himself was a wonderful dog, and being by a very purely-bred black pointer, was another instance of a violent out-cross and its results; for he, like Colonel Thornton's Dash, was not a success at the stud.

Let me repeat that to cross a pointing breed with a non-pointing breed, is to reduce in the offspring the pointing instinct by one half, and, therefore, very often in breaking these mongrels, the pointing that should come naturally, has to be taught by severe and laborious lessons. The same remark applies still more forcibly to backing, which is simple pointing on trust—without verification. The reason why the black breed of pointers at the present day surpasses the pied breeds in its instinctive knowledge of its work, is because it has not been crossed: fortunately its habitat was not in the shires, nor would a dash of tricolour have improved its complexion. Had all the breeds of pointers been kept equally pure, there would be fifty per cent. more pointers used in Britain to-day, but those wild, disobedient half-hounds are a 'vexation of spirit.'

Far be it from me to depreciate the foxhound, a perfect dog for his own work, and I should consider a fresh infusion of pointer blood into him just as objectionable as the converse; but I maintain that the pointer *ought* to be the more courageous and delicate-nosed of the two, considering the nature of his duties. For a pointer has to gallop for a longer time than a hound, and, on the moors, over much rougher ground; while this continuous galloping has to be done in cold blood before finding his game, not in hot pursuit of it. Then

## THE POINTER

as to nose, the pointer in his work has to, and does, catch the scent at a far longer distance than a hound ; for often have I seen the pack in cover, nearly surrounding some bush, in happy ignorance that a fox was there till he jumped up ' right among 'em.'

To compare the two breeds, I must borrow an illustration from the army. The foxhound is like a private soldier, well-made, active, strong, courageous, and by training obedient—but there it ends. He has no scope for intellect : he will be soon drafted as a ' skirter ' if he do not keep with the pack. On the other hand, the pointer, with all the talents of the hound and many superadded, resembles a scout. He works singly ; receiving orders, it is true, but depending on his own wits for the mode of carrying them out. In short, he has to persevere by himself in his quest, to act on his own initiative, and to use much craft that he may find without disturbing. And this, forsooth, is the animal, the product of generations of high-breeding, to be *improved* by a cross of the foxhound !

I am convinced from my own experience that the foxhound cross has proved disastrous to the sporting value of those families of pointers into which it has been introduced, as might indeed be expected when one considers the very different branches of sport in which the two breeds are used. I myself have tried many of these dogs, ' with a dash of the hound in them,' and have found, when they work, that they take much more breaking than pure pointers, being unruly, uncertain, jealous of backing, hare-chasers, and seekers after foot-scent in preference to body-scent. And I have also found a good many that are non-workers, being almost devoid of bird-hunting ambition, and so slack-mettled as to be practically useless. Of course there are brilliant exceptions, but they *are* exceptions, and even from such there is no certainty in breeding.

# ALIEN CROSSES

As regards the external signs of hound-blood in a pointer, in order that such a dog may be avoided for the stud, beware of the following—a narrow skull—an absence of 'stop'—a small, sunken, or oblique eye—a muzzle inclining downwards—a grave, sombre expression — coarse flews — low-set ears—a coat long, coarse, and, on parti-coloured dogs, the colours of different lengths—stern fuzzy-haired and gaily carried—round bone in the forelegs—short stiff pasterns—straight stifles—and cat-feet, *i.e.*, short toes and round full pads. For I believe that only when all these characteristics are absent from the parents, can one look forward with confidence to a litter level and representative.

As I have said before, some breeders, since the commencement of the show period, have been ashamed to confess to the cross with the hound; this is to be deplored because it prevents any accurate estimate being formed of the amount of hound-blood lurking in the pointers. The following story will illustrate the ease with which this fraud can be perpetrated, when a foxhound appearance is necessary to win in the ring. A certain breeder wished to try the effect of this cross, so accordingly he put his bitch to a hound, and three days afterwards sent her to a noted pointer sire. The pups were to the first service, but the pedigree was unimpeachable.

There are very few references to the cross with the greyhound, and no mention of bulldog, or bull-terrier, influence. The last-named dog was not developed in his present form till the 'secresy' period was in full force, so I can get no definite confirmation of my belief that the dog Don IX. had some of that blood. Both he and his descendants were prone to wide chests, ridiculously small tails, wedgy heads, small eyes, and vile tempers. The temper was the most difficult

## THE POINTER

to breed out; but if there were such a strain in them, its effects were far more easily eradicated than are the traces of the hound.

'Not only the various classes of hounds were used, but the assistance of the highly-bred greyhounds was deemed requisite; and though it was evidently found necessary to wash out much of his blood, yet the strain frequently manifested itself in the long rat-like tail, and other indications which cannot be mistaken' (*The Sportsman*, 1836, vol. iii., No. 4, p. 182).

The preceding is the most direct mention I can find of the greyhound cross, which, considering the numerous traces of it to be found in the modern dog, is remarkable, as I presume they are only present in him now through atavism: one cannot imagine any one resorting to this cross for show-ring purposes. Probably it would have an effect less permanent than that of the hound cross in modifying the character of the pointer; as the greyhound, though physically an entity imposing enough, in mind is but a cipher.

'Stonehenge,' in the 1856 edition, recommends, if a cross be necessary for the pointer, the use of a stout greyhound of a breed crossed with bull in preference to the foxhound, but I hardly think that many have adopted his suggestion; though, as far as concerns the bulldog blood, I have certainly seen suspicious 'kinks' in the tails of some pointers.

# CHAPTER VII.
## SHOOTING OVER DOGS.

I DO not expect to convert many unbelievers by this chapter on shooting over dogs, and I am not sure whether, in the present plethora of shooters, it would be even desirable to open the eyes of the multitude to its attraction. I believe that fondness for this style of sport must be innate; for there is a mysterious attraction in the sport, though it does not appeal to every constitution and is hardly to be defined in working-day prose. Where the soil is congenial this grace of perception bursts into flower sometimes early, sometimes late—now in the kennel-yard, now on the mountain-side. When was it implanted? None can tell that; but once established in a man's heart it can nevermore be uprooted.

But though it is hard to say who will become enthusiasts, it is pretty safe to prophesy that those who do not care for dogs, are not interested in nature, and dislike hard exercise, will never see where the fun comes in.

Probably the genuine gundog-lover has always been a rather rare personage. I suppose that in old times, when men had to use dogs in order to get any shooting at all, many employed them under unconscious protest as a necessary evil, taking no interest in the work or in the habits of the game, and, as now, being very impatient of anything that did not seem directly to promote slaughter. The legitimate descendants of these form the present noble army of shooters. But nowadays there must be many men with the temperament of

# THE POINTER

the true sportsman, who really have not had a chance of shooting over dogs, except perhaps at a pot-hunt over one slow, old animal. Of course there are a great many single dogs used about the country, but I am referring to the sport '*in excelsis*'—shooting over a fast brace on a grouse-moor.

By the way, this word *sportsman* has somehow got mixed up in a curious manner with the term *sporting-man*. The latter is applied by the comparatively modern Webster to 'a horseracer, pugilist, and the like,' whilst 'sportsman' is reserved for 'one who pursues, and is skilled in, the sports of the field ; one who hunts, fishes, and fowls.' But despite these definitions we are confused at present by hearing the title of sportsman bestowed indiscriminately on persons who bet at races without troubling themselves about the horses, who shoot pigeons out of traps for money, or who from behind butts assassinate grouse by the bushel, although one not on the wing they would hardly recognise, except in the tell-tale company of the bread-crumb. I think many middle-aged men are conscious of all this, as they generally tell me that they prefer shooting over dogs, and so perhaps they do—in the abstract! But very few of the younger generation can have ever seen the genuine thing, so when it is explained to them a few of the right sort may be fired to try it for themselves. There would be difficulties at first in the way of getting good dogs, good breakers, and good moors—but the sport is worth taking some trouble over.

Shooting over dogs is, I dare say, a bit selfish, unsociable, and unbusinesslike ; but how about salmon-fishing and stalking ! Mercifully, no ingenious person has yet invented a plan by which the individual prowess of the netters can be conspicuously illumined, or the rod might be put on the shelf as slow and too much trouble. Shooting driven birds is, I suppose, the glorification of

## SHOOTING OVER DOGS

marksmanship, one of the component parts of shooting, at the expense of all the others; but even if it be the cream of the sport, imagine a diet of cream! Personally I regard driving as suitable enough for some places and for some men not adapted to the rigours of dog-work, but I shudder to hear of good dog-moors being perverted into driving-moors, as the grouse only too readily change their habit of seeking concealment when disturbed, for that of at once taking to the wing; and then the moor is ruined. I feel sure that if sheep and peat-cutters were kept off moors, the birds would, in most places, lie sufficiently well till the end of the season; and though no doubt it would be expensive to exclude these undesirables, it would not be nearly so costly as preserving a deer-forest.

Some writers, who favour driving, have tried to draw comparisons between that pastime and shooting over dogs, as if they saw some similarity between the two. There is none, unless indeed a community of grouse, gun, and such-like, is regarded as sufficient to establish the relationship: but one might as well compare the sayings of Shakespeare and the *Sporting Times*! The spirit—the essence—is quite different. I have been amused by writers with smug relish contending that because you can increase the stock of grouse by driving, this proves it to be the right way to shoot them. An argument commercially sound without doubt; but they forget that similarly you can kill more fish with a net than with a rod, and can be surer of a gallop, and lots of jumping, with the drag!

Quantity before quality is no sportsman's proverb, and the condensation of four weeks' sport into four days' slaughter ought not to be desirable, unless there be cause for violent hurry: and hurry brushes the delicate bloom off all pleasure. Such an achievement may be useful to business men who snatch a fortnight's

## THE POINTER

holiday during the season, but surely sport in general may be free from the domination of the Stock Exchange. No! no! We will grant you, O gunners, the advantage in your bags, in your picnics, in your hospitalities, in your cheapening the food markets, in fact in everything—except the enjoyment of Sport with a capital S!

But as to the actual marksmanship over dogs, is it, as some pretend, too simple for experts? In no circumstances can it be so easy as that of shooting in line, though it may not present much difficulty, early in the season, to the gunner who steals ahead at the point, regardless of the feelings of dogs and men, and downs the first of the brood that may show a wing above the heather. But that is no more the true sport over dogs, than when a wretched pointer is worked in front of a line of guns and beaters. I am, however, inclined to doubt the transparent ease of shooting in good form to dogs, because, though I have seen many brilliant shots essay it, I have only known two men in twenty years who shot well enough over dogs, when the grouse were strong, regularly to take the foremost birds on their own side, without mangling them and without interfering with the other gun, and fine enough judges of pace to ensure there being a minimum of pricked birds.

To kill a brace of strong grouse rising wildly and going away from you, is a feat that requires great quickness of hand and eye; and nerves of iron are necessary for the strain of walking alongside the dog, watching his roading from the tail of your eye, and ignorant how, when, and where the birds will start up; you must also possess intuitive nimbleness in surmounting the inequalities of the ground, and you have to decide instantaneously on the birds that are yours. But let us turn from polemics to consider the infinite variety and delight of shooting over dogs.

## SHOOTING OVER DOGS

In the early season, when the grouse are lying well, how pleasant are the strolls with your friend, in cheery rivalry picking off the old birds at the rises, and discussing the work of the puppies as they fly over the heather buds that glint at the golden sunshine. I used the word *friend* advisedly, as unless you can lay hands on some one you know well, congenial, observant, and with his heart in it, you will do far better by yourself. I am now writing from the standpoint of a non-handler of the dogs, which personally I find more agreeable when shooting grouse, as I can see the work better so and can judge it more truly ; but working one's dogs has many charms, and breaking them, if one have the time, is even more fascinating.

After the first fortnight the co-operation of another gun becomes almost a necessity, when the season for hard walking and strict silence is developing, and when you have a bare margin to get there before the brood takes French leave of the most perfect dog ; but you can still approach from behind, getting plenty of glorious shots, and by this time, being in hard condition, you enjoy to the full the crispness of it all.

Then the last phase of the sport is also truly exciting ; but it must be entered into by only one gun, in company with one man to work the dog, and a gillie on the horizon to carry the game. Now is the time for the wiliest and wariest in your kennel, in this encounter to the death with the old cocks. When all goes well, you must not expect more than five brace in the day, but this compared to the meed of the deer-stalker is opulence. And, when you do get him, what a picture each one is—his legs muffled in white to the very toe-nails, his plumage a marbled harmony of all the browns and reds in nature's paint-box. Your dog, too, how he enjoys the sport! To him up-wind and down-wind are alike, old trump that he is! When he gets his steady

## THE POINTER

point, with nostrils on the stretch he is judging all the time of the quietude or uneasiness of his bird. He will guard it as does a collie his flock, rising to full height when escape is meditated in his direction, sinking to earth when the danger is past, sometimes even jesuitically blinking his point. Meanwhile you have to estimate, from your knowledge of your dog and his attitude, the distance of the game in front of him ; and from that and the lie of the ground, you must forthwith form your plan of campaign. Anyhow, you must skulk off, and, if there be a convenient peat-hag, you will probably crawl down it until by peeping you know you are right opposite the dog : then make steadily for his head. Many a bird is up and off without giving a chance, but none of you is discouraged, you simply try again. Some of these single old cocks prefer not to fly, they run instead ; and then such a search has frequently to commence as taxes all the qualities of both man and beast. Because this branch of the sport is often left to the keepers and is not well understood, I have tried to call due attention to it, but in this mere outline I have naturally been unable to do it justice—it would require a chapter to itself.

Still, of course, the chief glory of the sport is to shoot over a brace of raking pointers, matched for speed and style, sweeping over the rough places like swallows, and passing each other as if they were fine ladies not introduced. Let one of them get a point and the other will, as if connected by invisible wire, instantly point at him (*i.e.* back him); and as the pointing dog advances to make sure of the birds, the backer will do the same—often with an absolute mimicry of his leader's movements. When his master has come to the spot, how proudly will the first dog march him up to the game with outstretched neck, flame in his eye, and foam at his lip, while his companion watches from a distance with

## SHOOTING OVER DOGS

perfect self-control; and, when the birds rise, both dogs instantly drop to the ground, not to move till the game is gathered, and they are bidden to resume their search.

Then there is the chase of a running grouse across a bit of flow (marshy land), which for pure fun beats everything. The face of the flow is powdered with little lichen-covered hillocks, of the size and consistency of a bath-sponge; and among these the birds thread their way with such ease that they often run for a quarter of a mile or so. When your dog gets a point here, he trots on a bit, and you go floundering after him. Then he stands still, turns his head with an imploring glance, which expresses unmistakably 'I say, *please* come on.' You make a spurt. He runs forward only to wait for you again as you shuffle after him, and so on till up, with a chuckle, jumps the old bird about thirty yards behind you, having executed a well-conceived double, and you, quite out of puff, have a wild shot at him. And if he tumble, the dog and you worship each other in complete contentment, while you feel—there never was such a dog, there never was such a shot, and never such a sport as grousing in Caithness. But hit or miss, the sordidness of life is far from you; and you are free, and muddy, and happy!

The great beauty of a day's shooting is that a thousand unexpected events may occur, and variations innumerable. But I would not hint at them, even if I could, for I want my sympathetic readers to find them for themselves.

If I had my way, every twelfth of August, the day of the big bag, should fall on a Friday. Next day should be examination day for the puppies, shooting over them all singly: a day bright with anticipations and prophecies. Then Sunday to rest, to sort the young ones into future braces, and thoroughly to inspect them on the flags.

# THE POINTER

I will now subjoin some extracts from the sportsmen of the earlier half of last century, to show their temperament and feelings on these matters:—

'The grand and magnificent style of sporting, by which such slaughter is to be effected, is not such as could gratify the feelings and satisfaction of a keen and experienced sportsman. These kinds of gunners are well suited to the old saying, "never make a toil of pleasure;" from this language we may describe two kinds of shooters. The first is a man of fortune, surrounded with game-keepers (let us suppose the scene for the present in Norfolk), pointers, setters, &c., without number, *Manton* guns, and all in complete retinue, going out at perhaps twelve o'clock (the hour of indolent and feather-bed gunners) into the highest preserved covers in that county, where the game is so very tame that twenty birds may be killed in a few hours; their servants with clean guns ready, and, if necessary, loaded by them; and probably, if the dog of one of these *elegant* sportsmen is admired, or gains credit, if his master is asked his name, he makes for answer, "he really cannot tell you, but will ask his game-keeper." The second sportsman is that who rises early, and attends to his own appointments, guns, &c. Where is the sportsman that does not like a little pains or difficulty in finding game? A keen sportsman would as soon fire at crows, or barn-door fowl, as at game so plenty as on Mr. Coke's manors in Norfolk; besides this shooting is not the perfection that such a sportsman requires, that perfection exists, only in seeing the dogs perform, and do their duty; and not in slaughtering of game, but in seeing them *draw, back, and stand*, and above all, steady on the shot' (*The Shooting Directory*, by Thornhill, 1804, p. 399). 'In my opinion there is no pleasure in shooting of any kind, but where the faithful dog is a necessary attendant' (*id.* p. 411).

# SHOOTING OVER DOGS

'We do not admire that ground which resembles a poultry-yard. Grouse and barn-door fowls are constructed on different principles; the former being wild, the latter tame creatures, when in their respective perfection. Of all dull pastimes the dullest seems to us sporting in a preserve; and we believe that we share that feeling with the Grand Signior. The sign of a lonely inn in the Highlands ought not to be the Hen and Chickens. Some shooters, we know, sick of common sport, love slaughter. From sunrise to sunset of the first day of the moors, they must bag their hundred brace. That can only be done where pouts prevail, and cheepers keep chiding; and where you have half a dozen attendants to load your double barrels sans intermission, for a round dozen of hours spent in a perpetual fire. Commend us to a plentiful sprinkling of game; to ground which seems occasionally barren, and which it needs a fine instructed eye to traverse scientifically and thereof to detect the latent riches. Fear and hope are the deities of the moors, else would they lose their witchcraft. In short, we shoot like gentlemen, scholars, poets, philosophers, as we are; and looking at us you have a sight " of him who walks in glory and in joy, following his *dog* upon the mountain-side;" a man evidently not shooting for a wager, nor performing a match from the mean motives of avarice or ambition; but blazing away at his own sweet will' (Quotation from Christopher North: *Recreations in Shooting*, by Craven, 1846, p. 28).

'Grouse-shooting to the gunner is what the chase of the fox is to the zealous hunter of beasts. It is certainly attended with less danger, but it is infinitely more fatiguing, which, again, is compensated for to the lover of nature by the endless variety it presents, and to the sportsman by furnishing him with the objects he is in pursuit of' (*Encyclopædia of Rural Sports*, by Blaine, 1839, p. 309).

# THE POINTER

'In comparison with grouse-shooting and deer-stalking, all the other sports of this country are mere play. Grouse-shooting is the sport of all others exclusively British' (*The Shooter's Handbook*, by Oakleigh, 1842, p. 133). 'To the shooter in training, full of health and strength and well appointed, it is of little consequence whether game be abundant or not. The inspiriting character of the pursuit, and the wild beauty of the scenery, so different from what he is elsewhere in the habit of contemplating, hold out a charm that dispels fatigue. He feels not the drudgery! To him the hills are lovely under every aspect, whether beneath a hot autumnal sun or beneath the dark canopy of thunder-clouds; whether in the frosty morn or in the dewy eve; whether when, through the clear atmosphere, he surveys, as it were in a map, the counties that lie stretched around and beneath him, or when he wanders darkly on amidst the gloomy vapour that rolls continuously past him. The very sterility pleases. Scarcely is there a change of scene; silence and solitude —hill and ravine—sky and heather universally prevail. He beholds an unbounded expanse of heathery hills, by no means monotonous if he looks at it with the eye of a painter, for there is every shade of yellow, green, brown, and purple. The last is the prevailing colour at this season, the heather being in bloom. The invigorating influence of the bracing wind on the heights lends him additional strength; he puts forth every effort, every nerve is strained; he feels an artificial glow after nature is exhausted, and returns to the cot, to enjoy his glass of grog and such a *snooze* as the toil-worn citizen never knew' (*id.* p. 141).

'I cannot say that my taste leads me to rejoice in the slaughter of a large bag of grouse on one day. I have no ambition to see my name in the county newspapers as having bagged my seventy brace of grouse

## SHOOTING OVER DOGS

in a certain number of hours on such-and-such a hill. I have much more satisfaction in killing a moderate number of birds, in a wild and varied range of hill, with my single brace of dogs, and wandering in any direction that fancy leads me, than in having my day's beat laid out for me, with relays of dogs and keepers, and all the means of killing the grouse on easy walking ground, where they are so numerous that one has only to load and fire. In the latter case I generally find myself straying off in pursuit of some teal or snipe, to the neglect of the grouse and the disgust of the keeper, who may think his dignity compromised by attending a sportsman who returns with less than fifty brace. Nothing is so easy to shoot as a grouse when they are tolerably tame, and with a little choice of his shots a moderate marksman ought to kill nearly every bird that he shoots at early in the season, when the birds sit close, fly slowly, and are easily found. At the end of the season, when the coveys are scattered far and wide, and the grouse rise and fly wildly, it requires quick shooting and good walking to make up a handsome bag; but how much better worth killing are the birds at this time of the year than in August' (*Wild Sports of the Highlands*, by St. John, 1846, p. 26).

'It is time that the vulgar notion was exploded that to slaughter grouse alone constitutes a sportsman. If he has no other qualification than that, he must indeed be one of the very smallest calibre. A sportsman of the right stamp must also have an eye for all that is interesting and beautiful in nature, which adds to his pursuits their greatest zest' (*Remarks on the Decrease of Grouse*, Colquhoun, 1858, p. 6).

'The whole affair is a matter of display from beginning to end. Cram the bag as fast as you can, by every means, despite the sport, is the order of the day' (*id.* p. 13).

# THE POINTER

'Several relays of dogs are working, with their respective attendants, on different parts of the moor. Mounted on a strong hill-pony, the performer rides from one point to another; a loaded gun is put into his hands; every cheeper that can top the heather is made to count, and thus the hero of *a bird a minute* accomplishes his unparalleled exploit. A fair illustration of the love of notoriety more than the love of sport, which characterises the sons of the trigger in the present day. Newspaper shots are too rife amongst us. A large bag must be made by all means. Mr. This or Lord That has shot such a number, we must not be behind him. Just set nine-tenths of such show-off performers adrift on a strange moor, not overstocked with grouse, with a brace of dogs and an inexperienced gilly to carry the bag, and—excellent shots as I allow most of them to be—still see what a sorry picture they would cut in manœuvring their game' (*id.* p. 14).

I will now turn to the behaviour and treatment of the dogs on the moor, concerning which I have been fortunate enough to find most of the salient points in the writings of my predecessors.

'To ensure good sport the shooter must be provided with good dogs. However abundant game may be, there can be no real sport without good dogs; and, however scarce game may be, a good day's sport is attainable with good dogs by a person who feels what sport is, and who does not look upon filling the game-bag and loading the keepers with game as the sole end and aim of the sportsman's occupation. The mere act of killing game no more constitutes sport than the jingling of rhyme constitutes poetry' (*Shooter's Handbook*, by Oakleigh, 1842, p. 94).

'No species of shooting requires the aid of good dogs more than grouse-shooting, and in no sport does so much annoyance result from the use of bad ones.

## SHOOTING OVER DOGS

The best dog, perhaps, for the moors is a well-bred pointer, not more than five years old, which has been well tutored—young in years, but a veteran in experience' (*id.* p. 143).

'Grouse-shooters should separate and range singly: they should have no noisy attendants, nor any dogs that require rating. The sport cannot be carried on too quietly. *Only one dog as long as the heather is wet,* afterwards two, and in the afternoon three dogs. In wet weather one dog is quite sufficient' (*id.* p. 144).

'The very swift certainly miss *some* that a moderate galloper will pick up. But then the attitudes struck in a moment, with such infinite diversification, in the stabs of a fast dog, are more than a compensation for some casual unavoidable transits, and give a glow to the true, keen sportsman that the sight of 100 points made by a dull, trotting, slovenly brute in the common form cannot call up' (*Treatise on Field Diversions,* Symonds, 1776, p. 16).

'Have a horror of near rangers; they are the worst of all for moor-shooting. Of these—that is, pointers—hunt a brace at a time, it will be quite enough' (*Recreations in Shooting,* by Craven, 1846, p. 27).

At the same time beware of the opposite extreme, say I! On a well-stocked grouse moor, with defined beats, it is not only important to find game, but also to find it in proper sequence. I do not know of anything more prejudicial to both temper and bag than to find oneself saddled with one of those so-called 'natural gamefinders,' which is, as a rule, a euphemism for a headstrong, sky-ranging brute, with nose and pace, but lacking intelligence.

'I like to see blood, bone, and beauty combined in all the works of animated nature. Without the accompaniment of well-bred and well-broken dogs, shooting

## THE POINTER

is not sport; it is merely gun-firing' (*The Modern Shooter*, by Captain Lacy, 1842, p. 146).

'As nothing tends to beguile the fatigue of the shooter or keep up the life of a day's sport more than a change of dogs in the field, so is nothing more conducive to the preservation of the dogs themselves. How many dogs, from having been overworked, are done up in their prime! The best plan in changing dogs is to have a person meet you with them at an appointed time and place, and to send the dogs you have been working home again immediately in the same sheets which you strip off the fresh dogs, to be kennelled, groomed, and fed; because by this means the fresh dogs will be quite fresh, whereas, if kept in couples, following a party the whole morning, they will have been all along more or less on the fret from the report of the guns, &c.; and the dogs taken up in couples from work, and not sent home at once, are apt to chill, stiffen, and become stale and jaded; and, in fact, in bad weather, are more injured than if they had been kept at work the day through. Where the shooter goes out daily and stays out all day long, three changes of dogs will not be found too many to keep his kennel fresh; and some change there must be, or the appearance of his dogs, however regularly groomed, or nutritiously and bountifully fed, will soon prove him a bad kennel economist. It is absolute ruin to young dogs to keep them out too long a time' (*id.* p. 148).

More than one-half of the beauty of shooting, in my opinion, consists in the gallant style of ranging and in the beautiful attitude of the animals on point. I know full well that a dog may be a very good and handy one, with but small pretensions to appearance; but he who is ambitious of shooting in first-rate style must especially look to symmetry of form in his dogs. "Let them be handsome as pictures"' (*id.* p. 170).

# SHOOTING OVER DOGS

'All dogs for grouse-shooting should at all times be particularly steady; not a syllable should require to be spoken to them, but all done by hand-work, unless the whistle be occasionally used as a signal for them to turn, grouse being the most sensitive and the soonest disturbed of all game (*id.* p. 199).

'A little departure "in bold disorder" from rigid or formal rules, a little roaming on the moors, adds zest to the sport, albeit, at times, the bag may be somewhat the lighter for it. That man who, enjoying the cool elasticity of the mountain breeze, and walking on a carpet of purple heather, is yet withal bent on slaughter only, may be a good shot, but he is a tasteless sportsman' (*id.* p. 203).

'I frequently range down-wind for grouse, and invariably so in boisterous weather, for then the birds often lie closer and keep their heads down, and can therefore neither see nor hear you so well; you also have a much more distinct sight of them with the wind at your back than when it is blowing a moorland blast full in your face and eyes. Many sportsmen never think of going on the moors after August, or September at the latest; whereas, if the birds have had a tolerable respite, as frequently is the case, they are much more easily found by the dogs in October than during dry, sultry weather; will often lie on a fine day, especially one succeeding a black frost; and in point of size, fullness and beauty of plumage, and excellence of flavour, are incomparably superior to the birds of earlier date' (*ib.*).

To the remarks of Captain Lacy on the advantage of down-wind questing, I can only add that you should accustom your dogs, almost from the beginning, to work down-wind when necessary; as in beating a moor, nothing is more tiresome than fiddling about for the wind, in place of steadily going on trying for grouse.

# THE POINTER

Besides, the dogs very soon take to it, and it materially develops their intelligence; but on running into a brood they should always be scolded, even when you do not think them culpable.

'The best way [when a bird falls] is not to allow the pointer to move, but to have a dog of the proper kind for the sole purpose of retrieving the game; a dog for this purpose should bring well, have a good nose, and very little disposition to hunt' (*Observations on Dog-breaking*, by Floyd, 1821, p. 20).

This advice by Floyd (the game-keeper of Sir J. Sebright), to have some other dog to retrieve the game, is, I think, indisputable nowadays if really high-class work be desired; as the pointer, lying dropped during the process of picking the game, gains that pause for cool reflection which he enjoyed formerly during the re-charging of the muzzle-loaders: he is also freed from the temptation to unsteadiness engendered of actual contact with the game. For this office, I myself use small spaniels, which sit back while I go up to a point, and, at a whistle, hasten up to collect the fallen. I had believed this plan an invention of my own before I read the above passage and later still found the recommendation of the German, Von Fleming (1749). (See Chapter I. of this book.)

'When a dog stands (and it is seen by the point that he is sure of his game), the master should stand still also; the general stillness settles the dog more firmly to his point, and the birds are always the more likely to lie. If the gunner is young and impatient, hurrying up, as many of that description frequently do, it hurries the dog also, and not only makes him eagerly impatient, but the game in the confusion probably rises out of shot; or, what is equally productive of mortification, he gets up to the point so flurried and out of breath that he finds it impracticable to take regular

## SHOOTING OVER DOGS

aim; and when he erroneously conceives he does, the bodily tremor he is in renders the shot in nine times out of ten ineffectual' (*Sportman's Cabinet*, by Taplin, 1803-4, p. 98).

Some breakers have an irritating and game-scaring way of speaking or of making encouraging sounds to the dog when he is roading his birds. This should never be allowed by the master; nor should the heather round a dog be stirred with stick, foot, or other weapon. The man must not do the dog's work, or it will soon spoil the dog. The stickiest puppy can be easily taught to walk on boldly by keeping an old dog on a lead, and when the youngster gets a point, coupling them together. And as a free style of roading is necessary both for the success of the sport and the nerves of the sportsmen, every pointer while quite young should be perfected in this accomplishment.

'I caution gentlemen always to keep their own dogs scrupulously to themselves, and to have a set allotted to strangers; for many good sportsmen differ in their manner of treating their dogs; some care not how their dogs behave, provided they can get shots. I conceive the great pleasure and elegance of shooting depends on the good order in which the dogs are kept' (*Sporting Tour*, by Colonel Thornton, 1804, p. 163). An excellent counsel never to be departed from!

And now a few words about the sportsmen themselves, as we are on the subject of behaviour.

In the first place, never have more than two guns in one party when shooting grouse over dogs, or the pleasure will be spoiled and the pointers demoralised. 'Three in a party are dangerous, besides being too many for sport,' says, in 1832, the author of *Hints to Grown Sportsmen* (p. 20).

As a jealous shot is a curse at this kind of sport, promoting ill-feeling and retaliation, besides hindering

# THE POINTER

the bag, the Rules for this kind of shooting ought to be strictly observed :—

'The prudent and the patient who shoot in company will be found circumspect and consistent in every motion ; they will neither of them take aim at the first bird which happens to rise (to be confused by those who follow), nor fix upon a bird upon the left-hand when his companion is on that side ; the right-hand man and the left should invariably adhere to birds going off on their own sides, but when their flight is made in a direct line forward, circumstances must regulate and justify proceedings accordingly' (*Sportsman's Cabinet*, by Taplin, 1803–4, p. 28).

'If two gentlemen shoot together, each should wait patiently till a bird rises on his own side ; if it does not rise on his side, he should never fire, or at least not until his friend has fired and missed. Should only one bird rise, the shot belongs to the person on whose side it rose' (*Shooter's Guide*, by Thomas, 1819, p. 254).

'Let your first barrel be placed upon any bird on your own side, that is within a fair distance, reserving a near bird for the second shot' (*Hints to Grown Sportsmen*, 1832, p. 22).

Before you commence the day's shooting agree with your friend whether you are to be the right or the left-hand gun, and then stick religiously to that order : it will save much confusion.

If the birds are at all tickle, and you have to wait during the roading of the dog, be sure that you never stand still, but keep on marking time with your legs as if still walking. Nothing frightens birds more than to see a man standing about—to them it signifies discovery. When walking by the side of your roading dog, keep level with his tail, about five yards to your own side of him. Watch him that you may not walk on to ground towards which he is bearing, and when

## SHOOTING OVER DOGS

he does turn your way, stop walking at once, and steadily mark time. Keep with him during his entire march, never abandoning a point as barren, before the dog has given it up ; and do not cut corners from laziness, but only when such a process is unavoidable. Of course all these remarks have double force when you are working puppies, in which case you ought neither to shoot a hare, nor at any bird that has not been pointed.

'There are shooters who acquire an unsportsmanlike habit of firing at a covey immediately as it rises, before the birds are fairly on the wing, and thus, without aiming at any individual bird, bring down two or three. And sometimes they will make a foul shot by flanking a covey ; the birds being upon the wing, come upon them suddenly, and make a simultaneous wheel ; they take them on the turn, when, for a moment—and but for a moment—half the covey are in a line, and floor them rank and file. These are tricks allied to poaching, and almost as reprehensible as shooting at birds on the ground' (*Shooter's Handbook*, by Oakleigh, 1842, p. 112).

I will quote some additional passages of importance, germane to the foregoing :—

'But it may not be amiss to remark, in this place, that to beat a country properly the sportsman should not go straight forward, but should form a zig-zag figure in traversing the ground, taking care to give the dog the wind as much as possible; nor should he be afraid of beating the ground over twice, where he has reason to believe there is game' (*Shooter's Guide*, by Thomas, 1819, p. 254).

'In pursuing this game [grouse] if, when the dogs are set, the shooter perceives the birds to erect their heads and run, he may be pretty certain that they will not lie very well during the course of that day; and

## THE POINTER

the only mode by which he will be able to get at them is to make a circle of about sixty or seventy yards round them, with a careless eye, and the dogs standing staunch at the time, till you get ahead of the birds; when they perceive you before them and the dogs behind them, they will squat to the ground and lie close; when you observe this, step gently towards the dogs and the birds in a straight line; between you and the dogs they will lie till you get within twenty-five or thirty yards of them, by which means you are certain of a shot; when, by following them up with the dogs, and running, not once in ten times do you get within shot, and at the same time make the birds much wilder the remainder of the day' (*The Driffield Angler*, by Mackintosh, 1821, p. 196).

'The grouse-shooter should be long in training before the season, so as to be able to master his ground, and carry his gun, without much personal inconvenience. He should ride or drive to and from the shooting-ground, for, if he is unable to undergo the labour comfortably, he will by no means feel at home on the moors' (*The Shooter's Handbook*, by Oakleigh, 1842, p. 134).

I do not think that this subject of shooting grouse over dogs would be adequately treated without some mention of the every-day habits of grouse, ignorance of which would place one very much at the mercy of chance.

'To find the birds when, satisfied with food, they leave the moor to bask in some favourite haunt, requires both patience and experience, and here the mountain-bred sportsman proves his superiority over the less-practised shooter. The packs, then, lie closely and occupy a small surface on some sunny brow or sheltered hollow. The best-nosed dogs will pass within a few yards and not acknowledge them; and patient

## SHOOTING OVER DOGS

hunting, with every advantage of the wind, must be employed to enable the sportsman to find grouse at this dull hour. But if close and judicious hunting be necessary, the places to be beaten are comparatively few, and the sportsman's eye readily detects the spot where the pack is sure to be discovered. He leaves the open feeding ground, for heathering knowes and sheltered valleys ; while the uninitiated wearies his dog in vain over the hill-side' (*The Shooter's Handbook*, by Oakleigh, 1842, p. 139).

'Grouse do not fly with the wind on all occasions, but whenever they happen to do so, their flights are longer than when they face it ; and, when going across wind, their flight has ever a tendency to the lee side. Whatsoever species of game he is in pursuit of, the shooter will do well to keep on that side of the hill which is protected from the wind. The favourite haunts of grouse, when undisturbed, are those patches of ground where the young heather is most luxuriant. They avoid rocks and bare places, where the heather has been recently burnt. It is in young heather where grouse most frequently feed. They are seldom found in the very long, thick heather that clothes some part of the hills, until driven there for shelter by shooters and others. It is early in the morning, and towards evening, that grouse are to be found in young heather. During the middle of the day the shooter should range the sunny side of the hill, and avoid plains' (*id.* p. 146).

'As a rule it may be observed that all game, when raised, are apt to settle on lower ground' (*Recreations in Shooting*, by Craven, 1846, p. 25). 'Storms or high winds make them very wild ; the best way to approach them then is from below ; they cannot see you so plainly as when descending from ground above them' (*id.* p. 26). 'You must not beat over the same line

## THE POINTER

too often ; if constrained ever so much for want of room, not more than twice a week ' (*ib.*)

I have noticed that grouse, as a rule, feed downwind, *i.e.* keep on moving in the same direction as the wind, while partridges feed in the opposite direction. So while the latter are always easy to deal with, grouse may be sometimes exceedingly difficult for an inexperienced dog. He may likely get into the middle of a brood and point at the hindmost members of it (or even at their fresh scent) ; while the leaders, having moved on beforehand, are unsuspected by him at his back and, if he fidget at all, are in great danger of being flushed. In the morning and evening, therefore, be on the look-out, as you approach, for birds to rise from behind your dog.

Concerning partridge-shooting, I almost agree with Oakleigh (*Shooter's Handbook*, p. 134), that it is, ' compared with grouse-shooting, a comparatively tame and uninteresting amusement.' But in spite of this opinion, he has left us the following most accurate and valuable account of the habits of the bird.

'The habits of the partridge should be studied by the shooter. In the early part of the season, partridges will be found, just before sunrise, running to a brook, a spring, or marsh, to drink ; from which place they almost immediately fly to some field where they can find abundance of insects, or else to the nearest cornfield or stubble-field, where they will remain, according to the state of the weather, or other circumstances, until nine or ten o'clock, when they go back. About four or five o'clock they return to the stubbles to feed, and about six o'clock they go to their jacking-place—a place of rest for the night, which is mostly in aftermath, or in a rough pasture-field—where they remain huddled together till morning. While the corn i standing, unless the weather be very fine or very wet,

## SHOOTING OVER DOGS

partridges will often remain in it all day. When fine, they bask on the outskirts; when wet, they run to some bare place in a sheltered situation, where they will be found crowded together as if basking, for they seldom remain long in corn or grass when it is wet. Birds lie best on a hot day. They are wildest on a damp or boisterous day. The usual way of proceeding in search of partridges in September, is to try the stubbles first, and next the potato and turnip-fields. Birds frequently bask among potatoes or turnips, especially when those fields are contiguous to a stubble-field' (*Shooter's Handbook*, by Oakleigh, 1842, p. 104).

'When a covey separates, the shooters will generally be able to kill many birds, but late in the season it is seldom that the covey can be broken. In the early part of the season, when the shooter breaks a covey, he should proceed without loss of time in search of the dispersed birds, for the parent bird begins to call almost immediately on their alighting; the young ones answer, and in less than half an hour, unless prevented by the presence of the shooter and his dogs, the whole covey will be reassembled, probably in security, in some snug corner where the shooter least thinks of looking for them. As the season advances, birds are longer in reassembling after being dispersed. It is necessary to beat very close for dispersed birds, as they do not stir for some time after alighting, on which account dogs cannot wind them till close upon them. When a bird has been running about some time, dogs easily come upon the scent of it, but when it has not stirred since alighting, no dog can wind it until close upon it, and the very best dogs will sometimes flush a single bird. The length of time that will transpire before a dispersed covey will reassemble, depends too on the time of the day and state of the weather. In hot weather they will lie still for several hours. A covey dispersed

## THE POINTER

early in the morning or late at night, will soon reassemble. A covey dispersed between the hours of ten and two, will be some time in reassembling. A covey found in the morning in a stubble-field and dispersed, will next assemble near the basking-place. A covey dispersed after two o'clock, will next assemble in the stubble-field at feeding-time. A covey disturbed and dispersed late in the afternoon or evening, will next reassemble near the jacking-place' (*id.* p. 106). By attention to the above maxims I have many a time prophesied the whereabouts of birds, to the confusion of the keepers.

It is evident that the etiquette of partridge-shooting was settled very early, as we have Mr. Page writing on it in 1767 :—

'Two persons in the field with guns are better than more at partridge-shooting, who should with patience pay due attention to each other. When your dog points, walk up without any hurry, separating a few yards, one to the right and the other to the left of your dog. If a covey springs, never shoot into the midst of them, but let him on the left single out a bird which flieth to the left, and him on the right a bird to the right, that you may not interrupt each other, nor both shoot at the same bird and readily let fly at the first aim. If a single bird is sprung, let him take the shot to whose side it flies' (*Art of Shooting Flying*, p. 87).

And Mr. Howlitt testifies to the existence of brilliant shots, despite all disadvantages in those days, for he writes :—

'There are, however, some few sportsmen in England of such keen eyes that they can distinguish the cocks [partridges] from the hens when the covey rises from the ground, and so expert as to make it the pride of their dexterity to kill not more than a brace of hens

## SHOOTING OVER DOGS

in one day's sport' (*Essay on Shooting*, by Howlitt, 1789, p. 288).

Of course in the twentieth century, in an England so highly farmed, with its pastures drained, cornfields shaven, and turnips planted in drills, we cannot expect the same sport over dogs as our ancestors enjoyed in their rushy meadows, knee-deep stubbles, and turnips sown broadcast. One can have, however, even in the present day, a very good time among the partridges by the exercise of a little intelligent strategy.

Two shooters are better than one in most countries, because of the hedges ; and your retinue may well consist of your keeper, of a marker, and of a man to carry game, cartridges, &c. Oakleigh says of markers :—

'When birds are abundant, markers are a nuisance ; when scarce, a marker may be serviceable. When birds are scarce it is no loss of time to follow a marked bird, but when plentiful the shooter should not deviate from the line he has chosen' (p. 150). But I venture to believe that our author rather underrates such an assistant, whom as a rule I have found useful, except where there are too many birds to work dogs at all.

In the fields, it is easy to combine the working of one's own dogs with the shooting over them, since the grey partridge from its habit of moving up-wind when on the feed, from its indisposition to run far unless wounded, and even from the nature of the cover in which it is found, is a much more obvious bird than the grouse.

There are, no doubt, many wonderful moments in partridge-shooting. For instance, when the covey springs up all round you, as if by magic, in a whirling, chattering hurry-skurry ; or when, in a redolent clover-field, a brace of pups, at the very prime of their powers, will strike point after point on the stragglers of a scattered covey, while you respond by accounting for every fugitive.

In the present days of sowing in drills, to beat a turnip-field is the hardest task that you can set a naturally fast dog, and if he acquit himself with credit, you can be sure of possessing an animal of high intelligence and sporting value, for the birds are inclined to run down the drills, and if the dog be noisy in striding over the turnips, they will frequently take wing : in fact, to get points at them requires a combination of tact with brilliant nose, which but few dogs possess.

Colonel Hawker, in 1814, explains how, in an open country where the partridges were deemed unapproachable, he chartered a pony, and as soon as birds rose he galloped after them : he was thus upon them before they had recovered breath for a second flight (*Instructions to Young Sportmen*, ninth edition, p. 165). And, similarly, under almost every condition, it is possible to dodge the partridges or to prevent them from dodging you, if you only take the trouble. It would be both tedious and useless to detail any local methods for circumventing partridges, as successful tactics must vary so much in different districts. But there is one plan that is applicable in most cases, *i.e.* before beating a good-sized turnip-field, to send some one to the windward end of the field with instructions to keep on making a clapping noise, as this will cause the birds to run up into the roots, to separate, and, of course, being between two dangers, to lie better.

A word about artificial kites. These may be, I dare say, sometimes necessary when grouse are packed ; but partridges, I find, instantly take to the fences, and so the shooting of them over dogs is spoiled. Again, their terror is so extreme that it is sickening to witness ; though grouse, from being accustomed to the occasional sight of a falcon, are not so alarmed.

## SHOOTING OVER DOGS

Birds emit very little scent under the kite, for they tuck their feathers round them as tightly as possible and so prevent the emanation. I do not believe that the moderate use of a kite drives the birds off a beat, but personally I do not care for this style of shooting, and I would only adopt it as a last resource. On a windy day I have found it rather useful to show a kite along a boundary, to prevent the grouse from flying in that direction.

## CHAPTER VIII.
## BREAKING.

THERE is such a wealth of wisdom glittering among the pages of so many early writers on the breaking of dogs that, even by rigorous limitation of quotations, it is difficult to keep this chapter within reasonable bounds. For, of course, it is necessary to quote the most important sayings of the old Masters, since only by a careful study of their methods can we hope to emulate their results.

To facilitate the comparative reading of these maxims, I have arranged them chronologically without any interpolated comments :—

'You shall beginne to handle and instruct your dogge at foure monthes olde, or at six monthes at the uttermost, for to deferre longer time is hurtfull, and will make the labour greater and more difficult to compasse. Make him most loving and familiar with you, so that hee will not onely know you from any other person, but also fawne upon you and follow you wheresoever you goe, taking his onely delight to be in your company. You shall not suffer him to receive either foode or cherishing from any man's hands but your owne onely ; and as thus you grow familiar with the whelpe, and make him loving and fond of you, so you shall also mixe with this familiarity a kinde of awe and obedience in the whelpe, so as he may as well feare you as love you ; and this awe or feare you shall procure rather with your countenance, frowne, or sharpe words, than with blowes or any other actuell

# BREAKING

crueltye, for these whelpes are quickly terryfied, and the vyolence of torment not onely deprives them of courage, but also makes them dull and dead-spirited; whereas, on the contrary part, you are to strive to keepe your dogge (which is for this purpose) as wanton as possible. When, therefore, you have made your whelpe thus familiar and loving unto you, you shall begin to teach him to coutch and lye downe close, terrifying him with rough language when he doth anything against your meaning, and giving him not onely cherishings but foode (as a piece of bread or the like, which it is intended you must ever carry about you) when he doth anything according to your will' (*Hunger's Prevention*, by G. Markham, 1621, p. 268).

' When all these things aforesaid are perfectly learned, it is to be imagined by this time the whelpe will be by this time at least twelve monthes of age, at which time (the season of the yeare being fit) you may very well adventure to goe into the field and suffer him to raunge and hunt therein' (*id.* p. 273).

' And see that he [the puppy] beat his ground justly and even, without casting about, or flying now here, now there, which the mettle of some will do, if not corrected and reproved' (*The Gentleman's Recreation*, by N. Cox, 1686, p. 44).

' You must be very constant to the words of Direction by which you teach him, chusing such as are most pertinent to the purpose, and those words that you first use do not alter, for dogs take notice of the *sound*, not of the *English*, so that the least alteration puts him to a stand. For example, if you teach him to couch at the word " couch," and afterwards will have him couch at the word " down," this will be an unknown word to him; and I am of opinion that to use more words than what is necessary for one and the same thing is to overload his memory and cause forgetfulness in him'

# THE POINTER

(*The Gentleman's Recreation*, by R. Blome, 1686, p. 169).

'Quartering the ground and dropping are the pure effect of art in repeated lessons from the teacher. But when we see a dog (by some accident betrayed beyond his common sett) slip back to his usual distance; that must be all sagacity—all Self' (*A Treatise on Field Diversions*, by R. Symonds, 1776, p. 11).

'There is great beauty in quartering the ground well' (*id.* p. 80).

'A breaker ought to be half way before the dog is arrived at the extremity of his beat, and should always keep in the centre of his hunt, to make him describe equal distances on either hand. Being in the middle of the spot intended to be beaten, the master should walk briskly forward (as soon as the dog has passed him) some fifteen or twenty yards, according to the strength of the breeze more or less, and be ready, when he has reached his *ne plus*, to call him over fresh ground; otherwise, should he keep his stand, the dog will be apt to beat up too close to him, and return almost in his own tract, or clear but little ground. Some dogs I have remarked that would lead out one way and turn in the other. This arises from the breaker's keeping at one end of the work, where only he can give a true direction; whilst at the other the dog is by himself, entirely at liberty to do as he likes. I have taken notice of others that would make their turns right, yet when they came near, on their passage, would sink and get behind, not choosing to pass in front. This arises from fear, by whatever way occasioned, to remedy which, when you perceive him beginning to swerve, face about upon him directly, and speak to him in friendly voice, "Hey on, good lad!" &c., and when he finds he cannot get out of your eye, and that no danger or displeasure is incurred by a

## BREAKING

direct passage, his fears will cease, and his beats be made with propriety and freedom' (*id.* p. 81).

'Correcting falsely is doing what we cannot easily undo, and encouraging a fault is undoing all we had done before. By watching him so strictly, we may discover even his *Intention* from certain gestures, and by an instantaneous crack of displeasure frequently suppress it' (*id.* p. 93).

'It is very idle to be in a hurry with young folks; give time to see if they will fix themselves; the breaker may fix them improperly; a dog does no hurt, unless he springs; then is the time to rebuke, and not before. The *dog only* must be the judge of his own distances; to check, therefore, while he is fairly and cautiously drawing is driving him from himself; and giving directions to the creature you should expect to receive them from' (*id.* p. 96).

'A dog *once well broke* is *always broke* in the hands and under the eye of Judgment. To aim at taking game whilst the dog is imperfect is the way to have him *ever* be so' (*id.* p. 99).

'In training, both [whip and words] are absolutely necessary, the first yielding gradually to the latter; but I can never allow that dog to be perfect that requireth either. The whistle only is requisite, and the waft of the hand' (*id.* p. 104).

'Many will back at the second or third time of going out; but they are of a flat nature, and generally turn out *mere watchers*, that never strive to stretch ahead, as the sailors say, but content themselves with a negative goodness. Such are of no kind of service in company, only thickening the porridge and adding to the parade. Singly they may be useful dogs' (*id.* p. 112).

'He [the tutoring dog] should be of two or three years' hunt, tender-nosed, bold in point, without the

# THE POINTER

least motion. That is, in short, he should be as compleat as we can find one. His name should be as distant in sound as may be from the other's. You can encourage the old dog and rebuke the young' (*id.* p. 113).

'A dog that will draw up to his fellow, or near enough to catch the effluvia and no further, does not incommode or disappoint of a shot: but there is not that grace—that beauty—that elegance—that "je ne sais quoi," in a group of pointers packed together within a rod of ground, as in the same attitudes severally dispersed, sympathising from different quarters. The dog that *finds* is affected into attitude by his *nose*; the *backer* by his *eye*' (*id.* p. 114).

'If he is stubborn and unruly, it will be necessary to make use of the *trash cord*, fastening to the collar of the dog a rope or cord of about twenty or twenty-five fathoms in length, and then letting him range about with this dragging on the ground' (*Essay on Shooting*, by R. Howlitt, 1789, p. 252).

'In order to accustom him to cross and range before you, turn your back to him, and walk on the opposite side; when he loses sight of you, he will come to find you, he will be agitated and afraid of losing you, and will, in ranging, turn his head from time to time to observe whereabouts you are. The next step will be to throw down a piece of bread on the ground, at the same moment taking hold of the dog by the collar, calling out to him, "Take heed." After having held him in this manner for some space of time, say to him, "Seize!" or "Lay hold!" Repeat this lesson until he "takes heed" well, and no longer requires to be held fast to prevent him from laying hold of the bread. Never suffer the dog to eat either in the house or field without having first made him "take heed" in this manner. At the next lesson, take

## BREAKING

your gun, charged only with powder, walk gently round the piece of bread once or twice, and fire instead of crying "Seize." The next time of practising this lesson, walk round the bread four or five times, but in a greater circle than before, and continue to do this until the dog is conquered of his impatience, and will stand without moving until the signal is given him. When he keeps his point well, and stands steady in his lesson, you may carry him to the birds' (*id.* p. 253).

'The best way is to study the temper and disposition of the dog, and to conduct yourself accordingly in the application of correction' (*id.* p. 260).

'It is common not to begin to enter pointers till near a year old, because using them very young shortens their speed. Suppose there is truth in this maxim, and your dog should not hunt altogether so fast, a sufficient amends will be made for his want of swiftness, by hunting more carefully, nor will he run upon birds nor pass them unnoticed, as dogs which run very fast are apt to do' (*The Sportsman's Dictionary*, H. Pye, 1790, p. 360).

'Pointers, however well they may have been bred, are never considered complete unless they are perfectly staunch, as it is termed, to "bird, dog, and gun," which uniformly implies, first, standing singly to a bird or covey ; secondly, backing, or pointing instantly likewise, the moment one perceives another dog to stand ; and lastly not to stir from his own point at the rising of any bird or the firing of any gun in the field, provided the game is neither sprung nor started, at which he made his original point' (*The Sportsman's Cabinet*, by W. Taplin, 1803-4, p. 91).

'A tolerably well-bred pointer puppy may have the groundwork of all his future perfections theoretically implanted in the parlour or kitchen of the dwelling-

## THE POINTER

house before he once makes his appearance in the field' (*id.* p. 92.)

'When first entered it should be alone, and with a sportsman whose experience has convinced him young dogs should, from the earliest moment of their initiation, be taught to traverse every yard of the ground in proper lengths and at equal distances, so that no part should be left unbeaten; and this should be effected with as few words and as little noise as possible. Short, verbal, but expressive signals; low, vibrative, encouraging whistles; and the occasional waving of one hand or the other to the right or left are all that's necessary or useful; more does mischief' (*id.* p. 93).

'When a brace of pointers or more are hunted, they should alternately cross the same beat by meeting and passing each other, taking additional ground at each turn, but should not beat the same ground in a parallel direction.

'When a young dog is once made steady to bird and gun, broke from the natural desire to chase his game, and rendered obedient to every signal it is necessary for him to know and observe, then is the proper time to entertain him in company; that he may avail himself of advantages to be derived from hunting with older and more staunch or experienced dogs than himself. Previous to this introduction (when hunted alone), so soon as he knows his game, and is energetically anxious in the pursuit of it, feel for the wind, and let him have as much in his favour as the form of the field and circumstances will permit. So soon as he comes to a point a pause should ensue, and he should be permitted to enjoy it; not a buz, a word, an exclamation should escape by which he might be agitated to action; the necessary injunctions to caution should be tremulously vibrated upon the ear till the

## BREAKING

fire of his eye, the distention of the nostril, the elated loftiness of the aspect, and the seeming spasmodic affection of his whole frame (produced by the effect of the olfactory irritability), afford ample proof that the game is indisputably before him. This is the critical and awfully affecting moment, when the feelings of both are worked upon, and it is also the very moment when the most philosophic patience is necessary to be observed. Now is the time, if the game luckily lies, to advance nearer by degrees, but with all possible precaution of silence and deliberation. When time sufficient has been employed to confirm his steadiness, the game may then be walked up, and whether fired at or not, the first consideration is to prevent his chasing ' (*id.* p. 94).

' It is most advisable that a pistol or gun should frequently be fired over him in order to make him know the shot, for many young dogs, on the report of a gun, are so alarmed that they run away, and with the greatest difficulty, only after a length of time, are brought to be reconciled to it ' (*Shooting Directory*, by R. Thornhill, 1804, p. 56).

' Care must be taken not to stop them too soon, as it will be necessary to allow them for some time to chase the game previous to stopping them, particularly if it were long before they began to notice them ' (*id.* p. 57).

' You will find by experience that when a young one chases his game, and begins to know what he is about, he will sometimes, on coming up to it, make a sudden stop, and then run in on the birds. At this time, therefore, it will be the most proper to begin to stop him, and you must not only exert yourself, but take every advantage you can in favour of the dog, such as taking the wind and hunting him against it.

' When you cast him off to hunt either to the

## THE POINTER

right or left as your judgment and experience will decide, walk slowly, making the dog cross you backwards and forwards, hunting across the field from hedge to hedge, every now and then advancing yourself sixty or a hundred yards, always keeping the wind in his favour, and when you wish to cross make use of your hand—the less noise you make, the steadier he will hunt, and will consequently look for the signal; whereas, if you hunt him with your voice, he will hear you and scarcely ever turn to look for you or at you' (*id.* p. 58).

'A dog that does not bear the whip is easily *cowed*, and this often makes young ones *blink* their game, and a dog that *blinks* his game can be of little use to any sportsman. This is most frequently caused by beating dogs severely, who become so frightened at the very sound of your voice as to make them lie down. What we call *blinking* amongst sportsmen is when a dog finds his game and is spoken to, he draws off and runs behind you, and often without being spoken to, on finding the game, comes in close to your heels. Gentle means will be found always to have better effect than harsh. A sportsman should be very cool, especially in breaking young dogs; he will find himself always more successful in being so; and let every sportsman be cautious not to throw a stone at his dog' (*id.* p. 59).

'When your dog finds game, which you will easily perceive, go up to him, walking slowly, but never run, for if he sees you run, it is natural for him to follow the example, and then he will spring the birds' (*id.* p. 60).

'Young dogs are apt to *rake*, that is, to keep their noses too long on the ground, scenting, puzzling, which is a very bad custom and injurious to them, when you must have recourse to a puzzle-pin or peg' (*id.* p. 61).

'In breaking young dogs the compiler recommends

# BREAKING

making them always *clap*, or stand their ground, on first finding their game. It is not right, if the birds move, that the dog should attempt to do so until his master comes, or desires him, for if he does, if the birds do not lie well on that day, when they see the dog following them they will run until at last they are forced to take wing ; and, on the contrary, if a dog stops or *claps*, supposing the birds are disturbed and run, they will soon stop again, not finding themselves pursued, for it may be remarked, and it is an incontrovertible fact, that if a dog rakes and follows the birds, with his nose close to the ground, they will instantly take wing. However, to conclude this subject, a wellbred pointer will point naturally, and will only require practice and attention from his master in his first season' (*id.* p. 64).

'Eight young dogs are as many as one man can possibly manage, or should encounter at a time, and if he does his duty he will have but very few moments unoccupied. In the spring of the year he may continue out the whole day, but, as the weather becomes warmer, his excursions should be confined to morning and evening, and for the month of June and the first three weeks of July gentle exercise should be the chief objects of his attention' (*Angling, Shooting, and Coursing*, by R. Lascelles, 1811, p. 145).

'Words should at all times be used with the greatest caution, and a real good dog ought never to require them ; your hand must direct all his movements, and in every situation be the only interpreter ; I expect my dogs will always drop when I hold it up, and take whatever course it may otherwise direct them ; for this reason *no dog* should ever be allowed to go out of sight, and a *young one* never out of hearing. In whatever situation a dog sees a bird—running, flying or dead—he should instantly drop, and not move

# THE POINTER

an inch, till you have gone to the spot yourself' (*id.* p. 146).

'As soon as a dog points steady and true, the next thing you require of him is to back well; and if he is taken out in company with others, this, in its first stage, he will soon learn. That is, he will stop when he sees another do the same, and move on again accordingly: such, in the common acceptation of the term, is called backing; but much more is required to render it perfect. If I have four dogs out, and one of them makes a point, two others, we will say, are in a situation to see and back him instantly, which the third is prevented doing, from some intervening obstacle; in this case stop, and do not move until all are steady; either let him range until he backs to the point, or, if more convenient, drops to your hand. As you approach the dog first mentioned, all the others should very cautiously do the same, though many people would have them still keep their places till called to. In my opinion the beauty of a pointer is in being steady, and yet with all his natural spirit; to be as gallant as a foxhound, and as docile as a child; to know what he ought not to do, and never refuse doing what he may be ordered.

'It should be an invariable rule in breaking, and at the beginning of the season when birds lie well, to allow young dogs to lead up to their game; but as they become wilder, and in more critical situations, it is more prudent, perhaps, to give the reins to an old dog. There is something so beautifully characteristic in the sight of four steady pointers going well up to their game, that it is impossible, either on canvas or paper, to give a just delineation of it. And here I cannot too severely reprobate that restless anxiety of some sportsmen, which induces them to think that their sagacity, in this respect, is more penetrating than their com-

# BREAKING

panions'; and that the retreat of a bird is more likely to be discovered with the point of a gun, than the natural instinct of sense. It is from such bad and stubborn habits that all dogs are ruined, and in the end appear to have completely changed their condition; you must expect that, if a pointer is not allowed to exercise his right of search, he will very soon become indifferent to it, and after making his point leave the remainder entirely to his master (*id.* p. 147).

'At the end of May I leave off taking out my dogs till the middle of July, except for occasional exercise, when I enter upon the more serious process of moor-breaking. To a certain extent my young ones are all steady, at least so far as pointing or backing, and being free from chasing; all the higher qualifications they have got to learn, but more particularly that of footing. A partridge, except wounded, and this we have not had yet to deal with, seldom runs a great distance, and usually up-wind, so that a dog rarely finds any great difficulty in accomplishing his purpose: on this account it is that pointers are so strangely puzzled when they are first brought upon the moors. A grouse, and particularly the male, will frequently run down-wind, amidst the strongest heath and over the wettest bogs, for nearly half a mile; so that it not only requires sagacity, but the most steady perseverance to make him out well. A dog that has been broke upon the moors is as different from another as one animal can possibly be. You there see the nature of a pointer in all its best excellence; with a range of ground which his utmost wishes can scarcely occupy, and with an opportunity of taking advantage of the wind, at every turn and in every situation, he freely confides in the superiority of his own powers, unfettered by the constant interruption of a fence on the one side, or a dry unprofitable fallow on the other. Nothing will sooner induce a dog

## THE POINTER

to forget, or rather to break through, the rules of discipline he has already been taught, than his first essay upon the moors; and although he may previously have been as steady as a rock, yet when he suddenly finds himself in the midst of a brood of grouse, the cock cackling and running one way, the hen another, and the young ones getting up in every direction, it is generally fear, if he does keep true to his point, which predominates over inclination. You cannot then encourage him too much; language, properly used, is worth all the whipcord in the world; it will both encourage and correct, and will sooner bring an animal under the proper degree of subordination than the most severe flogging. You should endeavour to prevent a young dog chasing on the moors, by every means possible; for if he once begins, there are so many temptations for him to continue it, especially in a backward season, when birds are small and their flight slow and short, that all your previous labour will be thrown away' (*id.* p. 149).

'My plan is, always to hunt those parts first where I am pretty certain of finding no game; this will give a dog an idea of his ground, and also, in some degree, cool that high metal with which he first sets out. I then change my beat, let go an old dog, and take up the others. The first point is generally decisive; and if it be at a brood, will materially assist you; let your dog go very cautiously; and, to prevent any bad consequences, each should have a collar on, with a piece of strong cord attached to it of about two yards in length, with a loop at the end to lay hold of; give them the wind as much as you can, and be certain that they know what they are about before you disturb the brood. When the old birds begin running and calling, let them then have as full a view as possible, but without stirring an inch; and when the young ones get up, the same,

# BREAKING

but not, by any means, to allow them to observe where they afterwards drop. If the old cock should run to any distance, which he generally does, let your dogs foot him to the extremity of it, stopping them at the end of every ten or fifteen yards, to make them more cautious hereafter. Should you have no one with you, yourself must endeavour to mark down one or two of the brood, which is easily done, as they seldom fly above two hundred yards, before they have been much disturbed. In this case, let go your young dogs, and hunt them round the spot till they come upon the scent, and there allow them to stand for the space of five minutes; then follow them slowly up, and as you can guess almost to a certainty where the bird lies, if possible, take it under their noses, but having them so secure that you can let it go again without risk of being hurt. Should either make a snatch at it, correct him moderately; words, and a few gentle blows about the mouth, will probably quiet him; at any rate, first try the effect of lenient measures, and at all times proportion the degree of punishment to the excess of crime. After a few such precautionary measures you may loose your young dogs entirely; but I would not have you give them immediately too great a liberty to range, for fear they abuse the indulgence, and it is a dangerous maxim to trust too much to inexperience: in four or five days this forbearance will gradually cease; and at the termination of three weeks each will have acquired an instinctive confidence to qualify him for more useful purposes' (*id.* p. 151).

'The gentleman in the South undoubtedly has many advantages in the variety of game which in the course of the season is presented to him; but of the grandeur and style in which the diversion of shooting admits of being prosecuted amongst the hills of the north, for the somewhat too brief period during which, for a variety

## THE POINTER

of reasons, the pursuit is at all practicable, he can have but a very humble conception ; and for the means of creating perfection in the dog, the advantages are altogether on the side of the former [the sportsman in the North]. Let me add that, with a somewhat various acquaintance with different counties in the south of this island, although I have seen many dogs, to whom, without having had their noses elevated above the level of a partridge, it would be unfair to refuse the epithet of good, I have never witnessed one whom I could consider entitled to any very eminent distinction who had not in early life the good fortune to have his legs stretched, and his faculties expanded, on the moors' (*Kunopædia*, by W. Dobson, 1814, p. xxxi.).

' Endeavour to keep up the nose to pointer pitch ; for which purpose, where this grovelling propensity is too prevalent, it is not unusual to see recourse had to the " marvellous device " of the puzzle-peg ; but I must confess I never saw any good done by it ; on the contrary, the perpetual fretful interruptions to beat which it occasions, operate against the very principles of a radical cure. Where the circumstance arises, as is frequently the case, from a dulness of nose, which is obliged to seek for information downwards, or perhaps from some bastardising touch of derivation from a dog of an inferior trade, the proper employment of whose nose is on the ground, these are defects which will never be cured by splicing a bit of stick to the under-jaw, and you may as well let the half-bred creature grub on untormented in his own way' (*id.* p. 11).

' The rarest accomplishment of a dog, and not less valuable than rare, is *fine quartering*. You will observe, the great project is to procure a regular advance into the wind, at each end of his line of range, abreast of your line of march in the centre, and rather ahead of you, and then to cross direct to the call or whistle' (*id.* p. 17).

## BREAKING

'Nature and experience will instruct him in the performance of some of his other duties; but the habitual establishment of regulated range, the due performance of his evolutions, the quartering of his ground to all advantage, is the work of art, and must come from yourself alone' (*id.* p. 26).

'The dog who hunts his ground the truest will always find the most game' (*id.* p. 27).

'The great secret of making a dog *stand* is to *stop* yourself' (*id.* p. 35).

'Never pass a blunder unnoticed, nor a fault unpunished' (*id.* p. 78).

'Never avenge upon your dog your own errors in shooting. Neither let the giddy triumph of some fortunate shot atone for the heedless rattle by which he may have driven the bird within your reach, nor for any lawless violence by which he may further assist you in laying hold of it' (*id.* p. 79).

'Of necessity, there is a great deal of trouble, and of time lost, in working up a tender temper into a due consistency of conduct, and it seldom repays the toil bestowed in the attempt. I have already premised that, in the idea of establishing a kennel, I would have nothing to do with such a subject' (*id.* p. 93).

From the intricate business of tracking out an old grouse-cock among the broken hags, down to the still more equivocal chance for a second find of the little delicate land-rail,—it is of the last importance that a perfection in this lesson of "footing-out the game" should be solicitously taught and steadily adhered to' (*id.* p. 104).

'It cannot be denied, however beautifully perfect a dog may be made up as a single dog alone, that his education must be considered as only half completed, until he is rendered equally perfect in company' (*id.* p. 122).

## THE POINTER

'Our object is to call forth intellect, and to establish obedience upon principle' (*id.* p. 128).

'Now, my notions of education extend in the first instance to the dog's knowing what he is to stand for, and to bring him forward early in the more profitable business of independent inquiry. The stop which he has from instinct, more or less improved into a determined self-collected stand, makes the great characteristic difference between the animal whose superior talents we are endeavouring to cultivate into excellence, and the whole of the other inferior orders of the species; but although in itself indispensable, it is among the very least of the qualifications which go to the formation of a finished pointer' (*id.* p. 132).

'The few guineas that are usually given for what is termed "breaking in," would not pay for the shoe-leather worn out in doing justice to a dog of high courage and powers' (*id.* p. 139).

'Show me a dog *perfect at the down-charge*, and I will engage, in a very few days, to exhibit him to you equally firm, at the challenge of "take heed," to the point of another dog; and with all that cautious delicacy of approach, which constitutes good manners in society' (*id.* p. 150).

'The grand point is to teach him the method of finding his game by regularly and patiently quartering his ground. It may well be conceived a matter of no small difficulty to teach a young dog, first, how to comprehend, and afterwards to execute with punctuality and precision, the lesson of these various and regular crossings. And the reader is not to take it for granted that every pointer, however well spoken of, is an exact and able performer at this game; but whenever such is the case, the dog is of the highest character as a pointer; and the sight of two or three brace of pointers, regularly quartering their ground and *backing* each other, may be

# BREAKING

reckoned amongst the most interesting, grand, and wonderful' (*Sportsman's Repository*, by R. Lawrence, 1820, p. 118).

'We find twenty fine scenting dogs for one really fine quarterer' (*British Field Sports*, by W. Scott, 1820, p. 203).

'Much time will be gained, and a dog will be made much more perfect, by being kept for some time to the practice of quartering, lying down at the word, and turning to the whistle, without finding game, than by seeing partridges at first, without previous education, as is the usual practice' (*Observations on Dog-breaking*, by W. Floyd, 1821, p. 12).

'He will quarter better, because there will be no scent to induce him to deviate from his regular course, and he will not connect the dread of punishment with the scent of the partridges, which is in general the cause of blinking. All this, which is the principal part of breaking, may be done at any season, provided the weather be fine, for it is very injurious to young dogs to hunt them in the rain or during a high wind' (*id.* p. 13).

'When two or more dogs are at exercise and one dog is made to lie down, it should be a signal to all the others to do the same' (*id.* p. 18).

'Dogs may be daunted by the use of the whip, but it cannot explain to them (if I may be allowed the expression) what it is they are expected to do' (*id.* p. 21).

'All dogs are made shy by the use of the whip, but all dogs may be broken by the cord; it will never fail to daunt the most resolute, but may be so gently used as not to overawe the most timid' (*id.* p. 22).

'If it suit his convenience the shooter should frequently accompany the breakers when practising his dogs, he should direct them to make use of few words, and those words should be the same that he is in the

## THE POINTER

habit of using. A multiplicity of directions only serves to puzzle the dog, as a person speaking Irish, Scotch, and Welsh alternately would perplex a Spaniard!' (*Shooter's Handbook*, by T. Oakleigh, 1842, p. 94).

'*To-ho*, spoken in an undertone, when the dog is ranging, is a warning to him that he is close upon game, and is a direction for him to stand. There is no necessity for using it to a dog that knows his business. Spoken in a peremptory manner, it is used to make the dog crouch when he has run up game, or been otherwise in fault. *Down-charge*, is to make the dog crouch while the shooter charges. *Back*, is used to make a dog follow at heel. '*Ware fence*, is used to prevent the dog passing a fence before the gun. '*Ware*, is used to rate a dog for giving chase to a hare, birds, or cattle, or for pointing larks, or approaching too near the heels of a horse. *Seek*, is a direction to the dog to look for a wounded or dead bird, hare, or rabbit. *Dead*, is to make a dog relinquish his hold of dead or wounded game' (*id.* p. 95).

'Whenever speaking to a dog, whether encouragingly or reprovingly, the sportsman should endeavour to *look* what he means, and the dog will understand him. The dog has not the gift of tongues, but he is a Lavater in physiognomy' (*id.* p. 96).

'A well-bred dog will invariably backset instinctively. To backset instinctively is the distinctive characteristic of a promising young dog; indeed it is the only safe standard by which the shooter may venture to prognosticate future excellence. A dog's pointing game, and larks, the first time he is taken out is no certain criterion of his merit : but there is no deception in a dog's backing the first time he sees another dog make a point. It is a proof that he is a scion from the right stock' (*id.* p. 98).

'When punishing a dog, it is better to beat him

# BREAKING

with a slender switch than with a dog-whip. But whether a switch or dog-whip be used, the dog should be struck across, not along the ribs; or, in other words, the switch or lash should not be made to lap round his body, but the blow should fall on the whole length of his side. A dog should never be kicked, or shaken by the ears. When the shooter is unprovided with a switch or dog-whip, he should make the dog lie at his foot for several minutes, which the dog, eager for sport, will consider a severe punishment, and it is a sort of punishment not soon forgotten' (*id.* p. 98).

'The routine of dog-breaking is well explained below. We very much approve of the system there laid down:—

'"The first lesson, and the one on which the breaker's success chiefly depends, is that of teaching the dog to drop at the word '*down ;*' this must be done before he is taken into the field. Tie a strong cord to his neck, about eighteen yards long, and peg one end into the ground. Then make the dog crouch down, with his nose between his front feet, calling out in a loud voice, '*down.*' As often as he attempts to rise, pull him to the ground, and repeat the word '*down*' each time. When he lies perfectly quiet while you are standing by him, walk away, and if he attempt to follow you, walk back, and make him '*down*' again, giving him a cut or two with the whip. This lesson must be repeated very often, and will take some trouble before it is properly inculcated. When once learned it is never forgotten, and if properly taught in the beginning, will save an infinity of trouble in the end. He ought never to be suffered to rise until touched by the hand. This lesson should be practised before his meals, and he will perform it much better as he expects his food, and never feed him until you are perfectly satisfied with his performance." Extract from *New Sporting Magazine*, vol. v., No. 28, p. 256 (*id.* p. 99).

## THE POINTER

'The fact is, most shooters are content with a limited perfection in their dogs; and, again, so exceedingly scarce are dogs of pure breed—for it is not every high-bred dog that is a pure-bred dog—and superior training, that many who are fully persuaded within themselves that "the best dog in England" sleeps on their own premises, in reality, never so much as even saw a properly, so called, high-trained and thorough-bred dog in their lives' (*The Modern Shooter*, by Captain Lacy, 1842, p. 143).

'Indeed the art of real good dog-breaking appears to be one in which we moderns have retrograded' (*id.* p. 144).

'It is highly essential that young dogs especially should quarter their ground regularly to windward; they should, therefore, always be thrown off right and left up-wind, and be made to cross each other independently.

'Dogs, however well broken by a scientific trainer, when they get into a young shooter's hands will, for certain, take liberties with him, in a greater or less degree, unless he know how to manage them and to govern himself, and be a strict disciplinarian withal—from the very first never allowing a fault to pass without notice, reprehension, or punishment, according as it may deserve the one or the other—and never chastising them in anger, or with too great severity' (*id.* p. 151).

'If a young shooter commence his career with the best broke dogs—and it is his best plan—he never can endure to look at bad ones afterwards. But if, on the other hand, he commence with tolerable dogs, such as one generally sees, he will become reconciled to imperfection, will likely enough—for it's a monstrous contagious vice—turn as great a sloven as the animals themselves, become a sort of anyhow-shooter, and possibly, at last, degenerate into an arrant pot-hunter.

# BREAKING

Such a one, to be sure, may call himself, and think himself, a sportsman, but in reality has no more claim to that title than his erratic dogs; and, moreover, has as much conception of the genuine relish of shooting in first-class style, as a clod has of the genuine relish of *real* turtle soup. Nothing can be more delightful than sporting with good dogs, nor more discouraging and disgusting than having ill-bred or badly trained ones to accompany you' (*id.* p. 154).

'Command of temper is one of those virtues which is absolutely a *sine quâ non* in a dog-breaker' (*id.* p. 157).

'But little, if any, of the voice, and a very sparing use of the whistle; for there is nothing like *shooting in silence*' (*id.* p. 159).

'All the best breakers with whom I am acquainted use the long cord at first, and in some instances, where the animal is very refractory, the spiked collar. But unless a dog be exceedingly headstrong—and if he be, keep him not—the check-cord alone will be found sufficiently coercive' (*ib.*).

'Never beat a dog after he has done wrong, but as nearly in the act as possible. When you punish, have him upon a training-cord, and do not loose him till he has become reconciled to you. Should you let him go before, he will very likely skulk. Coil the line round your hand, and keep him at heel for some time, and give him his liberty by degrees. If you observe any signs of skulking, fasten the line to a stake and leave him behind you for a field or two. Then return, and if he seem cheerful, give him a piece of biscuit and caress him. Let him then off, but still fast to a cord; as soon as he beats freely you may remove it altogether' (*Recreations in Shooting*, by Craven, 1846, p. 142).

From the foregoing passages alone, an excellent

# THE POINTER

theory of breaking is to be constructed; though the works of so many different brains, during a period extending over two centuries, demand thoughtful assimilation, after flavouring them with practical experience of the conditions of to-day.

How wise, for example, are the remarks of kindly Gervase Markham on the relations to be cultivated between the dog and his master! And a mine of wisdom for breakers is Symonds's book, from which I have loaded myself with many a nugget.

Symonds much prefers the dog, when backing, to remain motionless when he first catches sight of the point; while Lascelles, another of the giants, makes his dogs (working four of them together) assemble with him at the point, and together march on to the grouse. Personally, I consider Symonds's method, which is followed nowadays at the Trials, to be much more beautiful, less likely to engender riot, and undoubtedly the right one for partridges; but on the moors the Lascelles system certainly has its advantages, when the grouse separate as they run on, or an 'old cock slopes off for a half-mile excursion. When, however, Symonds writes of quartering as 'the effect of pure art' and sets up a violent contrast between docility and sagacity, his conclusions do not seem to me quite soundly based. For even if quartering, when acquired, be solely mechanical, the will and the power to learn it—in a word, the docility—must proceed directly from sagacity. I will give an illustration of this. I had a pointer, an almost perfect quarterer by nature, which I ran at the Trials about ten years ago. Now, the Trials were at that period much debased, and Judges preferred a few slap-dash, far-ahead points to many homely ones by the systematic exploring of sides and corners. So my dog did not win much. One day my old breaker asked me, though with tears in his eyes, if

# BREAKING

he might 'spoil Tap's quartering, as he can't win without it.' I, rashly enough, gave him leave: the 'spoiling' was duly carried out, and afterwards Tap won many big prizes. But, wonderful to relate, though at Trials he would evermore flash about in the admired eccentric, when out shooting he would revert instantly to the fine quartering that was his birthright. In his case, at any rate, quartering was the offspring of sagacity.

Lascelles, who was the first to write exhaustively on grouse-shooting, and whose knowledge can only have been equalled by his originality and power of expression, becomes very sarcastic over those men who themselves, by springing the birds, are apt to usurp the prerogative of their dog. Taplin and Dobson contribute much that is of interest, but they have not the linguistic command of a Lascelles, and are apt to be flatulent. Dobson's remark, however, about the tendency to praise your dog when you kill, for the same conduct that you would punish if you had missed, is as keen as it is true.

Lacy, the prophet of working trials, also foreshadows the Kennel Club Stud Book in his exhortation to discriminate between 'high-bred' and 'pure-bred' pointers. And he draws attention to the action and reaction of slovenliness in work, interchanged between dog and man, when the latter has no idea of the 'relish' (excellent word!) of shooting in proper style.

I will now give a few plain, general directions of my own to enable any novice himself to break his pointer puppies, provided he have patience and a love of dogs. They are, of course, only intended to start him in this fascinating pastime, and are supplementary to the rest of this chapter; but, as far as they go, they are practical, for they are fruits of my actual experience.

# THE POINTER

First of all, it is important that you select your pups according to the principles of my fourth and fifth chapters. In which case you will have to deal with some purely bred pointers of intelligence and hereditary experience, which will respond to your efforts and will be endowed with an easy gallop, wanton tails, and highly carried heads. All this is very important, as it is 'a weariness of the flesh' to attempt the education of a cross-bred, which means, in its most literal sense, *breaking* him. So if your pups do not soon show some signs of awakening instinct, or if, unbidden, you find them frequently at your heel, by all means get rid of them—you have got hold of 'wrong uns.'

The elementary instruction of pointers, equivalent to the A B C, is shared by them with many others of the canine race that are required to be useful, or even agreeable, companions; and it is out of their love of his society that man is able to teach them the three rudimentary principles of obedience—to come when called, to walk at heel when told, and to lie down at command.

The education of a pointer is divided into two stages—the preliminary or mechanical, and the final or instinctive, the former being without, the latter with, game.

You will easily teach a four-months-old puppy *to answer* when called by name or whistle, and it is a good plan to associate such early lessons with his meals. As soon as he has mastered this, teach him to '*heel*,' which also presents no difficulty. Commence the process by walking down a narrow pathway with a switch in your hand. Say '*heel*' to the puppy, and whenever you can see his nose flick it, repeating the word. At the conclusion cry '*hold up*,' and encourage him to gallop away from you. Biscuits are an appropriate reward all through the mechanical course.

# BREAKING

Teaching the youngster *to drop* is a more difficult matter, and it takes time and patience; for nothing short of perfection will suffice in this, the keystone of the puppy's future development. You must not think his dropping is complete, till he will throw himself instantly to the ground, when going fast, on hearing the word '*down*,' or on seeing your hand raised above your head, and till, at command, he will remain couched while you go out of sight. For the attainment of which the method of Oakleigh, already placed in this chapter, is suitable; and be especially careful that, during the early lessons, the pup be fastened with a long cord, as if he once escape you it will cause him unfortunate doubts of your omnipotence.

His training will next embrace *backing*, for which you will loose in a field two or more puppies together, allowing them to range, and dropping one when the others have their backs turned. By shouting at these if they turn without taking notice, you can soon induce them to drop like stones on catching sight of a dog that is 'down.' This accomplishment, though a very easy one for a puppy that drops smartly, is of great importance as, taught thus, the dog later on will feel no jealousy in backing points on game; and even continued false-points will not annoy him.

You must now proceed to make each puppy *quarter* his ground, which is the last subject in his preliminary course; but before this, you must have begun to make him watch, and obey, the signs of your hand. It is a good plan, whenever you think he has for the moment forgotten you, to change your direction, to get nimbly out of sight, and if possible to hide yourself; as the puppy, on missing you, will be in despair till he has found you, and this manœuvre repeated once or twice will keep him always watchful and attentive.

Choose an oblong field, where there is no likelihood

# THE POINTER

of game, and walk up the centre of it. Hold the dog up, and every time he reaches either fence, whistle to him, and beckoning with your hand run a little way towards the other side, encouraging him by your voice. When he has passed you, push forward yourself till he turns at the fence, and then you must repeat your previous behaviour. At first you will have to strive hard to prevent his turning inwards at the extremity of his cast, and thus coming back over ground that he has previously beaten; so, when he makes a wrong turn or is about to pass behind you, you ought at once to face about, that you may transpose his futile cast into a correct one, and not to resume your advance till he has gone by you. Gradually you must accustom him to turn without the whistle, to be guided by your hand alone.

In beating a field the best 'pattern' to aspire after, with a view to future brace-work, is as below. The plain black line marks the range of one dog, the dotted line that of the other; this pattern is to be repeated until the whole of the ground is beaten:—

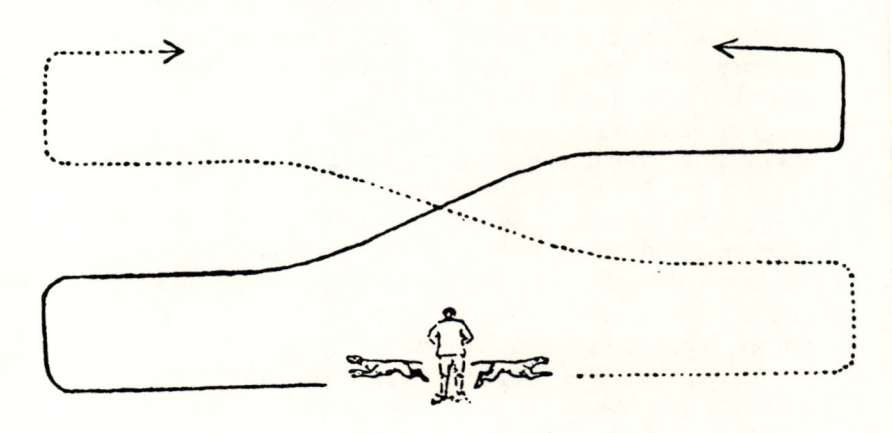

# BREAKING

At this point the mechanical training concludes; and, even in the foregoing exercises, much will have to be regulated and modified to suit the individual character of the pupil. But when he is properly grounded in the five preliminaries, there need be no delay before commencing his instinctive development on game, and the unfolding of his powers will take place smoothly and gradually: he may become a great genius, and he cannot fail to be an honest, useful worker.

Any one, with patience, ought to be able to teach an intelligent puppy the rudiments, but let us halt on the threshold of the second part of his education, to consider the kind of human influence that is likely to conduce to the production of an eminent dog.

A good pup is very spirited, very sensitive, very innocent; and it is necessary to make him obedient under any temptation, without crushing his common sense or damaging his sense of responsibility—to break his wilfulness without breaking his spirit. You must handle him firmly but tenderly to avoid knocking off the bloom, you must guide so imperceptibly that he will fancy that in obeying you he is pleasing himself  To accomplish this requires, of course, much sympathetic feeling with dogs, which is probably a natural gift; but it is at the root of all fine breaking, and possession of this gift distinguishes the artist from the mere mechanic.

A yearling pointer, especially when a tip-topper, is very high-strung, so he must not be needlessly startled or irritated. Never throw a stone at him, nor shout suddenly when near him, nor crack a whip, nor hurry him back into kennel with your foot.

Never use the whip when the dog is already ashamed of himself—but rate him soundly, and shake him if necessary.

## THE POINTER

Never let a fault go unrebuked, even when it is extenuated by circumstances—such as a flush downwind, or the being led away by bad example: a dog is no casuist, and his mind fails to understand nice distinctions.

Never use the whip when you have lost your temper, and, when you *do* flog, mind you have hold of the dog, and make it up with him before you release him.

But there is another mode of punishment more generally useful than the whip. For a serious fault, you can peg the puppy firmly to the ground and then go out of sight for a while. The great advantage of this plan is that while the culprit will cry piteously during his desertion, instead of being cowed at your return he will be overjoyed to welcome you.

Then there is the *trash-cord*, which is, however, more of a preventive than a punishment. With this blessed invention, which is worth more than all the rest of the breaking dodges put together, you can equally well school natures shy and self-willed. It is simply a cord fastened to the collar of a dog, and trailed after him; but its virtues are infinite. It need only be ten feet long, or you can make it fifty with a furze bush at its end: used as a leading-string it will bring confidence to the backward puppy at his point, and it will sober the most harum-scarum by the indefiniteness of its 'sphere of influence.'

The final stage of a puppy's education has now to be considered, and in superintending this you must remember all the time that you are trying to develop his instinct, not to impart to him some brand-new knowledge: in fact you are in command only to foster and bring to light his latent talents. For instance, when, at his first introduction to game, he seems for the nonce to forget his preliminary education, let him have

# BREAKING

his fling, let him skim about everywhere, chasing all that flies. Do not check him, only keep him hard at it, till his own sense rescues him. Do not try to force him to point or drop, till at last, when he is tired, you see him making a hesitating sort of point. Then is your chance! Get up to him as quickly as you can without running, and when once you manage to get hold of the end of the cord, and by his side you march up to the birds, you have done with your nondescript puppy, and another Pointer is born!

Be sure, after he has steadied to his points, that you never try to help him at them by whistling, or by otherwise cautioning him. He must learn from experience how near he may go; and even from the first he must obviously know more about it than the officious breaker. Your duty is to scold him when he *has* flushed birds, and to drag him roughly back to the spot, where, after the event, you know he should have waited.

At this stage your anxieties will practically cease, for the previous training of your pupil will make what remains quite simple for him.

His practice of dropping to hand, you must now extend to wing, fur, and shot; to accomplish which you will have, for a few times, to cry '*down*' at the sound of a shot and at the appearance of hare and partridge, but he will soon acknowledge them of himself.

Purely bred pointers are not addicted to chasing hares. Of course most pups will at first have a gallop or two after them, but these are not serious chases with nose to the ground and musical accompaniment. Such ebullitions of youthful gaiety need not be severely punished, they will soon die out: but avoid hares until your pup is staunch on partridges. '*Raking*,' or snuffling about with the nose on the ground, is very offensive when a habit: it is a result of either bad breeding or

# THE POINTER

bad breaking. Never allow a puppy to begin snuffling. When he will not judge game with his head high, force him to leave its vicinity: this will quickly teach him to make up his mind. Puzzle-pegs I have found quite useless; a lofty carriage of his head at the gallop, like turning the nose to the wind, must be innate, and cannot be taught. There is no doubt that a dog that rakes frightens the birds far more than a 'high-flier,' because, I suppose, they are certain that the former is after them, while they fancy that the other one has not discovered their proximity. A dog of this high principle will soon get to know by the scent when the partridges are tickle, and he will become cautious in due proportion.

Always, if possible, commence your pointers on partridges, as, if broken on the stronger-scented grouse, they will never take kindly to other game: similarly you must begin with snipe, if you want your dog to be fond of them. Spring is as a breaking time preferable to autumn, for, if broken on coveys, the nose of the puppy will not become so acute, and he may neglect single birds. His scenting-powers will constantly improve with practice and, under skilled direction, are capable of much development. I have known dogs, as they lost their eyesight, to attain an almost miraculous fineness of nose.

Do not let your scholar sniff about the hedges; and make him from the beginning understand that, if there *are* treasures therein, they are not for him. But it is absolutely right for a dog to run close along a line of fence when he is to windward of it, as by this move he secures the entire field for his operations. No dog should be allowed to break fence, to precede his master into another field; and when you are getting over an obstacle, he must wait and follow. In his preliminary lessons he will have been taught the secret of single

# BREAKING

quartering, and a brainy pointer will soon teach himself how to vary his pace and proportion his parallels, according to the scent of the moment.

It is necessary for grouse-shooting that a pointer be free and devoid of stickiness in roading birds, not needing further encouragement than the close companionship of the shooter. When, at first, a puppy shows reluctance to advance on his game, slip a band round his neck, and gently pull him along. If, however, he do not gain confidence, take with you an old dog on a lead, and at the youngster's points, yoke the two together, and thus, with the brace, make out the birds. But do not be satisfied till the puppy will, without assistance, work out and spring the game. Neither speak nor chirrup, nor pat him during the whole process, much less stir with your foot the cover in front of him, as such behaviour will foster in him a fatal laziness. All sensitive puppies dislike the shock of springing their birds; but if indulged in this weakness, farewell to those golden watchwords of the sportsman—*Swiftness* and *Silence.*

A similar mistake to the last mentioned is to encourage with flatteries a puppy whenever he happens to point; as, if this appeal to his vanity do not establish in him the vice of false-pointing, he will be satisfied to stand, as soon as he smells that game is somewhere about, without troubling to locate his birds—a disagreeable habit at all times, but in brace work intolerable.

Do not treat high-couraged dogs to a sniff at the game when killed, as a rule it unsettles them: the taste of the scent, or the knowledge that birds have fallen, is sufficient reward. But, of course, when a puppy is nervous, it is well to let him mouth a bird once or twice.

In working two pointers as a brace, make them quarter their ground independently (see diagram, p.

## THE POINTER

216), never allowing them to follow one another or to be near together, for much evil-doing may result from their juxtaposition; and they will be inclined to forget their duty in rivalry, if they do not wittingly lead each other astray. If, in their work, one of them stop to relieve himself, insist on the other dog couching until the brace can start again with equal chances; and when one makes a point, the other also must at once stiffen in acknowledgment and must immovably await the moment to couch, when the birds rise from the point of his companion. In breaking a brace, when you are going up to a point, lend three-fourths of your attention to the backing dog, to see that he do not leave his place; and in starting the brace again after the point, always give the precedence to the backing dog. One reason for this is that it will put him again on an equality with the pointing dog; another is that he may learn never to draw on, nor to move without leave: it is neglect of this observance on the part of the breaker that often makes old dogs creep on so disagreeably, when at the back.

When the game has been sprung, do not permit the pointing dog to nose about the haunt, or the backing dog ever to approach it. But, after keeping them at the down-charge for two minutes, hold them up, and let them quest afresh.

If necessary, in the beginning of your lessons, you may peg down the backing pup, or you can cause a lad to stand near him, to preclude the possibility of his approach towards the pointing pup; for you must not alarm the one on his point by rating the other. If, however, you have been careful in your preliminary lessons, you will not have to resort to such expedients: much less, as some persons do in their endeavours after steadiness behind, will you have to keep your pupils alternately at heel.

# CHAPTER IX.
## KENNEL MANAGEMENT.

IF it be worth while to own pointers at all, the master ought to make himself thoroughly acquainted with their management in kennel; for that establishment must be in a precarious state where he is not familiar with at least as much canine lore as his servants. And this knowledge is so easy to acquire! A little observation, a little thought, a little reading, and a little common sense will soon make any man conversant with the essential treatment of gundogs, from which most perils can be averted by scrupulous attention to elementary rules of health in their housing, their diet, and their exercise. And though in surgical cases and accidents he will be wise to summon a certified veterinary surgeon, he will himself be the best of consulting physicians for his own kennel, as the *doctoring* of dogs certainly needs specialised attention, for it is quite distinct from the treatment of horses and cows.

In the first place I will tackle the housing question, which deals with the actual structure of permanent kennels. These should occupy a sheltered site with a southern aspect, the floors of both houses and yards being placed on sealed arches, to ensure perfect freedom from damp. I find that the most commodious formation is that in which the main kennels are in a long row, while, behind them, a passage runs their whole length and is covered by the same pitched roof as the sleeping chambers. This passage is useful for the exercise of sick dogs, &c., and the walls can be gar-

## THE POINTER

nished with storage cupboards and kennel apparatus. In front of each kennel there must be a yard of corresponding breadth and about twenty-four feet long, to which the dogs have access at pleasure. These yards are to be inclosed by high iron fencing, with the bars bare to the ground in the front, but protected from the neighbouring yards by corrugated sheeting on the sides, to the height of four feet: the whole to be surrounded by a paddock of about one acre, inclosed by some outer fence too high to be scaled.

In addition to the ordinary kennel buildings, there must be a store-room for provisions, bedding, travelling-hampers, &c.; a boiling-house, detached from the main block, containing two iron coppers for the cooking of food; the hospital, joined on to the boiling-house, so as to receive warmth from the proximity of the caldrons; a range of miniature kennels and yards for the bitches to pup in; two bitch-houses and yards, isolated by a high wall, for bitches in season; and a house with playground (not less than thirty yards square) for the puppies in late autumn and winter, to be placed between the bitch-houses and the rest of the buildings.

If is a good plan to have your kennelman's house among the kennels; and necessary that it should be at farthest within earshot. Let all the drains be surface ones, then there will be no possibility of evil accumulations; and if possible, have a supply of water running through the kennels, the water troughs being placed as high above the level of the floor as compatible with the comfort of the dogs. As to the fittings, let every bit of woodwork within reach of the dogs be from the first edged with zinc. This, in the long run, will save expense, and the dogs will never acquire the habit of gnawing. The sleeping-benches had better be of seasoned oak, raised about sixteen inches from the ground, and not in actual contact with any wall; their four-

## KENNEL MANAGEMENT

inch sides must be detachable, so that the whole bed may be taken to pieces, to admit of periodical cleanings and dryings in the sun. If the dogs get into bad habits and pollute their bed, a rooflet of wire-netting is useful to prevent them from standing upright there.

There should be two ventilators of a foot square, with shutters, placed high up on the wall and opposite to each other, one opening into the outside air, the other into the passage; this will ensure a thorough draught above the dogs' level in hot weather, and the power of regulating the temperature at all times. Besides these there must be, of course, a glazed window for light, and low down in the door leading from the yard to the dormitory an egress hole, of about twelve inches by fifteen, which must be kept open except in illness or in very severe weather. It is also a good plan to support, on iron pillars one foot in height, the greater part of that wall of the dormitory which adjoins the yard, and to fit the space below with wooden shutters, which can be turned back during extreme heat and for the regular swillings out.

I think that concrete makes the best floor both for the buildings and the yards, for though large slabs of slate are warmer, there are necessarily interstices, which after a time become insanitary; tiles share this disadvantage, with the addition of being cold and slippery. But, whatever the flooring, from the back of the dormitories to the front of the yards, let there be one very gentle and continuous slope.

Quite as important as the housing of your dogs is their feeding, for anything amiss in the food itself, or in the manner of administering it, will soon produce skin diseases and all kinds of ills.

The adults should be fed only once a day, preferably in the late afternoon, which is conducive to their resting quietly during the night and to preparing

# THE POINTER

them for the season in Scotland, where they cannot have their food till even later. Young dogs, if thin and of light build, should have in addition a light breakfast, and so, also, should all bitches in pup. It is better at mealtime for the dogs to assemble outside the gate leading to the boiling-house yard, so that when the food has been poured into the long troughs there, they can be called in one by one; the preference being given to those that are delicate feeders, while those that are greedy and of gross habit are left till the last.

To keep a kennel of dogs in level condition, constant vigilance is necessary; but, because this uniformity is within the power of any kennelman, there can be no safer criterion of his trustworthiness.

The principal ingredients in the food for sporting dogs are flesh, cereals, and vegetables. Flesh, both raw and cooked, is good for dogs, but in the former state it must not be employed so often as in the latter. In cool weather, or when dogs are working hard, a liberal allowance of meat will benefit them, as it is their natural food. There is a superstition that flesh will engender the mange; but, as a matter of fact, it is not half so causative as the farinaceous stuffs. Horseflesh, if boiled, will do very well for dogs, as also will the cows or sheep that may die in the neighbourhood, provided they are not victims of any noxious disease. My private opinion is that unless actual poison be the cause of death in cattle, any carcase *while fresh* may be used in the kennel with impunity, but in this matter it is better to err on the side of caution. The refuse of the slaughter-house, also, forms a condiment wholesome and convenient for kennels situated near a town.

As regards the cereals, which form the staple of a dog's diet, the changes must be often rung on wheat-meal, oat-meal, and rice. Barley-meal and Indian-meal I do not like. The former is too heating; while the latter,

## KENNEL MANAGEMENT

besides possessing the same fault, causes accumulations of fat in the inside. I will back a course of feeding on Indian-meal to infect any kennel with the mange, unless strong corrective treatment be simultaneously employed: it is false economy to make use of it for dogs.

Wheat-meal and oat-meal are very wholesome, but care must be taken that they be sufficiently cooked. They should be boiled for about an hour, being stirred frequently all the time, and afterwards they should be poured into large shallow pans to cool. When the pudding is properly made, it will stiffen as it becomes cool, so that you can cut it with a knife, and none of it will stick to the sides of the pan.

Rice, also, should be boiled for an hour, as it is very hurtful unless thoroughly softened. It is a capital change during the summer, but it had better not be given to young puppies, as it is traditionally supposed to produce rickets in them. The pudding, in cool weather, need only be boiled twice a week, but during summer it must be freshly made every other day, or it will turn sour.

Then there are the various kinds of manufactured biscuits—Liverine, Carta Carna, Spratt's, &c.—each one of them valuable for a change, but more expensive and less nutritious than plain home-made food. I am well aware that many servants nowadays favour these artificial foods, as a saving of trouble to themselves; but neither man nor dog can be well nourished on the products of a factory alone, although the mischievous system of percentage may blind the eyes of some kennelmen to the fact.

Tallow-greaves, well boiled, are useful for giving savour to the pudding when the meat supply is short, as dogs are fond of them.

Vegetables in some form are necessary for the health of the domestic dog, and nearly all of them

## THE POINTER

agree with him. Cabbage, spinach, nettles, onions, beetroot, carrots, Jerusalem artichokes, mangel-wurzels, and potatoes are excellent for the purpose, and doubtless besides these many others that I have not tried. The mangel, however, excels all others in usefulness, being in season at a time (after Christmas) when garden stuff is scarce; it is a famous purifier of the blood, and dogs eat it with gusto. Roots and tubers should be thoroughly washed and trimmed before being introduced into the meat-caldron, where all kinds of vegetables should be boiled until soft enough to be pulped and mixed with the other food.

Let your dogs dine every day off a compound of the following ingredients :—One-half of cold pudding, made as I have just described ; one-quarter of hot meat, with its broth, cooked till it leaves the bones readily ; one-quarter of vegetables, boiled and pulped. But, of course, the proportions must be varied according to the season of the year, the amount of work being done, and the appetite and general condition of the animals themselves. And you can with advantage add occasionally one or other of such appetizers as greaves, kitchen scraps, skim-milk, treacle, and salt herrings. And writing of these last reminds me that, though most of the authorities have denounced salt as injurious to dogs and all flesh-eating animals, I have never found anything but good result in my kennel from its moderate use, both as a seasoning and a medicine.

I cannot conclude this dissertation on the feeding of pointers without introducing some very apposite remarks on the subject by Oakleigh, who seems to have been master of the minutest details in all that concerns the world of sport.

'The best regular food for the sporting dog is oatmeal, well boiled, and flesh, which may be either

## KENNEL MANAGEMENT

boiled with the meal or given raw. In hot weather, dogs should not have either oatmeal or flesh in a raw state, as they are heating. Potatoes, boiled, are a good summer food, and an excellent occasional variety in winter, but they should be cleaned before being boiled and *well dried* after, or they will produce disease. Roasted potatoes are equally good, if not better. The best food to bring dogs into condition, and to preserve their wind in hot weather, is sago, boiled to a jelly, half a pound of which may be given to each dog daily, in addition to potatoes or other light food, a little flesh meat or a few bones being allowed every alternate day. Dogs should have whey or butter-milk two or three times a week, during summer, when it can be procured, or, in lieu thereof, should have a tablespoonful of flower-of-sulphur once a fortnight. To bring a dog into condition for the season, we would give him a very large tablespoonful of sulphur about a fortnight before the 12th August, and two days after giving him that, a full tablespoonful of syrup of buckthorn should be administered, and afterwards twice repeated at intervals of three days, the dog being fed on the sago diet the while. There should always be fresh water within reach' (*Shooter's Handbook*, p. 102).

These hints for bringing a dog into working condition are simple to follow and very valuable, either as they stand, or modified according to each one's notions.

It must not be inferred from the rarity of quotations in this chapter, that in my researches I have found no valuable works on the housing and feeding of dogs. For, from the earliest times and in all languages, such treatises abound; in fact, they really take up an almost disproportionate space in canine literature. But, undiluted, they seem a wee bit out of date, not exactly suitable to the present day; so I

# THE POINTER

think that it is better on such subjects to give my own experience in my own language.

Having finished my description of suitable housing and feeding, I will consider the rest of the treatment requisite for the preservation of pointers in perfect health and condition, a state that is always denoted by the peculiar mellowness of their coats—a sort of creamy gloss—which is unmistakable.

Proper food and proper accommodation will not give the desired results without being supplemented by *cleanliness, exercise, and attention.*

The inner surface of the entire kennels must be whitewashed with lime and water, as a matter of routine, every August when the dogs are away, with, of course, additional lime-washings after any outbreak of disease.

Beds should be scrubbed once a week in summer, although once a month will suffice in winter, for fear of damp. Fine wheat straw is the best bedding for winter and at most seasons: it should be changed every three days. In the height of summer, however, the bare boards are more comfortable. A supply of sawdust is very useful about a kennel; but peat-moss I do not like, as it stains the coats and soon becomes verminous. Condy's Fluid, Sanitas, or some similar disinfectant, should be freely sprinkled, especially in hot weather.

The iron caldrons, the food-troughs, and the water-vessels should be thoroughly cleaned twice a week in winter, and every other day in summer.

The floors of the kennels should be swilled down every day, and at all times the kennelman should keep a spade and bucket handy, to remove any excrement he may see in the yards.

Perfect dryness and freedom from draughts, with a fair amount of warmth, are essential to the well-being

## KENNEL MANAGEMENT

of pointers. But let this warmth result from substantially-built kennels and dry bedding, rather than from artificial heat. In England, stoves and hot-pipes are unnecessary, and even injurious, as indeed are all coddling contrivances for healthy dogs; though the small portable stoves of the Atmospheric Churn Company, 119 New Bond Street, and some large oil-lamps, are useful in kennels for heating purposes, when there are invalids, or bitches pupping in winter.

The kennelman should commence operations at six o'clock in the summer and at seven in winter, and he should get his kennels clean and in order before breakfast. While he works, he should let all the dogs into the paddock, but *at no time* should he go away, even for a moment, leaving the dogs by themselves, loose in the paddock.

After his breakfast he should take his charges for the daily run, which should be, as a rule, two hours with the bicycle at a rate not exceeding eight miles an hour. When the weather is unfit for this form of exercise, the dogs should be walked, in coupling-chains to check their getting into mischief at the slower pace. About four o'clock they should have dinner, and, immediately after this, half an hour's saunter about the paddock. And if, the last thing at night, they are again let into the paddock for ten minutes, no doubt the man will find his labours lightened in the morning.

A fortnight before going to Scotland the daily exercise should become rather more rigorous—longer hours, longer distances, at a slightly increased pace. On their return from a day's work on the moor, after a brisk rub-down and a foot-bath of salt and water, the dogs should be promptly served with a supper both hot and tempting. Be sure also to exercise them well the day after hard or wet work, otherwise their limbs will stiffen. Even at your shooting-lodge, do not put

# THE POINTER

more than five in one kennel; and at home, when comparatively idle, the number ought never to exceed four, otherwise casual disputes may easily have a tragic termination.

There is nothing more crippling to the suppleness of a pointer, or more detrimental to his temper, than to chain him up; and you will promote his health if you can prevent his requiring much washing. By your strict attention to the cleanliness of his surroundings, he will, as a rule, keep himself all right, and the pointer in a state of nature is the most healthy, as well as the most beautiful. The latter is a reason for not washing him before a show, as in the ablutionary process he is robbed of his glossy bloom, and a dead bluish-white is substituted. But, though washing is obviously unavoidable sometimes, the chalking of his coat for the show-ring is downright faking—it ought to be punished accordingly. Indeed, healthy beings, whether ladies or dogs, require no powdering; and so if you bestow on a hearty dog two or three rubbings with the bare hand, to bring up his muscle and remove any dead hairs that may be clinging to him, he will be at his best.

If vermin, such as fleas, lice, ticks, &c., have to be got rid of, plunge the dog into some sheep-dipping compound (Cooper's will do or Jeyes' Fluid diluted), but be careful to keep his mouth and nose out of the liquid, as it is poisonous.

The intimate connection of nose and ear makes it imperative that the latter be kept clean, and free from wax and offensive matter, if only for the preservation of the scenting powers. Once a week all pointers should have their ears sponged out with tepid water, carefully dried, and a little canker-lotion introduced as a preventive: at the same time, they should also have their nails trimmed and examined.

# KENNEL MANAGEMENT

In your kennel passage you can keep the necessary appliances, such as chains, couples, collars, leads, and muzzles. Of these last, besides the ordinary stock, you should have a surgical one to prevent a dog from biting at a sore: it is something like a horse's muzzle, being a rigid, leathern cylinder with air-holes. Others that are useful are to prevent the puppies, when led by a boy and waiting their turn at breaking-time, from snuffling on the ground out of pure impatience and so laying the foundations of a fatal trick. These must be spoon-shaped, of very stiff, zinc-bound leather, projecting about two inches beyond the nose, and well turned up at the end. They lie under the jaws, are kept there by straps above the 'spoon,' and are connected with the neck in the ordinary manner. There must also be a supply of sheets, which are light, waterproof rugs to protect the body, when the dogs are waiting about in rough weather; a measuring stick for ascertaining heights at shoulder; a weighing machine; and half-a-dozen kennel coats for visitors. The travelling hampers of various sizes had better be made with gabled tops, so that during journeys other boxes cannot be piled on the top of them; and instead of willow, which is to dogs a palatable dainty, they should be made of bamboo, which is by no means so inviting for a nibble.

And now for a few words about a very important operation in most kennels—the production and rearing of the puppies.

I have found that old sires beget just as vigorous stock as young ones, though it is preferable for the dam to be in her prime. But do not suffer any bitch to have pups until she has been shot over for one season, not only because of the fatuity of blindfold breeding, but also because, until habits of work become fixed in her, motherhood will generally leave her lazy

## THE POINTER

and soft for evermore. I am supported in this by Columella who wrote, nearly 2000 years ago, that if you allow dogs to breed before they are a year old, ' it eats away their bodily vigour, and causes their mind to degenerate ' (*De Re Rusticâ*, book vii. chap. xii.).

Mate your breeding animals any time when the female is thoroughly in earnest. But if she be a doubtful breeder, or if the dog be old, keep the pair of them without food for twelve hours, and let each have a run for a quarter of an hour, before the union takes place. Tardif, also, counsels that ' both dog and bitch be made to fast the day before ' (*Chiens de Chasse*, 1492, p. 8).

Bitches often fail to breed from an acidity of the uterine membranes, which is fatal to the spermatozoa of the male. It is advisable, therefore, to give the doubtful breeders a vaginal injection of one-quarter ounce bicarbonate of potash in half a pint of warm water, half an hour before coition.

When the impregnated bitch is fit to be released from her necessary seclusion, she may be exercised with the others as usual, till half her sixty-three days of gestation are accomplished; after which she must be gradually restricted to a slower pace, and finally to wanderings about at her own will. She ought not to be exposed to the chance of shocks and collisions with the flying yearlings, and on the fiftieth day, at the very latest, she must move into her pupping quarters. For the rest of her pregnancy, she is to be given a teaspoonful of castor oil twice a week; and she is to be allowed to pup on a wooden bed with sides of at least four inches. The pupping bed should be prepared as follows: first a layer of carefully spread hay, then a piece of sacking or old carpet, nailed to the wooden sides, then more hay. This is the only occasion on which I advocate the use of hay, as it is apt to breed

## KENNEL MANAGEMENT

vermin; but it is necessary for new-born pups, as straw is much too hard and rough, and peat-moss gets into their throats and lungs.

If there be no sign of the bitch pupping on the proper day, do not be disturbed; for as long as she seem tranquil, all is well—even for a week. Avoid giving either sedatives on the one hand, or abortifacients on the other; but if any abnormal symptoms appear, at once send for the Vet., unless you have some trustworthy surgical talent nearer home.

Let some one watch over the pupping bitch, and sit up with her for the two succeeding nights, till the youngsters grow strong, as, if they are worth breeding at all, they are worth taking pains about. Hundreds of puppies are sacrificed yearly—some frozen, others flattened to death — during those two momentous nights.

If the blood be very precious, you will try to arrange for a foster-mother to be in readiness for any supernumeraries; but, for different reasons, you may find yourself obliged to select from the new-born litter, as it is fatal to the well-being of the pups to leave more than six of them on the mother. In such a case, I preserve those with the longest necks, the biggest heads, and the finest tails. The methods that have come down from classical times, of choosing the heaviest and, when a little older, the last to commence to see, are quite intelligible, as these are, of course, the best nourished and strongest of the new-born family; but it is more difficult to accept as an axiom that the mother will carry the best one back to her bed before the others, since the owner and she may look at her offspring from an entirely different point of view! There is, however, another old-fashioned plan for which I have a great respect, though I have never yet absolutely verified it from experience: it is to hold up

# THE POINTER

the new-born pointer puppy by the tail, and the farther back he stretches his forelegs behind his ears, the better shoulders he will have by-and-by. Certainly puppies under this treatment differ considerably in their powers.

Remember that any medicine given to the bitch while suckling will also affect her family, and that if one of them have a sore navel, you can cure it by rubbing on a little turpentine twice daily.

When the whelps commence to run about, they should have their noses dipped daily into a saucer of warm milk thickened with 'plasmon,' as, if their mother cannot give them a bellyful, they will soon commence to lap. The addition of ' plasmon ' to the milk enables them to receive sufficient nourishment without undue distension—recent analysis having shown that the milk of the bitch is about three times richer than that of the cow. This enrichment of the milk should be continued for a full fortnight after weaning-time. Dose them with small pills of worm powder at weaning-time (about six weeks after birth), and continue this treatment regularly once a fortnight, whether they appear to want it or not. If the bitch when weaned have her milk still upon her, it must be drawn from her by hand once a day, and her udder must be rubbed afterwards with vinegar (or brandy) and sweet oil in equal proportions. A teaspoonful of bicarbonate of soda in a wineglass of water is another excellent lotion with which to bathe swollen and tender udders.

I cannot do better than reproduce the following useful remarks on feeding :—

' Puppies should be fed at regular hours four times a day, with the same food (milk or broth, thickened with flour or fine meal) as was given them before weaning, gradually adding a little cooked meat as they grow. In three or four months they will eat the same food as grown dogs, but they require to be fed three

## KENNEL MANAGEMENT

times a day till they are six months old, and twice a day until they are a year old' (*House Dogs and Sporting Dogs*, by Meyrick, 1861, p. 130).

If the weather be mild and bright, the bitch, when her whelps are a fortnight old, can be promoted to a wooden kennel on wheels, with one side detachable, placed on some sunny grass-plot. This position is of the utmost importance, because the younger the puppy the more gristly the limbs, and the more incapable of supporting much weight; and if this immature bone have to stand as a pillar between a heavy body and a hard, unyielding floor, it will very soon become twisted and warped. As Lascelles says :—' His feet pressing nothing but turf will more effectually assist his growth, and remove the apprehension of disproportioned or distorted limbs' (*Angling, Shooting, &c.*, 1811, p. 142).

To assist in keeping the legs of the puppies straight be sure at first to put a hassock of turf at the entrance of the kennel, so that they can trot out and in again without any climbing; and instead of their being lifted up by their forelegs, insist on the skin at the back of the neck being made use of for this purpose. But frequently the puppies are born too early in the year to admit of their being planted out immediately; for the benefit of such, therefore, cover the floors of some of the bitch-kennels with what is known as cork carpet, which, when cemented down and given three coats of paint and varnish, makes a tolerable substitute for the springiness of turf, and can be swilled down in the same manner as the concrete. Treading on this, with an occasional sniff of fresh air at mid-day, when the upper half of their door is thrown open, the early pups contrive to escape malformations till they are liberated by the arrival of spring weather.

At one time I used to put my pointer puppies out to walk at the neighbouring farmhouses, but I found

## THE POINTER

that their health often, and their behaviour always, suffered for it. So I constructed some small paddocks at a distance from the kennels, and since then I have had all my young ones brought up at home. I find that, so reared, they are bolder and more obedient, and that, when breaking-time comes round, one has to deal with minds unversed in iniquity.

In their play-grounds it is beneficial to put some lumps of old building-lime that have been tempered by time and weather. The puppies in crunching them eat a good deal of the lime, which promotes bone.

In treating of diseases, the last branch of this subject, I dare say I shall shock many readers by my Spartan point of view ; but if by constant ransackings of the Pharmacopœia, you do manage to prolong the life of some weakling, building up for him a sham constitution with tonics and what not, you are really doing a disservice to the breed in general. You may have succeeded in a clever bit of doctoring, you may even have saved a star for the show-ring, but at the same time you have added one more to the radically unfit, and you have provided another agent for the multiplication of tainted stock. In breeding dogs we must learn of Nature, accept her law of the survival of the fittest, and not try to upset her order with our drugs ; thus the clever breeder will succeed, not by flying in her face, but by quietly following in her footsteps ; for he knows that a sure way to ruin his kennel will be to introduce the blood of these fascinating wastrels. If, after having been reared with all care, a dog remain sickly, by all means destroy him, he is a danger to the breed. I have been often amazed, in glancing at the agony columns of the doggy papers, to read anxious inquiries how, for instance, to prolong the pains of chronic disorders of the stomach, or how to keep life flickering in hydrocephalous monsters.

## KENNEL MANAGEMENT

But though I have neither the power nor the wish to prescribe for inveterate maladies, I will try to recount those acute disorders that are curable, together with remedial treatments that I have myself tested. In this veterinary essay, I do not attempt to be scientific—only practical and helpful.

*The Distemper*, although the most common, is also the most mysterious of diseases. Though highly infectious, it is thought to be incapable of spontaneous generation. It attacks head, lungs, bowels, and nerves, but it seldom assails two of these simultaneously with equal violence. Its very name is generic aud vague, simply meaning *the* disease, while in French, similarly, it is called '*la maladie*,' and so far it has practically evaded the diagnosis of the Faculty.

Concerning its origin, T. Watson, writing in 1785, says: 'The Distemper.—This has not been known in England above twenty-six years' (*Instructions, &c.*, p. 116), which is confirmed by Colonel Thornton's 'The distemper in dogs has not been known much more than forty years. It appeared in France for the first time in 1763; it began in England and spread all over Europe' (*Sporting Tour in France*, 1806, p. 244).

And yet in nearly 140 years no one has found a specific for this scourge, though I, among many others, have tried every well-attested ancient recipe, and every well-advertised modern nostrum (including inoculation threads) in the hope of discovering one.

At length, however, I have learned that the best way to fight it is by discarding all quackeries and by relying mainly on an even temperature and good nursing. The distemper must be taken at its commencement to make sure of saving the dog, which must be shut into a room free from draught and of an absolutely even temperature day and night. The temperature had better be about 60° Fahrenheit, but

## THE POINTER

whether hotter (in summer) or a little cooler, it must not vary in the least. Dogs kept in cottages generally succumb, from lying by day close to the fire and getting chilled at night without it.

As a rule the first symptom of distemper in a dog is a cough, attended by running at eyes or nose ; there is also a characteristic smell about the sufferer. On the first suspicion, give the dog a pill of one grain of Calomel and two of Tartar Emetic, which you may afterwards continue every other morning ; and at once relegate him to the hospital. If his nostrils be much affected, sponge them occasionally with vinegar or any antiseptic, diluted with warm water. The hospital, too, must be dusted constantly with disinfectants, and, of course, must be kept as clean as practicable without the use of water. The patient, as long as there is much fever, must be fed principally on milk, to be advanced to broth, and eventually to solids as soon as his temperature will allow. If he will not take nourishment, he must be promptly drenched with it before he loses his strength. If he be weak, he must have eggs beaten up ; if very weak, some brandy or port must be added to them. If the bowels be too loose, arrowroot boiled in milk is useful, but if bad diarrhœa have to be stopped, give twenty drops of Chlorodyne in a teaspoonful of brandy and water, the dose to be repeated and increased if necessary.

The patient must not be let out of hospital on any pretence, till he have entirely lost his cough and his temperature be normal. A dog's blood is normal at from 100° to 101° Fahrenheit, and it can be tested by the insertion of a clinical thermometer in his rectum, for four minutes. These veterinary thermometers are bought from Arnold & Co., 26 Smithfield West, London, E.C.

When the distemper has reached the head, as evi-

## KENNEL MANAGEMENT

denced by the dog having fits, there is but little chance of saving him; still, I should try a blister at the back of the head, or a leech inside the ear as a forlorn hope. This terrible development, however, is fortunately rare, except in cases of the virulent distemper contracted at Shows; and a rule should be made never to exhibit dogs till they have had this disease normally at home. If chorœa, or St. Vitus's dance, supervene to the distemper, the dog will never become quite sound again; but as it is not hereditary, if reasons be sufficiently cogent, a twitching dog can be kept to breed from, though he will be a perpetual eyesore among your team.

*The Yellows*, or *Jaundice*, is usually caused by a chill on the liver, often caught during an attack of distemper that from its mildness is unsuspected, though sometimes it is induced by eating tainted flesh: it is one of the most dangerous of canine complaints. Its first symptoms are the listlessness of the dog, combined with an offensive breath, and a buff tinge on the inside of the lips, which quickly intensifies into a vivid yellow and spreads to the palate, eyes, and external skin. It is a rare disease among well-cared-for dogs, and I cannot lay claim to much experience as regards the efficacy of the following recipes, though the only severe case that I did cure was treated with the first of them. The second and third I have not yet had opportunity to try: they are variants of the same idea, and come with first-rate credentials from sources distinct and trustworthy.

No. 1.—Put one good handful of Barberry Bark into a quart of strong ale, boiling. Administer three tablespoonfuls three times a day, adding a teaspoonful of Sweet Nitre to each dose.

No. 2.—Castile Soap, 2 drachms; Oil of Turpentine, 30 drops; Oil of Carraway, 20 drops; Calomel,

## THE POINTER

15 grains; Powdered Rhubarb, 40 grains; Aromatic Confection, 1 drachm.

No. 3.—Castile Soap, 6 drachms; Oil of Juniper, 20 drops; Prepared Calomel, 12 grains; Powdered Rhubarb, 2 scruples; Aromatic Powder, 1 drachm.

Both the above prescriptions enjoin a thorough mixing of the ingredients, and then ultimate division into six pills, one of which is to be given for six mornings, followed at an interval of two hours by a teaspoonful of Castor Oil.

The general nursing for the yellows should be the same as for the distemper.

*Pneumonia, or Inflammation of the Lungs*, may be detected from the rapid and difficult breathing, which sounds rough and harsh to your ear placed against the side of the patient. It is always accompanied by a high temperature. This attack is brought on by taking cold; but the dog may generally be saved by rubbing well into the chest, and behind the shoulder, a strong mixture of turpentine and mustard, and by, every hour, administering in a little water alternate doses of four drops of Aconite, of the ordinary or second strength (if of the 'mother tincture,' only two drops), and a blend of ten drops of Ipecacuanha Wine and ten drops of Paregoric. It is imperative that not a single dose shall be missed until the breathing is easier and the temperature on the decline. The general nursing for pneumonia must be the same as for the distemper.

*Influenza*, which is indicated by drowsiness with a very high temperature, attended by a cough, must be nursed with every precaution, as the least chill will induce pneumonia itself. It can be treated, while acute, with ten-grain doses of Salicine every three hours, preceded by a dessertspoonful of Castor Oil at the commencement of the attack. The dog must be

## KENNEL MANAGEMENT

kept in hospital till his temperature has subsided, and all his morbid symptoms have disappeared.

*Kennel-lameness*, a distressing complaint analogous to rheumatism, cripples and stiffens all the limbs, and renders the body tender to the touch. People say that it is promoted by the nature of some soils; but I think that dry kennels, attention on their return from work, and plenty of regular exercise, will prevent dogs, in most places, from becoming its victims.

Give the sufferer, before food in the morning, a red-herring with two drachms of Nitre rubbed into it, and feed him two hours afterwards. In the evening, give him one drachm of Camphor, made into a ball. This treatment, repeated every three days and combined with plenty of slow exercise (enforced, if necessary), will restore any ordinary case to comparative soundness, but I have never yet seen a dog recover altogether his suppleness and dash.

*Worms.*—These mischievous parasites are the bane of a sporting dog's existence, and there is no method of preventing them, except by the periodical administration of a vermifuge. Their presence is suggested by a great variety of signs—thinness, want of appetite, voracity, fits, lassitude, a dazed expression, a rough coat with no nature in it, scraping the hindquarters along the ground, and many others. In fact, when you are puzzled by strange symptoms in a dog, if you give him a smart dose of worm medicine, ten to one the mystery will be solved.

These parasitic worms are of several kinds, but I need hardly enumerate them, as the old-fashioned medicines—areca nut and turpentine—will usually expel them all, without exception. I have heard it said that these remedies are hurtful to the dog, but they have never harmed any of mine, though all take them regularly; and they are the most efficient vermifuges

# THE POINTER

to my thinking, though variety is beneficial to dogs — in drugs as in everything. If you are giving the former, have the nuts freshly grated, and use a little water to knead the powder into a big bolus. Then push down the throat of the full-grown pointers, which have fasted for twenty-four hours, a piece the size of a sparrow's egg; while a morsel of the size of a pea, and a fast of four hours, will be enough for newly-weaned puppies. Give them a little Castor Oil about two hours afterwards, and, as long as may be necessary, repeat the treatment every five days. If turpentine be employed, a dessertspoonful is the full dose with a raw egg afterwards: be sure to administer turpentine in capsules, as otherwise it is apt to choke a dog. It is a good plan to alternate the two medicines.

While on the subject of giving medicine to a dog, let me suggest that, to gain safety and efficiency, you should, while opening his mouth, insert a portion of his lip between his upper teeth and your fingers, so that if he closed his jaws, or indeed struggled, he would be paining himself.

*Fits* sometimes proceed from over-exertion in an unprepared state. In this case you must give a teaspoonful of Epsom Salts every other day, with gradually increasing exercise and a sparing diet. Read the remarks on parasitic worms and distemper, in order to doctor fits that occur in connection with those causes.

*Diarrhœa* it is unadvisable to check, unless it is symptomatic of other and more grave disorders, as it is generally an effort of nature to throw off something injurious. Still if it persist and weaken the dog, a thirty-drop dose of Essence of Ginger or a like amount of Chlorodyne, in a little water, will usually give immediate relief; the dose to be repeated, if necessary, at three-hour intervals. Feed on arrowroot with boiled milk.

# KENNEL MANAGEMENT

*Mange.*—Skin-diseases, like worms, are of several varieties. But as, with the exception of the *follicular* variety which is regarded as practically incurable, all the skin-diseases, like all the worms, can be conquered by the same remedies, I shall, to be strictly practical, lump them all together under the term *Mange*. I am told that some breeds suffer from congenital eczema, but pointers are happily exempt from such a scourge ; and they will continue so, as long as incurably mangy specimens, when such occur, are put out of their misery.

I believe this formula for the extermination of mange to be almost a specific : it was one of my father's—old-fashioned, but deadly to all kinds of skin troubles. In its preparation, care should be taken to observe the proportions exactly, as Hellebore is not a drug to be measured by rule of thumb.

Mix together thoroughly one point of Train-oil, two ounces of Black Sulphur, and half an ounce of Hellebore ; to these add two tablespoonfuls of Turpentine. Shake this dressing before use, and rub it well into the skin of the dogs all over, while they are fasting. Wash it off at the end of three days, and repeat the treatment, if necessary, once a week. The above amount of the dressing is sufficient for three applications. The evening before give each dog a pill containing two grains of Calomel and two grains of Jalap. A variant of the foregoing, perhaps preferable as never staining the coat, is to mix Turpentine and Train-oil in equal parts, thickening with Yellow-sulphur to the consistency of thick gruel. Virulent mange is benefited by a varied treatment, so that an occasional rubbing with such excellent dressings as Mr. Peter Return's and Mr. Campkin's will accelerate the cure.

But as mange, in bad cases, is often connected with disordered blood, it should be attacked simultaneously

## THE POINTER

from the inside, with such alteratives and purgatives as Flowers of Sulphur, Sarsaparilla, Epsom Salts, or the blood mixture supplied by Messrs. Freeman (City Road, Birmingham); and during this treatment, the food of the dog must consist mainly of vegetables and such-like cooling fare.

The Yellow-sulphur preparation, in addition to its therapeutic qualities, is also invaluable as a preventive. For when a dog's coat is out of bloom, when he scratches a little, when he has fiery stains at the armpits, on the belly or between the toes, you must, according to the gravity of the signs, either dress him all over or touch up the suspicious places with the mixture. And, clean or foul, it will be well to dress and purge him completely, at least twice a year, in the spring and again on his return from the moors.

*Canker of the Ear* is another effect arising from over-heated blood: its two varieties, internal and external, require different treatments.

*Internal* canker is shown by the dog shaking his head slightly, holding his head on one side, and scratching the root of his ear; while a closer inspection reveals an offensive smell from the ear, and a dark-coloured deposit therein. After having thoroughly cleansed the ear from this with warm water, thoroughly dry it, and then work well into the head some canker lotion, to be procured from Mr. Campkin, chemist, 11 Rose Crescent, Cambridge. This will infallibly cure the dog in a few days, if you continue to wash, and afterwards to saturate, the root of the ear daily. Medicine and diet must be similar to those prescribed in the cure of the mange.

But though internal canker yields so readily to treatment, the *external* variety is much more difficult; in fact, where the disease is of old standing, it is almost incurable. Usually it first attacks the ear-tips, which become very hot and sore, lose their hair, and are shaken by the dog so violently that they bleed. The canker, if unchecked, soon eats away parts of the edge, giving it a tattered appearance, and finally the whole ear will become swollen and infected. Taken in an early stage, it can be cured by clearing off the scabs and applying bluestone, and afterwards anointing several times with Green Iodide of Mercury. Later on, when there is much shaking of the head, the ears will have to be confined in a cap, in addition to the foregoing treatment. If the ear be much swollen, setons of tow, fresh every day, will give relief.

*Affections of the Eyes.*—In cases of weakness, when there is a collection of mucus in the corners of the eye, with or without soreness of the lids externally, apply several times a day the following lotion : half-an-ounce of Goulard's Extract, eight ounces of distilled water. Boracic Acid lotion also is excellent to apply to suchlike inflammations. This weakness is often found after distemper.

When a film spreads over the eye, apply twice daily, with a camel's-hair brush, an ointment composed of one grain of yellow Oxide of Mercury and one drachm of Lanoline. If the case be obstinate, place once a week, in the outside corner of the eye, a few drops of a lotion made up of a quarter of a grain of Nitrate of Silver and one ounce of distilled water, and anoint as before with the ointment on the intermediate days.

*Sprains*, canine as well as human, must be reduced by fomentations, by cold-water bandaging, and by rubbing-in an embrocation like Elliman's or Veterinary Homocea.

*Wounds* should be at once washed with a lotion composed of one teaspoonful of Carbolic Acid and one pint of boiled water, and afterwards they should be covered by a piece of lint, thickly spread with Boracic

## THE POINTER

Acid ointment and secured in place by a bandage. It is well to keep a supply of flesh-needles and silk, suitable for putting in a stitch or two, if necessary.

Pointer puppies, especially if very purely bred, are rather subject to a swelling and inflammation of the occipital bone. It is often sore to the touch, and I have even known it to gather. It must not be interfered with, and it will gradually disappear, or be absorbed, as the head grows larger. I do not know the cause of it; but only the intelligent ones are so affected.

When it is necessary to disinfect in your kennels, the following will be found an effectual mode :—

Wash the floors, walls, and especially wooden beds, with a solution of Corrosive Sublimate (one in two thousand). After this washing has been completed, close up every nook and crevice in the place : paste paper over the cracks in the door, or stuff cotton-wool tightly into them. Then take a quarter pound of Flowers of Sulphur, put it, all of a heap, into an iron pan, and set fire to it by putting live coals on the pan. Keep the doors tightly closed for twelve hours, and afterwards whitewash or limewash the place.

When a dog is convalescent after an illness, a capital tonic for him is formed by one ounce of Phosphate of Iron, three ounces of Phosphate of Lime, four ounces of Glycerine, one quart of water. Dose : One table-spoonful, with one dessertspoonful of Cod-liver Oil, twice daily.

Cod-liver Oil is always useful amongst the puppies, and Parrish's Chemical Food can be given in conjunction with it to the delicate ; Benbow's Mixture, also, is a good tonic. But the quickest of all pick-me-ups for dogs of any age and size, I have found to be 'Dr. Williams's Pink Pills for Pale People,' and tabloids of Easton's Syrup.

As aperients, Castor Oil and Epsom Salts are both

# KENNEL MANAGEMENT

needed ; the former is more mild and suitable to give in conjunction with other medicines during illness, but it has an ultimate reaction towards constipation ; the latter is more irritating and abrupt, but it exercises a beneficial action on the blood and is preferable as a purgative for a robust dog. A little Salad Oil to follow, is very soothing to the bowels. Beecham's Pills, also, are efficacious, and from their portability they are very convenient in Scotland, the climate of which necessitates the frequent use of a medicine of this nature.

Sweet Spirit of Nitre is invaluable in cases of suppression of urine, as it immediately increases the action of the kidneys. It is a harmless drug, and is indeed an active power of good in most other illnesses. The dose varies from ten drops for a young puppy to one teaspoonful for an adult pointer, and it can be administered either by itself in water, or allied with similar amounts of Castor Oil and Syrup of Buckthorn.

Friar's Balsam is useful externally for healing wounds, as dogs will not lick it. Carbolic, Condy, Jeyes, Izal, and Sanitas, are all excellent as antiseptics and disinfectants.

Most drugs have a precisely similar effect on dogs as on human beings, and this facilitates doctoring in the kennel. The only exception that I remember is phosphorus, which I have found dangerous to dogs, as it produces very bad fits.

I have only attempted to describe the ordinary illnesses of dogs ; but even of these, as I said before, you can ward off the greater part by promoting healthy conditions in your kennels, and by keeping only healthy stock.

# LIST OF BOOKS

## CONSULTED FOR THIS WORK, ARRANGED CHRONOLOGICALLY & IN SECTIONS.

### CLASSICAL.

*Cynegeticon*, by Xenophon. B.C. 445–360.
*Peri Zoon* (*De Naturâ Animalium*), by Aristotle. B.C. 384–323.
*Cynegeticon, de Aucupio Fragmenta duo*, by Marcus Aurelius Olympius Nemesianus. About B.C. 283.
*De Re Rusticâ*, by Marcus Terentius Varro. B.C. 116–28.
*De Conjuratione Catilinæ, De Bello Jugurthino*, by Caius Sallustius Crispus. B.C. 86–34.
*Historiæ Naturalis Libri XXXVII.*, by Caius Secundus Plinius. Died A.D. 23.
*Historiæ*, by Publius Cornelius Tacitus. 1st century.
*De Duodecim Cæsaribus*, by Caius Tranquillus Suetonius. 1st century.
*Panegyricus Trajano dictus*, by Cæcilius Caius Secundus Plinius. 1st century.
*Cynegeticon*, by Gratius Faliscus. 1st century.
*De Re Rusticâ*, by Lucius Junius Moderatus Columella. A.D. 50.
*Cynegeticus*, by Flavius Arrianus. 2nd century.
*Cynegetica*, by Oppianus. 2nd century.
*Onomastikon*, by Julius Pollux. 2nd century.
*De Naturâ Animalium* (*Peri Zoon*), by Claudius Ælianus Prænestinus. 3rd century.
*Ars Veterinaria*, by Vegetius Renatus Publius. 4th century.
*De Re Rusticâ*, by Rutilius Taurus Æmilianus Palladius. A.D. 371–395.

# THE POINTER

### English.

*Le Art de Venerie*, by Guyllame Twici (ex MSS. Phillipps, No. 8336. Printed 1840). 1307–1327.
*Sir Gawayne and the Green Knight.* A Romance Poem. 1320–1340.
*The Maister of the Game* (MS.), by Edmund de Langley (Duke of York). 1341–1402.
*De proprietatibus rerum*, by Bartholomeus de Glanvilla. About 1360.
*Boke of St. Albans*, by Dame Juliana Bernes. 1486.
*Toxophilus*, by Roger Ascham. 1545.
*De Differentiis Animalium*, by Edward Wotton. 1551.
*The Booke of Falconrie or Hawking*, by George Turberville. 1575.
*Englische Dogges*, by Dr. John Caius of Cambridge. 1576.
*Hawking, Hunting, Fishing.* (Anon.) 1586.
*Britannia*, by W. Camden. 1586.
*Hunger's Prevention*, by Gervase Markham. 1620.
*The Anatomy of Melancholy*, by Robert Burton. 1621.
*Field Sports (Pictures).* (Anon.) 1650.
*Notes on Gratii Falisci Cynegeticon*, by C. Wase. 1654.
*The Countryman's Treasure*, by Jas. Lambert. 1676.
*Exercitationes*, by Walter Charleton. 1677.
*Ornithology*, by Francis Willughby. 1678.
*The Vermin Killer*, by W. W. 1680.
*The Compleat Gentleman*, by Henry Peacham. 1682.
*The School of Recreation*, by R. H. (Robt. Howlitt). 1684.
*The Gentleman's Recreation*, by Nich. Cox. 1686.
*Gentleman's Recreation*, by Richard Bloome. 1686.
*A Collection for Improvement of Husbandry and Trade*, by John Houghton. 1691.
*Synopsis Animalium*, by John Ray, S.R.S. 1693.
*The Whole Art of Husbandry*, by John Mortimer. 1707.
*The Compleat Sportsman*, by Giles Jacob. 1718.
*Athenæ Oxonienses*, by Anthony A'Wood. 1721.

# LIST OF BOOKS

*The Compleat Gamester*, by Richard Seymour. 1729.
*The Gentleman Farrier.* (Anon.) 1732.
*The Sportsman's Dictionary.* (Anon.) 1735.
*The Complete Family Piece.* (Anon.) 1736.
*Field Sports (Poem)*, by W. Somerville. 1742.
*The Complete Sportsman*, by Thos. Fairfax. 1760 (?).
*British Zoology*, by Thos. Pennant. 1766.
*The Art of Shooting Flying*, by T. Page. 1767.
*Pteryplegia (A Poem)*, by — Markland. 1767.
*A Treatise on English Shooting*, by George Edie. 1772.
*Treatise on Field Diversions*, by R. Symonds. 1776.
*The Sportsman's Dictionary.* (Anon.) 1778.
*Instructions for the Management of Horses and Dogs*, by Thos. Watson. 1785.
*Letters and Observations written on a short Tour through France and Italy*, by Peter Beckford. 1786.
*Cynegetica*, by W. Blane. 1788.
*Essay on Shooting.* (Anon.) 1789.
*The Sportsman's Dictionary*, by Henry Jas. Pye. 1790.
*British Quadrupeds*, by Thos. Bewick. 1790.
*The Sporting Magazine.* 1792–1870.
*British Sportsman's Dictionary*, by W. A. Osbaldiston. 1792.
*Travels in France*, by Arthur Young. 1794.
*Cynographia Britannica*, by Sydenham Edwards. 1800.
*General Zoology*, by Geo. Shaw. 1800.
*Cautions to Young Sportsmen*, by Sir Thos. Frankland. 1801.
*Rural Sports*, by Rev. W. B. Daniel. 1801.
*The Sportsman's Cabinet*, by W. Taplin. 1803.
*Sporting Dictionary and Rural Repository*, by W. Taplin. 1803.
*A Sporting Tour through the Northern Parts of England*, by Col. Thornton. 1804.
*Shooting Directory*, by R. B. Thornhill. 1804.
*A Sporting Tour through France*, by Col. Thornton. 1806.

# THE POINTER

*Plates*, by William Howitt. 1806 (?).
*Sports and Pastimes*, by Joseph Strutt. 1807.
*Advice to Sportsmen*, by Marmaduke Markwell. 1809.
*The Art of Improving the Breeds of Domestic Animals*, by Sir J. Sebright. 1809.
*The Complete Sportsman*, by George Morgan. 1810 (?).
*Angling, Shooting, and Coursing*, by Robt. Lascelles. 1811.
*The British Sportsman*, by Samuel Howitt. 1812.
*Kunopædia*, by William Dobson. 1814.
*On Shooting*, by Col. Peter Hawker. 1814.
*To All Sportsmen*, by Col. Geo. Hanger. 1814.
*The Sportsman's Directory*, by John Mayer. 1815.
*Complete Farrier and British Sportsman*, by Richard Lawrence, V.S. (*alias* John Scott). 1816.
*The Complete Sportsman*, by T. H. Needham (*alias* T. B. Johnson). 1817.
*The Shooter's Guide*, by R. Thomas. 1819.
*The Sportsman's Repository*, by Richard Lawrence, V.S. 1820.
*British Field Sports*, by W. H. Scott. 1820.
*Observations on Dog Breaking*, by William Floyd. 1821.
*The Driffield Angler*, by Alexander Mackintosh. 1821.
*National Sports of Great Britain*, by Thos. McLean. 1821.
*The Suffolk Sportsman*, by B. Symonds. 1825.
*Anecdotes*, by Pierce Egan. 1827.
*The Sportsman's Companion.* (Anon.) 1827.
*British Animals*, by John Fleming, D.D. 1828.
*Sportsman's Cyclopædia and Shooter's Companion*, by T. B. Johnson. 1831.
*Arrianus (The Younger Zenophon) on Coursing*, translated by W. Dansey. 1831.
*Hints to Grown Sportsmen*, published by Hatchard. 1832.
*The Field Book*, by W. H. Maxwell. 1832.
*Book of Sports*, by Pierce Egan. 1832.
*Letters from the Earl of Peterborough to General Stanhope in Spain.* 1834.

# LIST OF BOOKS

*The Sportsman*, vol. i. (Anon.) 1835.
*Dictionary of Sports*, by H. Harewood. 1835.
*British Vertebrates*, by Rev. Leonard Jenyns. 1835.
*The Sportsman or Veterinary Recorder.* (Anon.) 1836.
*Observations on Instinct of Animals*, by Sir J. Sebright. 1836.
*British Quadrupeds*, by Thos. Bell. 1837.
*The Shooter's Manual*, by Jas. Tyler. 1837.
*Encyclopædia of Rural Sports*, by D. P. Blaine. 1839.
*Natural History of the Dog*, by D. P. Blaine. 1840.
*The Rod and the Gun*, by Jas. Wilson. 1840.
*Reliquiæ Antiquæ*, by T. Wright and W. Halliwell. 1841–43.
*Shooter's Preceptor*, by T. B. Johnson. 1842.
*The Shooter's Handbook*, by Thos. Oakleigh. 1842.
*The Natural History of Dogs*, by Charles Hamilton Smith. 1843.
*The Sportsman's Library*, by John Mills. 1845.
*History of the Dog*, by W. E. L. Martin. 1845.
*Recreations in Shooting*, by Craven. 1845.
*The Dog*, by Wm. Youatt. 1845.
*The Modern Shooter*, by Captain Lacy. 1846.
*Wild Sports of the Highlands*, by Charles St. John. 1846.
*History of the Romans under the Empire*, by Dean Merivale. 1850.
*The Sportsman and his Dog*, by H. B. Hall. 1850.
*Scottish Sports and Pastimes*, by H. B. Hall. 1850.
*Manual of British Rural Sports*, by Stonehenge. 1858.
*The Dog*, by Stonehenge. 1859.
*The Book of Field Sports*, by H. D. Miles. 1860.
*The Dog Fancier.* (Anon.) 1861.
*House Dogs and Sporting Dogs*, by John Meyrick. 1861.
*The Varieties of Dogs*, by Philibert Charles Berjeau. 1863.
*Researches into the History of the British Dog*, by G. R. Jesse. 1866.
*An English Garner*, by Edward Arber, F.S.A. 1877.

# THE POINTER

*Early Drawings and Illuminations in the British Museum*, by W. de Gray Birch, F.R.S., and H. Jenner. 1879.
*British Dogs*, by Hugh Dalziel. 1879.
*Lex Salica, the ten Texts with the Glosses*, by J. H. Hessels and H. Kern. 1880.
*The Dog*, by Stonehenge. 1881.
*The Dog*, by Idstone. 1882.
*Dog Breaking*, by General Hutchinson. 1882.
*G. Walker's Costumes of Yorkshire in 1812*, by E. Hailstone, A.R.A. 1885.
*The Earl of Peterborough*, by F. S. Russell. 1887.
*Peterborough*, by William Stebbing. 1890.
*Modern Dogs*, by Rawdon Lee. 1896.
*The New English Dictionary*, by Murray. Still incomplete.

### FRENCH.

*Le Roman du Rou*, by Robert Wace (*Maistre*). 12th century.
*La Chanson d'Antioche* (*Chroniques des Croisades*), by Richard le Pèlerin. 13th century.
*Bibliotheca Mundi*, by Vincentius Bellovacensis. 13th century.
*Phébus des deduiz de la Chasse*, by Gaston Phœbus. 1387.
*Les Chiens de Chasse*, by Guillaume Tardif. 1492.
*Le Bon Varlet des Chiens*, by Gaston Phœbus. Published 1507.
*La Chasse de Gaston Phœbus*. (Anon.) 1507.
*Lettres de Catherine de Medicis* (*édition de documents inédits*). 1533–81.
*La Nouvelle Agriculture*, by Pierre de Quinqueran de Beaujeu (Bishop of Senés). 1551.
*La Venerie*, by Jacques du Fouilloux. 1561.
*La Chasse du Loup*, by Jean de Clamorgan. 1576.
*Le Plaisir des Champs*, by Claude Gauchet. 1583.
*Charles Estienne's Maison Rustique, 1564*, translated by Richard Surflet. 1600.

# LIST OF BOOKS

*Histoire Universelle*, by T. A. d'Aubigné. 16th century.
*Liber Legis Salicæ Glossarium*, by F. Lindebrog. 1602.
*La Fauconnerie*, by Charles d'Arcussia. 1605.
*La Maison Champestre*, by Antoine Mizauld. 1607.
*Négociation du Marechal de Bassompierre, Ambassade en Angleterre.* 1626.
*Les Passions de l'Ame*, by René Descartes. 1649.
*La Venerie Royale*, by Robt. de Salnove. 1655.
*Les Ruses Innocentes*, by Francois Fortin. 1660.
*Traitté fort curieux de la Vénerie*, by Francois Antoine Pomey. 1676.
*Le Parfait Chasseur*, by Jacques Espée de Sélincourt. 1683.
*Comptes des Bâtiments de Roi sous Louis XIV.*
*Documents Authentiques et détails curieux sur les dépenses de Louis XIV.*
*Journal du Marquis de Dangeau.* 1684.
*Mélanges historiques et administratifs sous Louis XIV. et Louis XV.* (*Recueil* Canje).
*Mémoires de L. de Rouveroy, Duc de St. Simon.* About 1700.
*Amusemens de la Campagne*, by Louis Liger. 1709.
*Le Ménage de la ville et des champs*, by Louis Liger. 1712.
*Nouveau Traité de Vénerie*, by Antoine Gaffet. 1750.
*Regnum Animale*, by M. J. Brisson. 1756.
*L'Ecole de la Chasse*, by Verrier de la Conterie. 1763.
*Code des Chasses*, by Saugrain. 1765.
*Traité de Vénerie et de Chasse*, by Goury de Champgrand. 1769.
*Quadrupèdes*, by M. le Comte de Buffon. 1777.
*Mammalogie*, by Anselme G. Desmarest. 1782.
*Encyclopædie Méthodique.* (Anon.) 1782–1832.
*La Chasse au Fusil*, by G. F. Magné de Marolles. 1788.
*Traité de Vénerie*, by M. de Yanville. 1788.
*Dictionnaire des Sciences Naturelles*, by Frédéric Cuvier. 1804.

## THE POINTER

*Le Parfait Chasseur*, by Auguste Desgraviers. 1810.
*Traité Général des eaux et des forêts*, by J. J. Baudrillart. 1821.
*Journal des Chasseurs* (French Sporting Magazine). 1836–70.
*La Chasse au viel Grognart*, by M. L. Cimber. 1837.
*Les Anciennes Tapisseries Historiées* by Achille Jubinal. 1838.
*Essai sur l'éducation des animaux*, by A. D. Léonard. 1842.
*Histoire du chien*, by Elzéar Blaze. 1843.
*Le Chasseur au Chien d'arrêt*, by Elzéar Blaze. 1846.
*Dictionnaire des forêts et des chasses*, by Léon Bertrand. 1846.
*L'Esprit des Bêtes*, by Adolphe Toussenel. 1847.
*Captivité de François 1er (D. I. sur l'Histoire de France)*, by M. Aimé Champollion-Figeac. 1847.
*Cyclopædie d'Histoire Naturelle*, by J. C. Chenu. 1850–60.
*Chasseur Rustique*, by C. F. A. d'Houdetot. 1850.
*La Chasse à tir en France*, by Joseph La Vallée. 1854.
*Le Chien*, by Charles Dubourdieu. 1855.
*Vie de la reine Anne de Bretagne*, by Le Roux de Lincy. 1860.
*La Chasse et les Chasseurs*, by Léon Bertrand. 1862.
*Dictionnaire de la Langue française*, by E. Littré. 1863.
*Chasses et Voyages*, by M. Jules de C. (Cabarrus). 1863.
*Histoire physiologique et anecdotique des Chiens*, by Béné Révoil. 1867.
*Du Chien de Chasse*, by Baron de Lage du Chaillou (M. de Cherville). 1867.
*Histoire de la Chasse en France*, by Dunoyer de Noirmont. 1867–8.
*Le Chien*, by Eugène Gayot. 1867.
*Traité pratique du chien*, by A. Gobin. 1867.
*Mœurs, usages, et costumes au Moyen Age*, by P. Lacroix. 1873.

# LIST OF BOOKS

*Los Paramientos de la Caza, ou réglements sur la chasse en général, par Don Sancho le Sage, Roi de Navarre.* Published in 1180, translated by H. Castillon (d'Aspet). 1874.
*Les Chiens de Chasse,* by H. de la Blanchère. 1875.
Sid Mohammed el Mangali. *Traité de Vénerie,* by F. Pharaon. 1880.
*Les Chiens d'arrêt Français et Anglais,* by A. De la Rue. 1881.
*Le Chien,* by Alfred Barbou. 1883.
*Ouvrages sur la Chasse,* by R. Souhart. 1886.
*L'origine et l'évolution intellectuelle du chien d'arrêt,* by C. A. Piétremont. 1886.
*Races des chiens,* by Pierre Mégnin. 1889.

## GERMAN.

*De Animalibus,* by Albertus Magnus (Bishop of Ratisbon). 1193–1280.
*Das Buch der Natur,* by Konrad von Megenberg. 16th century.
*Historiæ Animalium,* by C. Gesner. 1516–87.
*Ein Neuw Thierbuch.* (Anon.) 1569.
*Rei Rusticæ Libri Quatuor,* by Conrad Heresbach. 1570.
*Venatus et Aucupium,* by J. A. Lonicer. 1582.
*Vogelstellen,* by Joh. Conrad Aitinger. 1653.
*Plates by John Elias Riedinger.* Born 1695.
*Jagd und Weidmann's Anmerkungen,* by H. F. von Göchhausen. 1710.
*Der Dianen Hohe und Niedere Jagd Geheimnisse,* by Johann Tänzer. 1734.
*Der vollkommene teutsche Jaeger,* by Hans F. von Fleming. 1749.
*Quadrupedum Dispositis,* by J. F. Klein. 1751.
*Notabilia Venatoris,* by H. F. von Göchhausen. 1751.
*Praktische Abhandlung von dem Leithund,* by Carl von Heppe. 1751.

# THE POINTER

*Der sich-selbst rathende Jäger*, by Carl von Heppe. 1753
*Forst und Jagd Historie der Teutschen*, by H. G. Francken. 1754.
*Der Jägerey*, by Joh. Jac. Büchtings. 1768.
*Beyträge zur Geschichte von Baiern*, by J. N. Mederer. 1777–1793.
*Thiere zu fangen*, by C. W. J. Gatterer. 1781.
*Hohe und niedere Jagd*, by Joh. Chr. Heppe. 1783.
*Jäger Practica*, by H. W. Döbel. 1783.
*Der Vogelsteller*, by Joh. Andreas Naumann. 1789.
*Handbuch der Jagd-wissenschaft*, by F. G. Leonhardi. 1797.
*Der Vogelfang*, by Joh. Christoph Heppe. 1797.
*Der Jagd- u. Hühnerhund*, by K. A. Kupfer. 1822.
*Forst und Jagd Wissenschaft*, by Dr. T. M. Bechstein. 1833.
*Lehrbuch für Jäger*, by Dr. Theodor Hertig. 1845.
*Die Federwild-Jagt*, by L. Ziegler. 1847.
*Der Vorstehhund*, by Fr. Oswald. 1855.
*Kaiser Maximilian I., Geheimes Jagdbuch*, by Th. G. von Karajan. 1858.
*Der Hühnerhund*, by A. Vogel. 1865.
*Der Hühnerhund*, by C. Herstatt. 1868.
*Handbuch des Jagdsport*, by Dr. Oscar Horn. 1882.
*Forst und Jagd Geschichte Deutschlands*, by Dr. Adam Schwappach. 1883.
*Züchtung, Erziehung und Arbeit der Gebrauchhunde*, by C. G. L. Quensell. 1883.
*Der Schweisshund und seine Arbeit*, by Ernst Drömer. 1887.
*Jagd- Hof- und Schäferhunde*, by E. Schlotfeldt. 1888.

### ITALIAN.

*Li Livres dou Tresor*, by Ser Brunetto Latini. 1260–1267.
*Il Convito*, by Dante Alighieri. 13th century.
*Bucolica*, by Baptist Sapagnuoli Mantuanus. 1448–1516.
*Aliquot aureoli vere libelli*, by Belisarius Aquaviva (Duke of Nardo). 1519.

# LIST OF BOOKS

*De Quadrupedibus Digitatis Viviparis*, by Ulysses Aldrovandi. 1522–1607.
*Venusini Canes*, by Joannes Darchius. 1543.
*De Canibus et Venatione*, by Mich. Ang. Biondo. 1544.
*De Venatione*, by Natalis Comes. 1551.
*I quattro libri della Caccia*, by Tito Giovanni Scandianese. 1556.
*Cynegetica*, by Pietro Angelio da Barga. 1561.
*De Aucupio, liber primus*, by Pietro Angelio da Barga. 1566.
*Gli Uccelli da Rapina*, by M. F. Sforzino da Carcano. 1568.
*Tractatus de Venatione, Piscatione et Aucupio*, by Dr. G. Mor. 1605.
*Le Caccie delle Fiere*, by Eugenio Raimondi. 1621.
*Ucceliera*, by G. P. Olina. 1622.
*La Caccia dell'Arcobugio*, by Cap. Vita Bonfadini. 1652.
*La Venaria Reale*, by Conte Amedeo di Castellamonte. 1672.
*La Caccia dello Schioppo*, by Nicolo Spadoni. 1673.
*La Cacciagione de Volatili*, by Giovanni Pontini. 1758.
*L'Uccellagione*, by Antonio Tirabosco. 1775.
*Trattate della Caccia*, by Bonaventura Crippa. 1834.

### SPANISH.

*Etymologiarum Libri XX.*, by St. Isidore (Bishop of Seville). 600–630.
*Libro de la Monteria del Rey D. Alfonso XI.* 1345.
*Libro de Caza*, by Principe Don Juan Manuel. 14th century.
*El Conde Lucanor*, by Principe Don Juan Manuel. 14th century.
*Libro de la Caza de las Aves*, by Canciller Pero Lopez de Ayala. 14th century.
*Tratado de Caza y Otros.* Anon. MS. (British Museum). 15th century.

# THE POINTER

*Aviso de Caçadores y de Caça*, by Pedro Nuñez de Avendaño. 1543.
*Tratado de Monteria y Cetreria (MS.)*, by Mossen Juan Vallès. 1556.
*El Peregrino en su Patria*, by Francisco Lope Felix de Vega Carpio. 1562–1635. -
*Discurso sobre el libro de la Monteria del Rey D. Alfonso XI.*, by Gonçalo Argote de Molina. 1582.
*Fueros y Observancias de Navarra.* 16th century.
*Dialogos de la Monteria.* Anon. MS. of the Escorial Library. 16th century.
*Origen y Dignidad de la Caça*, by Juan Mateos. 1634.
*Exercicios de la Gineta*, by Gregorio de Tapia y Salzedo. 1643.
*Arte de Ballesteria y Monteria*, by Alonzo Martinez de Espinar. 1644.
*Tratado de la Caza del Buelo*, by F. F. De la Escalera. 1654.
*De las Propriedades del Perro Perdiguero.* (Anon. MS. of Duke of Osuna's Collection.) 17th century.
*Arte de Cazar*, by Juan Manuel de Arelanno. 1745.
*Tratado de la Caza de las Perdices*, by Ramon Mauri y Puig. 1848.
*Investigaciones sobre la Monteria*, by Miguel Lafuente y Alcantara. 1849.
*Tesoro del Cazador.* (Anon.) 1858.
*Tesoro de los Perros de Caza.* (Anon.) 1858.
*La Aviceptologia*, by Jose Maria Tenorio. 1861.
*Fauna Mastologica de Gallicia*, by Victor Lopez Seoane. 1861.
*La llustracion Venatoria* (Periodical). 1878–1886.
*Biblioteca Venatoria*, edited by Gutierrez de la Vega. From 1879.
*La Caza* (work of reference), by Francisco de Uhagon. 1888.

# LIST OF BOOKS

*Los Perros de Caza Españoles*, by Gutierrez de la Vega. 1890.
*Paginas de Caza*, by Evero. 1898.

### VARIOUS.

*Geoponica*, edited by Emperor Constantine VII. (Byzantine.) 905-959.
*Cynosophion*, by Demetrius Pepagomenus. (Byzantine.) 13th century.
*Icones Variæ*, by Jan van der Straet. (Dutch.) 1600.
*Venatio Novantiqua*, by Janus Ulitius (Van Vliet.) (Dutch.) 1645.
*Systema Naturæ*, by Carl Linnæus. (Translated by Gmelin, 1792). (Swedish.) 1735.
*Historia Naturalis de Quadrupedibus*, by Johannes Johnstonus. (Icelandic.) 1755.

# INDEX

## A

'*Agutarius*,' a hare-hound. 4, 5
Aitinger (J. C.) on sport and pointing-dogs. 62, 69
Albertus Magnus, on partridge-dogs. 7
Alderwasley pointers. 78
Aldrovandi, on the brach. 17
  ,, on net-dogs. 51
Alien crosses. 147-162
Amos (Mr.) head-keeper at Douglas. 94
Angus (Mr.), his black pointer. 85
Anson (Colonel), his large bag over dogs. 87
Antrobus (J. C.), his pointers. 82
Appleby pointers. 78
Arelanno (Juan Manuel de), on the breeding and choosing of pups. 50
Argote de Molina, on '*ventores*.' 18
Armstrong (Edward), dog-breaker. 88
  ,, (John), dog-breaker. 87
Arquebuse, development of the use of, for shooting flying, 59, 60
Arran, Isle of, famous for its shooting. 72
Ashton (G.), crossed his pointers with foxhounds. 156
Auction sales of pointers, the earliest. 77
'*Aviarii*,' misuse of the term. 2

## B

Backing. 200, 215, 222
  ,, invented in England. 70
Bang (a pointer). 157, 158
Bang II. (a pointer). 157
Banjo O'Gymru (a pointer). 82
*Barbets*. 64
Bates (Jasper), owner of a dog called Don. 76
Baude, an Italian brach. 22
Baudrillart (M.), on doubled-nosed *braques*. 142
Beaujeu (P. de Q. de), on setting-dogs. 9, 54

Bedford, first working trials for pointers near. 99
Belle (a pointer), Mr. Lloyd Price's. 78
Bentinck (Lord George). 78
  ,, (Lord Henry), pointer-breeder, crossed foxhounds with pointers. 78, 81, 155
Bernes (Dame Juliana), on 'spaniels.' 12
Bible, the, and hunting-dogs. 1
Bichell (Baron), early use of the Spanish pointer in England. 25
Biondo, on hunting-dogs. 18
  ,, on the characteristics of pointing-dogs. 51, 116
Birmingham Exhibition. 83, 156
Biscuits for dogs. 227
Bishop (Elias) and his sons — dog-breakers. 88
Bishop (John), head-keeper to Mr. Pollock. 91
Bitches in pup, exercise of. 234
Black pointers, historical account of. 84, 90, 96
Blaine (D. P.), his misquotation about spaniels. 12
  ,, ,, on the pointer's characteristics. 121
  ,, ,, on grouse-shooting. 171
Blands of Kippax, their pointers. 79
Blaze (Elzéar), quotations from. 58-60
Blinking. 198
Blome (Richard), on shooting flying. 67
  ,, ,, on the breaking of dogs. 191
Board of Agriculture and quarantine. 103.
Bob (a pointer). Mr. Bird's. 84
Bonfadini, on the selection of brachs. 52
Bowhill dogs. 94, 95
Brace-stakes. 105
Brachs (short-haired pointing-dogs), their origin. 8, *et seq.*
  ,, early references to. 8, 15

# INDEX

Brachs, origin of the name.  15-18
„  definition of.  17
„  the Italian *bracchi*.  22, *et seq.*
„  the French *braques*.  23
„  characteristics of.  51
„  selection of.  51-53
„  double-nosed.  141
Brailsford (Mr.), gamekeeper to the Earl of Chesterfield and to Jeffrey Lockett.  86, 87
Brailsford (W.), dog-breaker.  86
„  on working trials.  98
„  on the pointer.  127
Breakers, some well-known dog-breakers.  86, *et seq.*
„  at dog trials.  111
Breaking of pointers.  190-222
Brearey & Co., auctioneers.  77
Breeding in-and-in, degeneration through.  137
Breeding, and selection.  137-146, 233, 234
„  alien crosses.  147-162
„  reduction of pointing instinct by alien crosses.  159
Brittany, origin of the hounds of.  21
Brodick Castle Sandy (a pointer).  73
Buccleuch (Duke of), his famous pointers.  94
Buffon, on the origin of pointing-dogs.  14
Bulled (Mr.), on the crossing of pointers and foxhounds.  157
Burn (C. M. P.), letter from.  155
Burton (Robert), on fowling.  67
Byrne (J. L.), on the '*Gorgas*.'  23

## C

Caius (Dr. John), first to describe the spaniel.  13
„  „  on setting-dogs.  64, 100
*Cane da rete*.  23
*Canis agaiæus*.  16
„  *odorus*.  16
„  *sagax*.  16, 51
Cannon Hall pointers.  74
Carlo (a pointer), Mr. Whitehouse's.  84
Castillon (M.), unreliability of his *Los Paramientos*.  5-7
Cat-foot, in pointers.  126, *et seq.*
Cereals, for dogs.  226

Chance, a Spanish pointer.  139
'Chapping the point.'  133
Characteristics of pointers.  115-136
Charles X.  58
Chesterfield (Earl of), famous kennel.  86, 87
'Chewing the scent.'  133
*Chien d'arrêt*, origin of term.  23
Chorœa, or St. Vitus's dance.  241
Clamorgan (Jean de), on setting-dogs.  54
*Code des Chasses*, extracts from, on sporting laws.  56, *et seq.*
Coinas (hats), their origin.  6, 7
Colquhoun, on grouse-shooting.  173
Columella, on breeding dogs.  234
Combermere (Lord), pointer-owner and judge.  92
Concrete, for kennel floors.  225
Constantine IV., Emperor, compiler of *Geoponica*—on dogs and partridges.  3
Contades (M. de), his present to Louis XIII.  55
Corbet (Sir Vincent), pointer-owner.  81
Cortachy Castle, black pointers at.  91
Cotes (Colonel), on the Woodcote pointers.  80, 83
Court (Dr.), a sporting experience of.  75
Coventry (Lord), pointer-breeder.  83
Cow, the, for partridge-catching.  62
Cox (N.), on the breaking of dogs.  191
Craven, author of *Recreations in Shooting*.  71, 175, 183
„  on a pointer's head.  122
„  how to select a pointer.  143
„  on the breaking of dogs.  211
Craw (James), gamekeeper to Lord Home.  95, 96
Crosses, alien.  147-162
Croxteth pointers.  80

## D

Dachshunds, instance from breeding.  144
Dan (a pointer), Duke of Hamilton's.  73
D'Arcussia, on brachs.  54
Dash (Thornton's), a cross between a pointer and a foxhound—characteristics of.  150-152
D'Aubigné, anecdote from.  54

# INDEX

Derby (13th Earl of), his famous pointers. 80
Descartes, example from setting-dogs. 54
Dhuleep Singh (Maharajah), 'the Black Prince.' 91, 94
*Dialogos de la Monteria*, on the killing of partridges over pointing-dogs and the training of the same. 29, *et seq.*
Diarrhœa, treatment for. 244
Diseases, treatment of. 239, *et seq.*
'Dished' face, in pointers. 123
Distemper, treatment for. 239–241
Dobson (W.), on pointers. 135
,, on the breaking of dogs. 203–206
Dodsworth (Sir E.), pointer-breeder. 80
Dog clubs. 99, *et seq.*
Dog shows. *See* shows.
Dogs, mentioned in early laws. 4
,, early laws on theft of. 4, 5
,, shooting over. 163–189
,, behaviour and treatment of, on the moor. 174, *et seq.*
Don (a pointer), Arkwright's. 155
Don IX. (a pointer). 161
Don José (a pointer). 155
Double-nose in pointers. 141
Down-wind questing. 177
Drake (a pointer), famous at field-trials. 128
Dudley (Robert), *Duke of Northumberland*, first trainer of a setter-dog. 13
Dunoyer de Noirmont (M.), on the French kings and their dogs. 55

## E

Ear, canker of the, treatment for. 246
Earl (Miss Maud). 124
Eaton Hall pointers. 82
Ecob (Mr.), dog-breaker. 88
Edenhall pointers. 79
Edge (Thomas Webb), his pointers. 78, 81, 82, 92
Edie (George), on the characteristics of pointers. 119
Edward VI., statute against 'Hayle shott.' 65
Edwards (Sydenham), on the pointer. 25
Edwards (Sydenham), on crossing pointers and foxhounds. 149, 150

Egan (Pierce) *Anecdotes*, quoted. 75, 86
Eglinton (Lord), pointer-owner. 93, 97
Egypt, methods of sport. 2
Elliott (Sir William), pointer-owner. 94
England, introduction of spaniels into. 10–14
,, introduction of pointing-dogs. 24–28
,, references to use of pointing-dogs and shooting - flying in. 65–70
English dogs, superiority of. 70
Espinar (Alonzo Martinez de), on sporting over pointing - dogs. 39, *et seq.*
Europe, pointing and setting - dogs originated in. 1
Evero, unreliability of his *Paginas de Caza*. 3, 5
Exercising of pointers. 231
Eyes, affections of the, treatment for. 247

## F

Faking. 48, 232
'Fancier,' description of a. 103
Falcon-dog or spaniel. 9
Falconry, Thomas Oakleigh on. 68
Falcons and setting-dogs. 68, 69
Feeding of pointers. 225, *et seq.*
Ferdinald, King, pointing-dog breeder. 140
Field trials. *See* trials
Fisher (George), trainer of pointers. 73
Fits, treatment for. 244
Flag-hoisting at trials. 112
Fleming (L. F. von), on hunting with pointing-dogs. 64
Flint (a pointer), Lord Mexborough's. 81
Floyd (William), author of *Observations on Dog-breaking*. 86
,, ,, on retrieving. 178
,, ,, on the breaking of dogs. 207
Foix, Comte de. *See* Phebus.
Forbes (D. M.), his black pointers. 95
Fouilloux (Jacques de), on '*limiers*.' 20
,, on the introduction of hounds into France. 20, 21
Fowling, early English writers on. 64–69
Foxhounds, crossing with pointers. 142, 149, *et seq.*

267

# INDEX

Foxhounds, comparison with a pointer. 159
,, disastrous crossing of pointers with. 160
France, introduction of spaniels into. 9, 10
,, spaniels from, introduced into England. 14
,, the *braques* of. 24
Francken (H. G.), on laws relating to dogs. 4, 5
François I. 22, 59
Frank (a pointer), ancestor of Hamlet. 83

## G

Garth (Sir Richard), his pointers. 83
Gaunt (Thomas), gamekeeper, his black pointers. 92
Gedling pointers. 87
Gell (Philip), of Hopton Hall, his pointers. 77
General (a pointer), Arkwright's. 155
*Gentleman Farrier, The*, on the Spanish pointer. 25
,, ,, ,, on shooting-flying. 68
German writers on pointing-dogs. 61, *et seq.*
Gesner, on pointing-dogs. 62
,, on the brach. 17
Goodricke (Sir Harry), his famous pointers. 79
Gordon (John), of Aikenhead, his black pointers. 92, 93
*Gorgas* (partridge-dogs) introduction into Spain—their extinction. 22
Graham (James), his kennel at the Trossachs. 92
Graham (Sir James), setter-owner. 87
Greyhounds and pointers used together. 75
,, crossing with the pointer. 162
Grouse, shooting of, over dogs. 164, *et seq.*
,, habits of. 182-184
,, (a pointer), Lord Eglinton's. 97

## H

Hamilton (Duke of), his breed of pointers. 72, 73, 90
Hamlet (a pointer), famous winner at shows and field-trials. 83, 157

Hampers, travelling. 233
Hare-brained trial dogs. 105
Hare-foot in pointers. 127, 128
Hares, chasing of, by pointers. 219
Harewood (H.), on the pointer's characteristics. 121
Harford (Summers), his black pointers. 93
Harris (John), a dog-breaker. 86
Hawker (Colonel), on partridge shooting. 188
Hawks and pointing-dogs. 63, 69
Hayle Shott, statute of Edward VI. against. 65
Heat system at trials. 108
Henri III. and IV., ordinances against setting-dogs. 56, 57
Henry VIII., statute against 'Crosbowes and Handguns.' 65
Hill (Noel), pointer-owner. 81
Holden (James), pointer-breeder. 78
Home (Lord), his pointers. 94, 95
Hopton Hall pointers. 77
Hound-pointers. 155, 156.
Hounds, original connection with pointing-dogs. 14-20
Howlitt (R.), on expert shots. 186
,, on using the trash cord. 194
Hunting-dogs, definition of. 17, 18
Hurt (Mr.), pointer-breeder. 78

## I

'Idstone,' author of *The Dog*, on a model pointer. 99
,, on crossing pointers. 156
,, on pointer's feet. 128
In-and-in breeding. 140, 144
Indian meal, danger of mange from. 227
Influenza, treatment for. 242
Instinct of pointers. 131-135
International Gundog League. 102
,, Pointer and Setter Society. 102
,, Pointer and Setter Society, its Trial laws. 109, *et seq.*
International Shooting-dog Club. 101
Ipsley Court pointers. 83
Italy, pointing-dogs of, 21, 22
,, the brachs of. 22, *et seq.*

# INDEX

## J

Jacob (Giles), author of *Compleat Sportsman*. 68
James I., present of setting-dogs to. 14
,, statute against setting-dogs. 66
Jaundice, treatment for. 241, 242
Johnson (T. B.), on Yorkshire pointers. 74
,, methods of training young pointers. 74
,, on the head of the pointer. 122, 127
,, on the selection and breeding of pointers. 140-142
,, on cross-breeding. 152
Judges, at dog-shows and trials. 104, *et seq.*
,, qualities necessary in. 107
,, undesirable types. 107
,, advice to, at dog-shows. 113
Judging at trials, various systems. 107, *et seq.*
Juno (a pointer), dam of Hamlet. 84

## K

Kate (a pointer), dam of Rap. VI. 95
Keepers, some well-known. 86, *et seq.*
,, Scottish. 90
Kennel Club, its demoralising influence on gundogs. 89
,, ,, its apathy regarding pointers. 99, 100
,, ,, its 'modified heat system' at Trials. 109
,, ,, and the degeneration of pointers. 156
Kennel-lameness, treatment of. 243
Kennelman's duty. 231, 232
,, house. 224
Kennel Management. 223-249
Kennels, famous English. 71, *et seq.*
,, structure and equipment of permanent. 223, *et seq.*
,, cleaning of. 230
,, disinfecting. 248
Kingston (Duke of), his pointers. 24, 28, 77
Kirke (Mr.), head-keeper to J. Graham. 93

Kirkland (Mr.), keeper to Lord Eglinton. 97
Kites, artificial. 188
Knowsley pointers. 80

## L

La Blanchère, on English dogs. 70
Lacy (Captain), on Sir John Shelley's pointers. 75
,, ,, on dog-breakers. 86
,, ,, on want of pointer societies. 102
,, ,, on the shape of the pointer. 124, 127
,, ,, on the ideal of a working pointer. 132
,, ,, on speed in pointers. 143
,, ,, on crossing hounds and pointers. 155
,, ,, on the treatment of dogs on the moor. 175-177
,, ,, on the breaking of dogs. 210
Lambert (Daniel), excellence of his pointers. 75
Lang (J.), gun-maker and pointer-breeder. 84
Langley (Edmund de), author of *Mayster of the Game*—on 'spaniels.' 12
Lascelles (R.), author of *Angling, Shooting, and Coursing*. 71, 77
,, on the pointer's characteristics. 120, 138
,, on crossing pointers and setters. 150
,, on the breaking of dogs. 199-203
,, on the care of pups. 237
Latini (Brunetto), on brachs. 7
Lawrence (Richard), on the origin of English pointers. 26
,, ,, anecdotes about pointers. 75-77, 151
,, ,, on the breaking of dogs. 207
Leash-hound. *See* Lymer.
Legh (George Cornwall), his pedigree-books. 82
Legh (George John), his pedigree-books. 82

# INDEX

Leighton (W.), keeper at Wynnstay. 82
*Lex Emendata*, on dog-stealing, etc. 4
*Lex Salica*, on hunting-dogs. 4
Lichfield (Lord), pointer-owner. 79
*Limiers. See* Lymer.
Lindsay (Mr.), head-keeper to Duke of Buccleuch. 92, 95
Lloyd (Mr.), head-keeper to Duke of Hamilton. 93
Lockett (Jeffrey), setter-owner. 87
Lodwick (Major), on the pedigree of 'Old Bang.' 157, 158
Lort (Mr. W.), advised the crossing of pointers and foxhounds. 156
Lothian (Marquis of), pointer-owner. 94, 95
Louis XIII., love for pointing and setting-dogs. 55, *et seq.*
,, the first in France to shoot flying. 60
Louis XIV., love for pointing and setting-dogs. 55, *et seq.*
,, ordinance against setting-dogs. 57
,, a good shot. 61
Lungs, inflammation of the, treatment. 242
Lymer or Leash-hound. 20.

## M

McCall (W.), gamekeeper, his pointers. 94
Mackenzie (John), gamekeeper, on the Duke of Hamilton's pointers. 73
Mackintosh, on grouse shooting. 182
Major (a pointer), Mr. Princep's. 79
Mange, causes of. 227
,, treatment for. 245
Mangel, the, as an article of diet for dogs. 228
Marchese Fortunato Rongoni (breed of brachs). 52
Markers, utility of. 187
Markham (Gervase), on fowling. 67
,, ,, on the breaking of dogs. 190, 191
Marolles (Magné de), on shooting with ,, ,, arquebuses. 59
,, ,, on shooting in line. 61
Martinez de Espinar (Alonzo), on partridge shooting. 39, *et seq.*
Mastiffs, crossing with pointers. 153

Mayer (John), gamekeeper and author of the *Sportsman's Directory.* 86
,, ,, on the pointer's characteristics. 120, 130
Meat, for dogs. 226
Medicines, for dogs. 238-249
,, how to administer. 244
Menerbe, its capture aided by a setting-dog. 54
Mexborough (Lord), his famous pointers. 79, 81
Meyenburg (R. A. von), on dogs. 8
Meyrick (John), on feeding pups. 236, 237
Millar (John), letter from. 96
Millar (W.), of Whitehill Kennels—his pointers. 96
Mitford (Admiral), his black pointers. 79, 84
Mohammed el Mangali, his treatise on hunting. 2
Molina (Argote de), author of *Libro de Monteria.* 18, 70
Mona (a pointer), Mr. Whitehouse's. 84
Montgomery (Sir Graham), his pointers. 95
Moor, the, behaviour and treatment of dogs on. 174, *et seq.*
Moore (George), pointer-breeder. 78
Mundys' pointers. 79
Musgrave (Sir R. G.), his breed of pointers. 80
Muzzles. 233

## N

National Pointer and Setter Society. 101
,, Society, and brace-stakes. 105
Navarre, Laws of, against poaching. 48
*Navarro*, title for both hounds and pointing-dogs. 19, 20, 37
Net-dogs. 51, 62
Netting, vicissitudes of. 68
Newcastle-on-Tyne, first pointer show at. 85, 98
Newfoundlands, crossing with pointers. 153
North (Christopher), on game-preserves and sport. 171
Nose, the, importance of, in pointers. 138, *et seq.*

270

# INDEX

## O

Oakleigh Thos.), author of the *Shooter's Handbook*, on Falconry. 68
,, ,, author and pointer-owner. 71
,, ,, on the selection of pups. 142
,, ,, on cross-breeding of pointers. 153, 154
,, ,, on grouse shooting. 172
,, ,, on sport. 174, 175
,, ,, advice to sportsmen. 181, 182
,, ,, on the habits of the grouse. 182, 183
,, ,, on the habits of the partridge. 184, *et seq.*
,, ,, on markers. 187
,, ,, on the breaking of dogs. 207-209
,, ,, on feeding sporting dogs. 228, 229
Occipital bone, inflammation of the. 248
Odlin (Mr.), gamekeeper and dog-breaker. 86
Old Bang (a pointer). 157, 158
Old Naso (a pointer). 157
Olina, author of *Ucceliera*, on the characteristics of the brach. 51
Oppianus, on hunting-dogs. 17
Orsay (Count d'), his large bag over dogs. 87
Osbaldiston (W. A.), author and pointer-owner. 27, 76, 119, 147
Osuna (Duke of), MS. belonging to. 49
Oudry, painting by, of pointing-dog. 23, 130
*Our Dogs*, quoted. 157

## P

Page (T.), on pointers. 26, 119
,, gun-maker and pointer-breeder. 84, 85
,, on crossing pointers and setters. 147
,, on the etiquette of partridge-shooting. 186
*Paginas de Caza*, on the '*aviarii.*' 2

Pape (W. R.), gun-maker and pointer-breeder—his famous black pointers. 84
*Paramientos, Los*, a spurious work. 5-7
Partridge-dogs. 15, 17
,, faking of. 48
Partridges, dialogue on killing over pointing-dogs. 29, *et seq.*
,, killing over dogs, by Martinez de Espinar. 39-48
,, to catch with the 'cow.' 62
,, hunted with pointing-dog and hawk. 63
,, the habits and shooting of. 184-189
Pastizzo (a brach). 52
Pegging down, of the backing pup. 218
Pennant (Thomas), quotation from. 26
Penson (Andrew), keeper at Woodcote. 80
Phebus (Gaston), *Comte de Foix*, author of *Deduiz de la Chasse.* 12, 53, 70
,, on the spaniel or falcon dog. 9
Pisanello, sketch by, of pointing-dog. 15
Pliny, and hunting dogs. 2
Pneumonia, treatment for. 242
Poaching, formerly in Navarre. 48
Pointer and Setter Society. 107
Pointer Club, the. 101
Pointer-fancy, the. 101
Pointers. See also *Brachs, Partridge-dogs, Ventores,* and *Pointing-dogs.*
,, ANCESTRY OF. 1-23
,, ORIGIN OF. 23-28
,, quotations from early English writers, showing the use of pointers in England. 64-69
,, superiority of English dogs. 70
,, LATER HISTORY OF POINTERS. 71-97
,, famous kennels and breeds. 71, *et seq.*
,, prices of. 76-78
,, demoralising influence of the Kennel Club on. 89
,, black pointers of Scotland. 90-97
,, blending of English and Scottish. 97

271

# INDEX

Pointers, bad outlook for. 97
,, SHOWS AND WORKING TRIALS. 98-114
,, Pointer Club. 101
,, Rules for judging at trials. 109-112
,, CHARACTERISTICS OF POINTERS. 115-136
,, figure and index. 118
,, quotations from early writers on the pointer's characteristics. 119, *et seq.*
,, the head. 122-124
,, the trunk. 124, 125
,, the limbs. 125-128
,, the tail, the coat, and the colour. 129-131
,, instinct for sport. 131-136
,, BREEDING AND SELECTION. 137-146
,, ALIEN CROSSES. 147-162
,, crossing with setters. 147, 148
,, English pointer produced from pointing-dogs of Navarre and Italy. 149
,, crossing with foxhounds. 149-161
,, crossing with greyhounds. 161
,, BREAKING. 190-222
,, KENNEL MANAGEMENT. 223-249
,, feeding. 225-229
,, appearance of, when in good condition. 230
,, cleaning. 230-232
,, exercising. 231
,, breeding. 233, *et seq.*
Pointing, natural. 133
Pointing-dogs, EARLY HISTORY OF. 1-70
,, a product of the Middle Ages. 3
,, first likeness of. 15
,, relationship to the hound. 15-21
,, origin of the name. 24
,, introduction into England. 24-28
,, dialogue on the characteristics and training of dogs for partridge-shooting. 28-39

Pointing-dogs, Martinez de Espinar on the training of. 39-48
,, choosing of pups. 49
,, characteristics favoured by Italian writers. 50, *et seq.*
,, French and German writers on. 53, *et seq.*
Pope, on pheasant-shooting. 69
Portland (4th Duke of), purchases at Edge sale. 78
Portland (5th Duke of), his pointers. 75
Portland (6th Duke of). 155
Potatoes, for sporting-dogs. 228, 229
Powys (H.) pointer-owner. 81
Press, in relation to gun-dogs. 104
Price (Sam), breeder of pointers. 158
Prices of pointers. 76-78
Princep (Wm.), pointer-breeder. 79
*Propriedades del Perro Perdiguero*, on the choosing of pups. 49
Punishment for dogs. 208, 209, 211, 217
Puppies, selection of. 49, 146, 235
,, breaking in of. 190-222
,, production and rearing of. 233-238
,, feeding of. 236-237
Puzzle-pegs. 198, 204, 220
Pye (H.), on the breaking of dogs. 195

## Q

Quail (a pointer), Sir E. Dodsworth's. 81
Quail-dogs. 62
Quartering. 192, 204, 206, 207, 210, 215, 216
,, at trials. 212
'Quartogenarian,' on pointer-dogs. 28, 134
Quinqueran de Beaujeu (Pierre de). 9, 53
Quiz (a pointer), Earl of Derby's. 80

## R

Rake (a pointer), Mr. Edge's. 78
Raking, or snuffling. 198, 220
Rap VI. (a pointer), Mr. Usher's. 95
Reid (William), gamekeeper at the Hirsel. 94
Renton Abbey Pointers. 79
*Retiarios*, dogs of the net. 51

# INDEX

Retriever Society. 102
Rice, cooking of, for dogs. 227
Roading. 179, 201, 205, 221
Romano (Cesare Solatio), sporting author. 59
Ruby (a black pointer), Mr. Usher's. 95

## S

St. Isidore, *Origines* of, mention of hunting-dogs 3
St. John (Charles), author of *Wild Sports of the Highlands.* 71
  ,,    ,, on cross-breeding of pointers. 155
  ,,    ,, on grouse-shooting and large bags. 173
St. Simon (Louis de), quoted on the dogs at the French Court. 55
St. Vitus's dance. 241
Sallust, and hunting-dogs. 2, 3
Salt, use of, for dogs. 228
Sancho (a black pointer), Lord Lothian's. 94
Saugrain (M.), extracts from his *Code des Chasses*, on sporting laws. 56, *et seq.*
Scotland, black pointers of. 90-97
  ,, the gamekeepers of. 90
Scott (Lord John), pointer-owner. 94
Sebright (Sir John), on the breeding of live-stock. 137
Sefton (Lord), his pointers. 80, 81, 130
Selia Price (a pointer). 158
Senès (Bishop of), on setting-dogs. 9, 53
  ,, on English breeders. 70
Serjeantson (G. J.), pointer-breeder. 80
Setters, account of, by Dr. Caius. 64
  ,, statute of James I. against. 66
  ,, characteristics of, by R. Symonds. 119, 120
  ,, crossing with pointers. 147, 148, 154
Setting-dogs, originated in Europe. 1
  ,, early picture of. 10
  ,, first training of, in England. 13, 14
  ,, early references to. 53-55
  ,, love of Louis XIII. and XIV. for. 55, *et seq.*

Setting-dogs, French laws against. 56, 57
Sforza (Caterina), on brachs and hounds. 18, 21
Sforzino da Carcano, on brachs. 18
Shakerley (Sir Charles), pointer-owner. 82
Shelley (Sir John), his famous pointers. 75
Shipley pointers. 79
Shooting flying, development of the art of. 59-61
Shooting over dogs. 163-189
Shows, and working trials. 98-114
  ,, first show for pointers. 98
  ,, degeneracy of pointers through. 99, 100
  ,, title of champion for pointers. 99
  ,, incompetent judges. 103, 104
Shrewsbury Society. 101
Single-stakes. 104, 105
Simpson (John), head-keeper to Lord Overtoun, his black pointers. 96
Slate, disadvantages of, for kennel floors. 225
Sleeping-benches, structure of. 224
Solatio (Cesare), on shooting flying. 50
Spadoni, author of *La Caccia dello Schioppo*, on the characteristics of the brach. 53
Spain, hunting dogs of. 8, 9
  ,, spaniels or falcon-dogs came from. 8-10
  ,, the *Gorgas*. 22
Spaniels or falcon-dogs, description. 9
  ,, origin of. 8-10
  ,, derivation of the name. 10, 14
  ,, introduction in England. 10, *et seq.*
Spanish pointers, introduction into England. 24-28
  ,,    ,, crossed with English breeds. 149-153
Speed, of pointers. 142
*Sporting Magazine*, on the pointer. 25
Sporting-man, and Sportsman. 164
Sporting Spaniel Society. 102
*Sportsman's Dictionary*, references to. 27, 28, 68
*Sportsman, The*, quoted on the training of pointers. 74, 75
  ,,    ,, on the characteristics of the pointer. 115, 117, 126, 127, 133

273

# INDEX

*Sportsman, The,* on the selection of pointers. 140
,, ,, on crossing pointers and setters. 148
,, ,, on Colonel Thornton's 'Dash.' 151
Sportsmen, etiquette when out shooting. 179–182, 186
Spotting system, at trials. 101, 108
Sprains, treatment for. 247
Stafford trials in 1866. 98
Stamford (Lord), pointer - breeder. 81
Stanhope (Colonel Spencer), on the Cannon Hall pointers. 73
Stanhope (Walter Spencer), pointer-breeder. 73
Statham (W.), his pointers. 78
Statter (T ), his pointers. 78
Stobo Castle, breed of pointers. 95
*Stock-keeper* quoted. 128, 157
'Stonehenge' on pedigrees of pointers. 81
,, on the judges at dog-shows. 98
,, on pointers. 101
,, on trials. 105
,, on the pointer's characteristics. 121
,, on crossing pointers and greyhounds. 161, 162
Strelley Hall pointers. 78, 79
Strutt (Joseph), author of *Sports and Pastimes.* 67
Stubbs (G.), delineations of pointers. 130
Sweep (a black pointer), Lord Home's. 94
Sykes (Sir Tatton), pointer - breeder. 74
Sylvia (a pointer), Sir E. Dodsworth's. 80
Symmetry in a pointer. 117
Symonds (R.), on the origin of the pointer. 26
,, ,, on the characteristics of setters and pointers. 119, 120
,, ,, on swift dogs. 175
,, ,, on the breaking of dogs. 192–194
,, ,, and quartering. 212
Symons (Sir Richard), purchaser of 'Dash.' 151

## T

Tane (a *braque*). 24
Täntzer, on pointing-dogs. 62, 63
Tap (a pointer). 159, 213
Taplin (W.), author of *The Sportsman's Cabinet.* 71
,, ,, on hurrying to a point. 178
,, ,, on sportsmen's etiquette. 180
,, ,, on the breaking of dogs. 195–197
Tardif, on relieving a dog's thirst. 53
,, on breeding. 234.
Tattersalls, auctioneers of pointers. 78, 83
Taylor (Tom), pointer - breeder and judge. 77
Thermometers, clinical, for dogs. 240
Thomas (R.), advice to shooters. 180, 181
Thornhill (R. B.), author of the *Shooting Directory.* 77
,, ,, on swift pointers. 135
,, ,, on crossing Spanish and English pointers. 148, 149
,, ,, on sportsmen. 170
,, ,, on the breaking of dogs. 197–199
Thornton (Col.). 69, 71–73
,, ,, on French sportsmen. 116
,, ,, on breeding pointers. 138
,, ,, first to cross foxhounds with pointers. 150
,, ,, on not lending dogs to others. 179
Thornycroft (Mr.), the sculptor, pointer-owner. 82
Tillemens, painting by, of pointers. 24
Tomes (Mr.), of Cleeves Prior, pointer-breeder. 83
Tonic, a, for convalescent dogs. 248
Trash-cord, the, use of in dog-breaking. 194, 207, 218
Trials.—TRIALS AND SHOWS. 79, 98–114
,, first working trial for pointers. 98
,, point-worship at. 105

# INDEX

Trials, various systems of judging and awarding. 107, *et seq.*
„ laws of the International Pointer and Setter Society. 109–112
„ flag-hoisting. 112
Trojans, introduced hounds into France. 21
Trossachs, James Graham's kennel at the. 91, 92

## U

Usher (Mr.), his black pointers. 85, 95

## V

Valles (Mossen Juan), on faking dogs. 48
Vegetables, for dogs. 227–229
Vendôme (Duc de), love for dogs. 55
*Ventores*, term for both hounds and pointing-dogs. 18
Venus (a pointer), Mr. Serjeantson's. 80
Vermin, to get rid of. 232
Vespasian, whether he introduced Spanish dogs into England. 11
Von Fleming, on using a spaniel with pointing-dogs. 63, 64, 178

## W

Walker (G.), *Costumes of Yorkshire*, quoted. 69
Walsh (Mr.), editor of the *Field*, and first dog-show. 85

Washing of dogs undesirable. 232
Watson (T.), on the origin of distemper. 239
Welfitt (Colonel), crossed foxhounds with pointers. 155
Wemyss (Earl of), his black pointers. 93, 95, 96
Westminster (Marquis of), dog-owner. 82
Wheat-meal, for dogs. 227
*Wheeble and Pitman's Magazine*, quoted. 76
White (James), head-keeper at Douglas Castle, his pointers. 93, 94, 96
Whitehouse (Mr.), of Ipsley Court, his pointers. 83
Whitfield (George), a keeper at Cannon Hall. 73
Woodcote pointers. 80
Worms, treatment for. 243, 244
Wotton (Edward), author of *De Differentiis Animalium*. 13
Wounds, treatment for. 247, 248
Wynnstay pointers. 82

## Y

Yellows, the, or jaundice, symptoms, and treatment for. 241, 242
York (General), American sportsman. 85
Yorkshire pointers. 73
Youatt (Wm.), on the pointer. 133

Printed in the United Kingdom
by Lightning Source UK Ltd.
126027UK00001B/38/A